} The Athens of America

D1211527

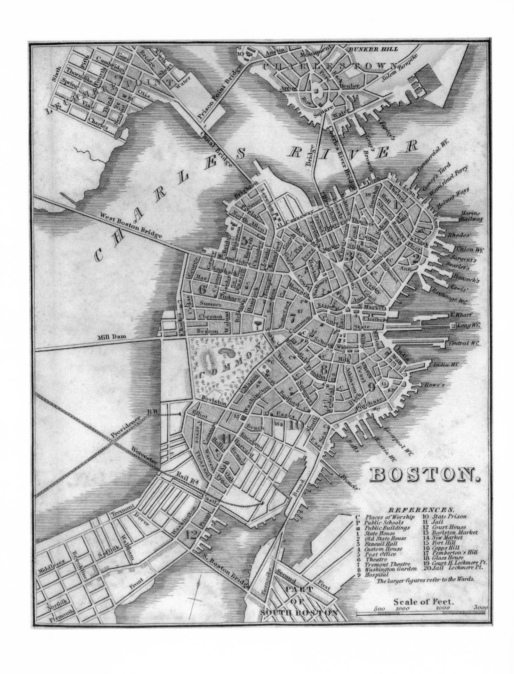

BOSTON.

REFERENCES.

C   Places of Worship   10 State Prison
P   Public Schools   11 Jail
☐   Public Buildings   12 Court House
1   State House   13 Boylston Market
2   Old State House   14 New Market
3   Faneuil Hall   15 Fort Hill
4   Custom House   16 Copps Hill
5   Post Office   17 Pemberton's Hill
6   Theatre   18 Glass House
7   Tremont Theatre   19 Court H. Lechmere Pt.
8   Washington Garden   20 Jail Lechmere Pt.
9   Hospital

The larger figures refer to the Wards.

Scale of Feet.

500   1000   2000   3000

PART
OF
SOUTH BOSTON

} *Boston, 1825–1845*

THE
ATHENS
OF
AMERICA

Thomas H. O'Connor

UNIVERSITY OF MASSACHUSETTS PRESS   Amherst & Boston

Copyright © 2006 by Thomas H. O'Connor

All rights reserved

Printed in the United States of America

LC 2005019233

ISBN 1-55849-524-x (library cloth ed.); 518-5 (paper)

Designed by Richard Hendel

Set in Adobe Minion by BookComp, Inc.

Printed and bound by Thomson-Shore, Inc.

Library of Congress Cataloging-in-Publication Data

O'Connor, Thomas H., 1922–

The Athens of America : Boston, 1825–1845 /

Thomas H. O'Connor.

   p. cm.

Includes bibliographical references and index.

ISBN 1-55849-524-x (library cloth edition : alk. paper)—

ISBN 1-55849-518-5 (paper : alk. paper)

1. Boston (Mass.)—History—19th century. 2. Boston
(Mass.)—Civilization—19th century. 3. Boston (Mass.)—
Social conditions—19th century. 4. Elite (Social sciences)—
Massachusetts—Boston—History—19th century. I. Title.

F73.44.O245   2006

974.4'6103—dc22   2005019233

British Library Cataloguing in Publication data are available.

Frontispiece: Map of Boston from H. S. Tanner, *The American Traveller, or, Guide through the United States . . .* , 8th ed. (Philadelphia: T. R. Tanner, 1842). Courtesy, University of Texas Libraries, Austin.

FOR MARY

with love forever

Contents

} *I*LLUSTRATIONS

Contemporary developments affecting the personal and professional lives of historians invariably cause them to reflect upon those various periods of history in which they conduct their research, looking for contrasts and similarities that might help them make sensible judgments and prudent decisions. The subject of the city of Boston has long been the central focus of my own historical research, and whenever significant changes take place in the city's traditional structure, they are almost certain to arouse my curiosity and interest.

At the turn of the twenty-first century, what seemed like an inordinate number of Boston-owned and Boston-based financial and literary enterprises were either taken over by corporations based in other parts of the United States or, with the rapid growth of globalization, located in other parts of the world. Early in 2005, for example, Gillette, a solid manufacturing company founded in 1901, and with deep roots in the Boston community, was acquired by Procter & Gamble, a consumer conglomerate with headquarters in Cincinnati, Ohio. A year earlier, the FleetBoston Financial Corp. was sold to the Charlotte, North Carolina–based Bank of America, and a short time before that, John Hancock Financial Services went off to Toronto, Canada. Before that, the *Boston Globe* had become part of the *New York Times*; two longtime retail establishments, Jordan Marsh and Filene's, disappeared from the Boston scene; the venerable Parker House, where Emerson, Longfellow, and other members of the Saturday Club met for dinner, became part of an international chain; the Shawmut Bank no longer existed as a Boston landmark. Even the Boston Safe Deposit & Trust Company, where leading members of Boston's financial establishment, popularly known as "The Vault," held their weekly meetings during the period of urban renewal, went off to somewhere in Pennsylvania. And in April 2005, the *Atlantic Monthly*, one of America's most celebrated magazines and a prestigious Boston institution since 1857, announced that it would move to Washington, D.C., signaling a serious loss in both literature and journalism.

For 147 years, according to Ellery Sedgwick, grandson of the journal's eighth editor, the values of the *Atlantic Monthly* emphasized the life of the mind, liberal inquiry, and intellectual engagement in moral and political issues. All that is no longer part of the Boston cultural scene.

The leaders and directors of these prominent financial and literary institutions were men who lived in Boston, whose enterprises were located in Boston, and who had always assumed a serious personal responsibility for the social, cultural, and intellectual life of their community. They not only contributed money, but they gave generously of their time, their talents, and their concern in establishing and maintaining those institutions that helped Boston retain its long-held reputation as "The Athens of America."

What all this means in long-range financial terms is well beyond my capabilities to determine. The changing tides in Boston's long and complicated economic history have demonstrated how new technologies can bring about profound changes in a very short period of time, and yet they also illustrate how Boston has always been able to respond to these changes in remarkable fashion. What does concern me, however, is what these changes and relocations will mean in terms of Boston's social, cultural, and intellectual future. As I read about all the companies and institutions leaving Boston, with their directors residing in New York, London, Singapore, and Tokyo, I must say I wonder who now will serve as the "treasurers of God's bounty" and represent the community as trustees of corporations, editors of journals, directors of hospitals, board members of museums, subscribers to the symphony, monitors of the charitable and welfare centers of the Commonwealth. Who will serve as the new leadership elite in shaping the future of the city?

In reflecting upon Boston's past history, *The Athens of America* is an attempt to demonstrate how, during the early part of the nineteenth century, a leadership elite, composed of men of family background, liberal education, and managerial experience in a variety of enterprises, used their personal talents and substantial financial resources to promote the cultural, intellectual, and humanitarian interests of Boston to the point where it would be the envy of the nation. Those who are familiar with the history of Boston are well aware that in those years the city was not only known as the "Hub of the Solar System," but was also heralded as the "Athens of America." For the most part, however, the references to the way in which Boston sought to re-create the idealized glories of ancient Greece have usually been associated with the accomplishments of the famous literati of Boston and Cambridge during that remarkable period that one historian has called "The Flowering of New England." Certainly, the celebrated writers and philosophers of that period—Emerson, Thoreau, Longfellow, Hawthorne, Whittier, Lowell, and the rest—were a significant part of the city's emerging reputation as a center of literature and learning. Unfortunately, however, that emphasis has too often obscured the more interesting fact that the city's efforts to transform the founding vision of the City Upon a Hill into a modern version of Ancient Athens was the result of a much larger community effort, involving a much broader cross section of Boston's citizenry.

In the aftermath of their successful struggle for independence from Great Britain, and the subsequent achievement of a national identity, Bostonians joined with their fellow countrymen in visualizing America as nothing less than the legendary torchbearer carrying the light of Western Civilization from the Old World to the New. Just as ancient Athens had been long regarded as the Cradle of Civilization, a well-ordered republic that fostered literature, learning, and the fine arts, many of Boston's leaders saw Boston as exercising that same role for itself, as well as for the nation as a whole. Not only did literary figures and scholarly philosophers see themselves as significant influences in this development, however, but so did physicians and lawyers, ministers and teachers, merchants and businessmen, mechanics and artisans, all committed to creating their own version of a well-ordered city whose citizens would be cultured and well-educated, where homes would be comfortable, public buildings impressive, colleges stately, and temples of religion appropriately inspiring. Like ancient Athens, Boston would be a city of great statesmen, wealthy patrons, inspiring artists, and profound thinkers, headed by members of the "happy and respectable classes," a leadership elite whose members would assume responsibility for the safety and welfare of the "less prosperous portions of the community" for their own benefit, as well as for the benefit of the city as a whole.

To accomplish this noble vision, to create what they felt would be an Athens in America, leading members of the Boston community, of all stations and all walks of life, joined in programs and projects designed, first of all, to cleanse the old town of what they felt were generations of accumulated social stains and embarrassing human failures, and then to create new programs and more efficient institutions that would raise the cultural and intellectual standards of all its citizens.

The Athens of America, then, is an attempt to survey the two decades of

Boston history, from about 1825 to 1845, in order to assess the broad range of social, educational, cultural, benevolent, and humanitarian reform activities consciously intended to make Boston an outstanding model for the future. This is not the result of original research in primary sources, but an attempt to synthesize the numerous excellent secondary sources, which have concentrated on specialized subjects and personalities associated with this period of American history. I have tried to draw together a complex series of individual topics into a single readable synthesis so that these two decades of intensive social and intellectual reform in Boston can be seen in a more comprehensive fashion, rather than in a series of separate and generally unrelated studies. In this manner, the ideal of an "Athens of America" can be viewed not only as a way in which Bostonians visualized their city as a significant influence upon the future of the United States, but also as a way in which Bostonians saw their city as a reflection of their own personal moral beliefs, social values, and intellectual accomplishments. This is the fascinating story of how Boston started out desiring to become the Intellect of America, and ended up trying to be its Conscience—only to find that at least half the nation wanted neither its intellect *nor* its conscience.

I am grateful to Paul M. Wright, editor of the University of Massachusetts Press, for encouraging the completion of this reflective work about early-nineteenth-century Boston history and for sponsoring it for publication. In 1976, Paul served as editor for *Bibles Brahmins, and Bosses*, the first book I ever wrote about the city, for the Boston Public Library's innovative NEH Learning Library Program. I am pleased to say that the intervening thirty years have only served to strengthen a close personal and professional friendship.

I have benefited from the enthusiastic support of Bruce Wilcox, director, Carol Betsch, managing editor, and the staff at the University of Massachusetts Press in the course of the production of this work. I owe a special word of thanks to Mary Capouya, copy editor, for the skill and perception with which she carried out the painstaking work of editing the manuscript. Lauren Mandel, library assistant at the Bostonian Society, was both efficient and gracious in making available to me the superb photographic resources of that illustrious institution that has done so much to preserve and advance knowledge about the city of Boston.

Thomas H. O'Connor
Chestnut Hill, Massachusetts

THE ATHENS OF AMERICA

CHAPTER 1 } *A New Day Dawning*

On January 8, 1788, a special convention of 364 delegates assembled in Boston in accordance with the order of the Great and General Court of Massachusetts to act upon the proposed Constitution of the United States. Late in the afternoon of February 6, 1788, after a month of heated and often acrimonious debate, the "grand question" was moved: Should Massachusetts ratify the Constitution? The final vote was 187, yes, and 168, no. By the narrow margin of nineteen votes, Massachusetts had become the sixth state to join the new Union.

The announcement that Massachusetts had ratified the Constitution of the United States almost immediately produced a wave of jubilation and good fellowship throughout the town of Boston. Even outspoken Antifederalists now pledged their support for the new framework of government. Abraham White, a delegate from the town of Norton who had opposed the change, announced that from now on he intended "to induce his constituents to live in peace under, and cheerfully submit to it." A gala reception had been arranged for the delegates in the Senate Chamber of the nearby State House, and during the festivities it was evident that the bitterness of the debates had been replaced by a general spirit of "joy, union, and urbanity." Everyone joined in toasting the happy occasion, and appeared to do so with sincerity and good will. "All appeared to bury the hatchet of animosity," wrote the correspondent of the *Massachusetts Centinel*, "and to smoke the calumet of union and love."

While citizens of Boston were celebrating the transition from the excitement of revolution to the stability of nationhood, a new cluster of leaders took over the direction of state and local affairs. With the forced evacuation of British administrators and Tory bureaucrats during the war, the resulting political vacuum was quickly filled by a group of well-known Bostonians who now moved up from the levels of financial wealth and social influence to positions of political power and legislative prominence. After the war, for example, John Hancock, one of the town's most successful merchants, became governor of the state in 1780, and continued to serve in that capacity until his death in 1793. Thomas Cushing, a close friend of Hancock and a former member of the town's Merchants Club, served as lieutenant governor from 1780 to 1788. Samuel Adams, who had failed in several business ventures before the Revolution, found political fulfillment as lieutenant governor from 1789 to 1793 and then, after Hancock's death, took over the role of governor from 1794 to 1797. James Bowdoin, who was active in postrevolutionary politics and served briefly as governor from 1785 to 1787, came from a distinctly mercantile background, as did Stephen Higginson and James Warren, who regularly opposed the Federalist policies of John Hancock. Elbridge Gerry had started out in the family shipping business on the north shore before making politics his career, and Thomas Handasyd Perkins continued to pursue his profitable commercial enterprises while becoming active as a Federalist legislator in the postwar years.

A number of small-town lawyers of local repute, too, found the postwar years a time of unparalleled opportunity for moving up into positions of greater power and influence since English jurists had left the scene. Josiah Quincy of Boston and Fisher Ames of Dedham found seats in the new United States Congress. Harrison Gray Otis, a young lawyer whose father had been ruined by the revolution, now went on to political prominence, first in the House and then in the Senate. Theophilus Parsons of Newburyport left his law practice in Boston to become Chief Justice of the Supreme Judicial Court of Massachusetts. And John Adams of Braintree, after serving as America's first minister to Great Britain, would shortly reach the pinnacle of success as Vice-President, and then as President of the United States in 1796. By the time the first national elections had taken place in the fall of 1788, and the new government of President George Washington was under way in the spring of 1789, a new political oligarchy had firmly established itself in power. In line with the orderly process of Federalism created at the national level by Secretary of the Treasury Alexander Hamilton, a new Federalist aristocracy in Boston was more than content to retain the class structure that had characterized their society over the past century and a half. Once they had driven out their British overlords and achieved national independence, they were satisfied that for all practical purposes the rebellion was over—their "revolution" was complete. Assuming that their colonial traditions—religious orthodoxy, social integrity, and political responsibility—would remain intact, they anticipated no further surprises. Hamilton's policy of government by "the wise, the well-born, and the good," combined with his "stake-in-government" principle that wedded the stability of the new nation to the prosperity of its financial leaders, were perfectly consistent with the views of those local Federalists who now directed the affairs of the town.

A new sense of national pride now pervaded the town, and already many of the old streets had been named after such Patriot leaders as Hancock, Franklin, and Warren, while others were changed to more appropriate titles. King Street now became State Street; Queen Street was changed to Court Street; Long Lane, where the Constitution had been ratified, was called Federal Street; and the wide road that ran through the main part of town across the neck was named after George Washington. Still tied to the wharf and the dock, Boston remained intensely proud and singularly parochial as it looked out to the sea and made plans to resume its previous maritime activities now that a measure of political stability had finally been established. In short order, the dockyards came alive, the shipyards opened once again, able-bodied workers returned to the town, and the vessels put out to sea. Between 1794 and 1802, according to the eminent maritime historian Samuel Eliot Morison, the size of the total merchant and fishing fleet in Massachusetts almost doubled; and by 1810 it increased another 50 percent. Aggressive Yankee skippers found ingenious ways of evading British trade regulations and renewing their lucrative trade with the West Indies. The Caribbean Islands supplied large quantities of cocoa, sugar, tobacco, and molasses, so greatly in demand throughout the Bay State. In return, Yankees supplied badly needed outlets for the codfish, whale oil, lumber, and rough manufactured goods of the entire New England region. In addition to the West Indies trade, Yankee whalers and fur traders found the eastern waters of South America a surprisingly lucrative source of commercial profits. When the outbreak of the naval wars between England and France during the late 1790s made a normal transatlantic traffic with European countries too hazardous, many Americans decided to open up new markets at Rio de Janeiro and along the River Plate for the exchange of such commodities as hides and lumber. More enterprising skippers made their way even farther down the South Atlantic coast, through the Strait of Magellan, and then up along the western shores of South America and into the waters of the Pacific to explore the rich China market.

During this same period, Boston vessels, loaded with copper, cloth, trinkets, blankets, and clothing of all sorts, were also making regular voyages along the west coast of North America to the Columbia River, along what is now the Washington–Oregon border. After bargaining with the native peoples of the region in exchange of their wares for otter skins and furs, they would sail across the Pacific, with frequent stops at the Hawaiian Islands and the Sandwich Islands, finally to dispose of their goods in China. Then they made their way home around the southern tip of Africa (there was no Suez Canal then) and across the stormy Atlantic with their cargoes of Chinese tea, colorful silks, and the delicate porcelain so much in demand by the well-to-do families back in Boston. The aromas of exotic spices wafted through parts of town, beautiful new fabrics were available for personal adornment, and even little monkeys became stylish as household pets.

The growing prosperity of Boston in the late 1790s was reflected in the growth of its citizenry and expansion of its living space. From an all-time low of 6,000 residents during the period of British occupation, by 1790 the population of the town had risen to 18,000. In 1800, it was recorded at 25,000, and by 1810, it had gone well beyond 30,000—a fivefold increase in only thirty-five years. Considering the fact that the town, now about two hundred years old, still looked like a small, half-inflated balloon attached to the mainland by a thin stretch of mudflats, this remarkable increase in population forced a series of changes, not only to accommodate the rising number of residents, but also to make up for the deteriorating conditions in the older parts of town. What had once been a small, pleasant, somewhat rustic, colonial seaport town was fast turning into an uncomfortably crowded and badly congested urban center. A number of well-to-do merchants, businessmen, lawyers, and retired sea captains had already started to move away from the cluttered, unsightly, and decidedly smelly district around the waterfront and the Town Dock. The prosperous began having new homes built farther away, in such areas as the South End and the West End, which soon became fashionable residential districts with substantial brick buildings and carefully cultivated gardens.

A young architect who was most instrumental in effecting many of the changes that came about during the late 1790s was Charles Bulfinch. Son of a prominent Boston physician, and a graduate of the Boston Latin School and Harvard College, the young man worked in a countinghouse before setting out for a two-year tour of Europe, where he was struck by the beauty and ingenuity of town planning in Paris. When he later visited England, he was also impressed by the architectural work of Sir Christopher Wren in London, as well as the stylistic designs of the Adam brothers in the town of Bath. On his return to Boston in 1787, he began to apply many of these ideas to the layout and appearance of his hometown in such a vigorous and comprehensive fashion that almost single-handedly he came close to transforming the whole tone and character of the town.

For a period of time, Bulfinch designed several handsome mansions in the West End for prominent citizens such as Harrison Gray Otis, Samuel Parkman, and Thomas Amory, who were anxious to move away from the congested waterfront district. He then went on to become involved in a number of local commercial enterprises, designing a series of warehouses, wharves, and shops along the waterfront district in the area of Long Wharf, at the end of State Street. In addition to individual structures, Bulfinch also experimented with more comprehensive real-estate developments. In 1793, in an area behind Summer Street, he built a block of connected town houses along Franklin Street in a curved unit called the Tontine Crescent. Seven years later, he built another row of attached town houses, known as Colonnade Row, that extended along Tremont Street directly across from the Boston Common Mall. Although Bulfinch lost money on both the Tontine Crescent and Colonnade Row, each of these commercial ventures served to redefine and reenergize certain parts of the town.

Perhaps the most distinctive and memorable addition Charles Bulfinch made to the Boston townscape was his design of the new State House, as well as his architectural influence on the subsequent development of the whole Beacon Hill area. After the Revolution, Bostonians had continued to use the old provincial Town House, on what was now called State Street, for the conduct of state business; but it was clear that the citizenry wanted a new state house of their own to which the memories and fixtures of British sovereignty were no longer attached. In 1795, two years after the death of John Hancock, town leaders purchased Hancock's pastureland on the slope of Beacon Hill as the site for a new state office building and selected young Bulfinch as architect for the project. In 1798 he completed his new State House, providing the town with an impressive red-brick building with white marble trim, a long flight of stone steps, a series of white Ionic columns, and an imposing dome that would eventually become a distinctive landmark for Boston.

Awareness that the new Capitol would be constructed on Beacon Hill immediately produced other changes in the rustic surroundings of nearby Park Street and Tremont Street, where hay carts rumbled and cattle still grazed.

Within a dozen years, sparked by the town's new postwar prosperity, the whole area was in the midst of rapid development that was transforming the old Puritan town of wood and thatch into a new Federal capital of stone and granite. One particularly dramatic change came about when a group of investors, calling themselves the Mount Vernon Proprietors, bought up the extensive Beacon Hill farmlands belonging to the well-known portrait painter, John Singleton Copley, who had gone off to England during the Revolution to avoid the painful family divisions that came from the separation from Great Britain. With Copley still on the other side of the Atlantic, the proprietors proceeded to use his extensive parcel of land to transform the southwest slope of the hill into a new residential district. After laying out a system of streets to accommodate blocks of town houses, in the summer of 1799 the investors lopped off fifty or sixty feet from the top of Mount Vernon with the use of small gravity cars that dumped the fill from the top of the hill into the waters at the foot of Charles Street. As houses began to go up in the new Beacon Hill development, the architectural influence of Charles Bulfinch once again became evident. In addition to the construction of individual dwellings for such prominent figures as Harrison Gray Otis and Stephen Higginson Jr., the young architect also constructed several town houses on Chestnut Street, with stables conveniently located in the rear.

Besides Bulfinch, several other architects contributed to the changing character of the town at the turn of the century. Asher Benjamin, for example, had come in from Western Massachusetts to add to the cluster of new buildings going up in the West End with his construction in 1809 of the West Church on Cambridge Street—a lovely Federal-style structure of red brick, with a belfry that terminated in a dome topped with a weather vane. Benjamin built a second church not too far away on lower Mount Vernon Street, at the corner of Charles Street—the Charles Street Meeting House—another brick structure with a belfry, dome, and weather vane. Also at this time, an Englishman named Peter Banner constructed the Park Street Church on the corner of Park and Tremont Streets, next to the Old Granary Burying Ground. The graceful white steeple of this Congregational church quickly became a landmark in the new area of the town and a permanent feature of Boston's architectural renaissance on the western side of Tremont Street. All these new private residences, public buildings, marketplaces, warehouses, town houses, and churches not only provided the old town with a neighborhood of sturdy and impressive structures, but they also emphasized the fact that Boston was moving into a more prosperous and substantial period of its historical existence. With a body of highly respected members of the local Federalist elite in control of public affairs, a rapidly increasing population swelling the size of the town, and a thriving mercantile economy fueling physical growth and reconstruction, the leaders of Boston had every right to feel that their own future was secure and that the town's permanence was well established.

Despite the confident national spirit, the upsurge in the local economy, the increase in population, and the new Bulfinch influence, there were very few signs that the town of Boston was preparing to move beyond its comfortable colonial traditions, or become anything other than the colonial seaport town it had always been. Even by 1800, observed the historian Henry Adams, Boston had changed very little "in appearance, habits, and style from what it had been under its old king." The town's notoriously crooked lanes and narrow streets were still paved with cobblestones and separated from the carriageways only by posts and gutters, according to Adams, and the lack of anything like adequate lighting made walking at night not only difficult but downright dangerous. Most of its citizens retained a town mentality, and still followed the lead of their old-time Federalists leaders who exercised considerable authority in debates, elections, and town meetings, not so much because of any organized party system, but as a result of their standing in the community as men of wealth, culture, and respectability. The town itself continued to be managed by selectmen, the elected instruments of the town meetings, whose "jealousy of granting power," as Adams put it, was even greater than their objection to spending money for what needed to be done.

Thus, the citizens of the town tended to follow the old ways and the old fashions as if nothing had changed. According to young Dr. John Collins Warren, who had just returned from Europe in 1800 to begin his practice in town, gentlemen in Boston still dressed in colored coats, figured waistcoats, short breeches that buttoned at the knee, long boots with white tops, ruffled shirts, and fancy wristbands, with cocked hats and powdered wigs for the older generation. Many years later, William Henry Channing still recalled how, as a boy, he would watch with awe as his seventy-year-old grandfather (Stephen Higginson) came down to breakfast every morning in his long robe, read his daily newspaper (quite literally the autocrat at his breakfast table), and then prepared to confront the world. After shaving himself with elaborate care, he would have his wife comb his hair, powder his wig, and then help him squeeze into his long black stockings and his short tight breeches. Suitably attired in his black frock coat, he would put on his broad-brimmed hat, grasp his gold-headed cane, and step out of his house and into his polished carriage to join his friends at the Exchange to discuss the latest return on their investments. It was a time when the leaders of Boston had every right to assume that God was in his heaven and that all was right with the world—and with theirs.

God may have been in his heaven, but increasingly, in a Boston that would change more rapidly than anyone could have imagined, that august and almighty figure was being viewed in a much different light from that of previous generations when a strict Calvinist theology had shaped the religious views of the Massachusetts Bay Colony. For generations, Congregational ministers had always preached a wrathful God of terrible judgment, a humankind born into sin and corruption, and a doctrine of predestination wherein God alone had already decided who would be saved (the "elect," the "saints") and who would be sent to the fires of eternal damnation (the "damned").

Increasingly, however, these dark and depressing predictions were unable to keep pace with the democratic spirit of the new nation, and with the natural optimism of a people who had carved a civilization out of the wilderness, defeated a world power, and secured their own national independence. Americans were extremely and rightly proud of the great things that they had accomplished and could no longer conceive of themselves as depraved sinners doomed to eternal damnation by the whim of a vengeful God. Similarly, in the new American Republic where citizens worked together in common cause and fraternal harmony, and where Almighty God was seen as a helpful and essentially benevolent figure ("In God We Trust"), it seemed there must be a more enlightened and democratic road to salvation, on which everyone would be able to enjoy the blessings of life and the promise of salvation. Somehow, the depressing views of mankind expressed by the likes of Cotton Mather now rang hollow to many Americans who had pledged their lives, their fortunes, and their sacred honor in defense of a public declaration that boldly announced that "all men" were created equal.

The progressive impulse away from the pessimistic concepts of Calvinist orthodoxy was influenced not only by the remarkable achievements of

American history, but also by the growing rationalism of the New Science that had begun to permeate much of the thinking and reading world. Throughout the early colonial period, there had been no question that God was the Creator of the universe, and the sole arbiter of the ways in which that universe worked. The darkness and the light, the sun and the moon, the oceans and the lands, the birds and the beasts, the first man and women, all came directly from the hand of God who had created everything, and who ruled over it all with personal direction and infinite care. Any extraordinary natural catastrophes—lightning, hurricanes, floods, droughts—were signs of the Lord's displeasure and usually called for periods of public prayer and days of fasting and abstinence. At the same time, episodes of sin and wickedness—melancholy, madness, witchcraft, diabolic possession—were also given a supernatural explanation, usually attributed to the work of Satan himself or various forms of witches, imps, demons, and other evil creatures who roamed the countryside seeking the corruption of souls.

By the early 1700s, however, some of the new and revolutionary scientific theories of Sir Isaac Newton (1642–1727) began to find their way into the American colonies, especially those with a high rate of literacy, raising unsettling questions about established orthodox beliefs. Although Newton conceded the fact that God had created the initial elements of matter and motion that constituted the universe, he also insisted that God had established certain natural laws that governed the universe and explained the way in which it operated. Newton claimed that human beings, through their own natural powers and scientific observations, could come to know and understand the natural laws (such as the laws of motion and gravity) that controlled the universe. In a colony like Massachusetts, where a number of prominent people were already involved in such scientific disciplines as astronomy and mathematics because of their obvious importance to the study of navigation, many of these new ideas were hospitably received. Some of those who followed Newton's theories were called "deists" because, although they still believed in the existence of God, they referred to him by such titles as the First Cause or the Grand Architect (the Declaration of Independence refers to "the Creator" and the "Supreme Judge"), convinced that after the initial act of creation, the Almighty no longer "interfered" with the natural operations of the universe or the mundane affairs of His human creatures. As a result of such ideas, many rationalists argued that something like Divine Revelation was not scientifically possible, and that the Bible, while still an inspirational document, could no longer be regarded as the literal word of God.

In accepting the importance of human reason, and conceiving of a truly Godly community that would operate in a rational, orderly manner in accordance with the natural laws designed by the Almighty, a new religious movement of the early 1800s sought to combine a traditional Christian orthodoxy with a more enlightened view of the human experience—liberal concepts that were perhaps best expressed in the local Boston area in the eloquent sermons of a local minister named William Ellery Channing. Born in the seaport town of Newport, Rhode Island, in 1780, Channing's grandfather had signed the Declaration of Independence, and Channing himself, as a boy of seven, was present when Rhode Island had ratified the Constitution of the United States. His optimistic view of human nature, therefore, was based in great part on his personal witness of what most of his fellow citizens regarded as the astounding success of the American experience. After graduating from Harvard College in 1798, and spending a year and a half as a tutor for a family in Richmond, Virginia, he then returned to Cambridge to work on his religious studies. Ordained to the Congregational ministry in 1803, Channing was installed as minister of Boston's Federal Street Church, where he remained until his death forty years later. Despite the strict orthodoxy of his early theological training, Channing was described by one writer as a "Broad Churchman" who accepted Christianity as a way of life, and wanted only to persuade others to follow in the same manner. He "breathed into theology a humane spirit," according to the inscription on the statue later erected in his honor in the Boston Public Garden. In his own reading of the Christian scriptures, Channing could find no justification for the old Calvinist–Puritan belief in a jealous and judgmental God, a debased and iniquitous humanity, or a form of predestination that limited salvation only to the members of the elect. "We cannot bow before a being, however great, who governs tyrannically," he declared preaching, instead, a gospel that emphasized the beneficence of God, the essential goodness and perfectibility of human beings, and the ability of all souls to attain salvation. "God has given us a rational nature," he wrote, "and will call us to account for it." Because they insisted on upholding the unity of God, instead of the more complex mystery of the Trinity that many of their members regarded as inconsistent with reason, Channing and his supporters were referred to as Unitarians.

Although Channing at first hesitated to form a new and separate denomination, the popularity of his liberal ideas, and the remarkable speed with which they circulated, led him to adopt the new movement and become its leader. In 1820, he published an article, "The Moral Argument against Calvinism," in which he defended his concepts as an essential part of the Christian tradition. He made clear that the debate over the question of the Trinity was not so much an argument about the nature of God, but more about the Calvinist doctrine of the depravity of human beings—a belief that Channing rejected entirely. "Man is God's child, made in his image and object of his love," he wrote; "his reason and conscience are divine witness to truth and light. . . ." A sign that the days of the old orthodox establishment were numbered came in 1805, when, after a heated argument among the Overseers, a Unitarian named Henry Ware was appointed to the Hollis Chair of Divinity at Harvard College, an indication that Congregationalism as a leading intellectual and theological force was fast becoming a thing of the past. In the course of the decade, nearly all the Congregational pulpits in and around Boston were taken over by Unitarian preachers. While the eloquent William Ellery Channing was enunciating his gospel of the "adoration of goodness" at the Federal Street Church, Nathaniel Frothingham was at the First Church; John Gorham Palfrey, historian and future Dexter Professor of Sacred Literature, served at the Brattle Street Unitarian Church; and Francis Parkman held forth at the New North. When the conservative Presbyterian minister Lyman Beecher moved to Boston in 1816, he expressed his disappointment at what had taken place: "All the literary men of Massachusetts were Unitarian; all the trustees and professors at Harvard College were Unitarian; all the elite of wealth and fashion crowded Unitarian churches." By the time the American Unitarian Association was formed in 1826, there were already 120 churches of the new denomination in Massachusetts, including 20 of the 25 oldest Calvinist churches in the United States.

At almost the same time that many old-time Boston families were bemoaning the disturbing changes taking place in their most cherished religious beliefs, the defeat of John Adams of Massachusetts and the overthrow of the Federalist Party in November 1800 by Thomas Jefferson and his Democratic–Republicans caused even further consternation in their conservative ranks. Many New Englanders feared that Jefferson's strong states'-rights views, together with his strict-construction views of Constitutional issues, would completely dismantle Alexander Hamilton's carefully contrived system of centralized national authority and orderly political structures. The Virginian's outspoken animosity toward a national banking system, his restrictive views on taxation and appropriations, his high regard for the agrarian way of life, and his outspoken opposition to "the mobs of great cities," and to manufacturing in any form ("let our workshops remain in Europe," he insisted) raised grave concerns about the effects Democratic national policy would have upon the financial future of New England. Jefferson's sympathy for developments in revolutionary France, his "atheistic" views concerning the traditions of Christianity, and his "radical" and "foreign" philosophies regarding the virtues of republican government raised serious fears that the political process would be overrun by masses of uneducated and inexperienced people who would ruin the American democratic experiment. Many New Englanders were predicting that the success of Thomas Jefferson and his political party, already increasing in power throughout the South and West, meant the inevitable end of the Bay State as an influential player on the national scene.

The worst fears of the Federalists concerning the pro-French foreign policy of the Republicans were realized in 1812 when, over their persistent protests, Jefferson's successor, President James Madison, successfully urged both houses of Congress to declare war against Great Britain. It was a conflict that maritime New England had feared from the start, correctly anticipating that, with the outbreak of fighting, English maritime power would sweep the seas clean of Yankee shipping and completely destroy the commercial economy that Bostonians had worked so hard to rebuild in the years after the Revolution. Federalist leaders throughout New England publicly opposed what they contemptuously called "Jimmy Madison's War" from the very start, and refused to supply either men or money to support a conflict they regarded as both unjust and immoral. The lower house of the Massachusetts General Court issued an address urging the American people to organize a new peace party and "let all other party distinctions vanish." Governor Caleb Strong followed up by proclaiming a public fast in order to atone for a declaration of war "against a nation from which we are descended and which, for many generations, has been the bulwark of the religion we profess." Most of the old Boston families supported the governor's antiwar stance, and members of the Harvard Corporation, including President John Kirkland himself, announced themselves in agreement with the antiwar position taken by most of the leading Federalist spokesmen in the area. Although a complete disaster did not occur at once, the British naval blockade gradually took its inevitable toll. By the close of 1813, only five American vessels had cleared from Boston Harbor, which was choked with some two-hundred-fifty vessels of all sorts swinging idly on their rusting anchor chains. British squadrons regularly patrolled the whole New England coastline, while enemy frigates set up headquarters at Provincetown and policed the area from Cape Cod to Cape Ann.

Now that maritime activities were no longer profitable sources of investment, Yankee merchants were forced to look elsewhere for new enterprises in which to invest the capital they refused to give to the government to fight the war. Many entrepreneurs shrewdly diverted their surplus capital to the manufacture of cotton textiles rather than continuing to invest in mercantile enterprises which no longer paid dividends. As a result of wartime scarcities, sections of the United States were now forced to go without various types of manufactured goods. Woolens for the white folks, homespun for the children, cotton for the slaves, sheets and shirts, dresses and trousers— all these products, and hundreds of others, were in great demand by consumers in all parts of the country. If there was a demand, New England was ready to supply it. Despite some false starts and early setbacks, a number of makeshift factories were constructed along local waterways, and before long the cotton textile industry expanded rapidly during the war years. "Wheels roll, spindles whirl, and shuttles fly," rhapsodized the *Connecticut Herald*, and a New York newspaper pointed with pride to the fact that President James Madison was seen wearing a coat that was manufactured in Springfield, Massachusetts. The number of spindles in New England had already surpassed the hundred-thousand mark when the United States' second war with Great Britain suddenly came to an end in January 1815.

What started out as a desperate but temporary wartime expedient, quickly turned into a permanent feature of the Bay State economy once the war ended. In 1821, Francis Cabot Lowell, Nathan Appleton, and Patrick Tracy Jackson moved out from their first location at Waltham and established new and much larger plants about 40 miles west of Boston, where powerful waterfalls were located along the Merrimack River. Here they set up a distinctive type of company town called Lowell, which included boardinghouses for the workers and elaborate forms of supervision of the young women (called the "Mill Girls") who came in from nearby farms to work in the factories. The acceptance of manufacturing as a permanent feature of

THE TEXTILE INDUSTRY

The British blockade of America's Atlantic ports during the War of 1812 forced Boston's wealthy merchants to divert their idle capital into textile manufacturing rather than into mercantile enterprises that no longer paid dividends. By the 1830s, what had started as a small, localized operation had mushroomed into a multimillion-dollar industry that utilized mechanical power, capital finance, and corporate management. (Courtesy, Bostonian Society/Old State House) the American economy was accomplished, not only because of the profits it generated, but also because of what was seen as its importance to national security. Letting our workshops "remain in Europe," as Thomas Jefferson had insisted for so long, sounded wonderfully idyllic—so long as there was peace. Once the country found itself at war for a second time with a major power like Great Britain, however, it was evident that the United States needed its own manufacturing system to provide the guns and goods necessary to defend itself. The War of 1812 had been a frightening demonstration of how national security was directly related to an independent industrial system. And when it was all over, even Jefferson was forced to admit, somewhat grudgingly, that "manufactures are now necessary to our independence as well as to our comfort."

The new factory system not only provided the Bay State with what would prove to be a multimillion-dollar industry, but it also helped create a new aristocracy of wealth and power as members of the old mercantile families of Boston, who had grown rich on the commercial profits of the West Indies and the Far East ("old money"), now began to merge with those who made their profits ("new money") in the manufacture of cotton cloth and fancy fabrics. By the late 1820s, there developed a cohesive group of about forty Boston families who became collectively known as the Boston Associates. Starting out with textile mills in Newton and Waltham, and then expanding their operations along the Merrimac River at places like Lowell and Lawrence, the Associates eventually took a commanding interest in virtually all the major textile industries in northern New England. By 1850, according to historian Robert Dalzell, they controlled about one-fifth of all cotton spindles in the United States. Not content with simply making money in textiles and shipping, the Associates invested their capital extensively in real estate, insurance, banking, railroading, and other enterprises. All the Boston banks, for example, with the exception of the Commonwealth Bank, were managed by members of the Boston Associates. The same men also directed the Boston & Albany, the Boston & Maine, the Boston & Lowell, and all other major railroad lines that radiated from Boston during the antebellum years. With their financial holdings and their extensive economic interests, it is not surprising that the Boston Associates came to wield considerable political control as well. They would dominate city government, control the State House, and see their conservative Whig interests in Washington ably represented by the state's two U.S. Senators, Edward Everett and Daniel Webster.

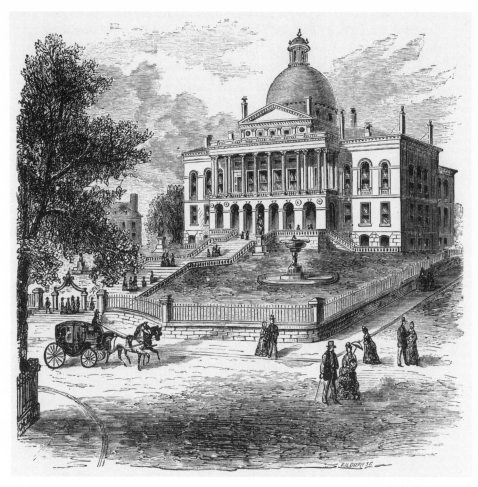

STATE HOUSE

The handsome new State House, designed by Charles Bulfinch and completed in 1798, generated the new and fashionable community of Beacon Hill. Taking up residence in the elegant red-brick houses in Louisburg Square and Mount Vernon Street, wealthy families like the Lowells, the Lawrences, and the Appletons further integrated their financial relationships through the powerful agency of kinship and marriage. (Courtesy, Bostonian Society/Old State House)

At the same time they were assuming a leading role in the business affairs of the Bay State, the Boston Associates further augmented their dominance through the powerful agencies of kinship and marriage. When he first set out to establish the Boston Manufacturing Company, Francis Cabot Lowell turned for support to his Cabot relatives, as well as to his wife's brother, Patrick Tracy Jackson, whose sister he would marry. John Amory Lowell's son married Nathan Appleton's daughter; Nathan Appleton became Thomas Jefferson Coolidge's father-in-law; young Amos Adams Lawrence married Nathan Appleton's niece. Partners in industry and colleagues in business, heirs to old shipping fortunes, and amassers of new factory money, they now became part of the same extended family circle, living in close proximity to one another in their elegant mansions on Beacon Hill. Out of what historian Samuel Eliot Morison has described as a marriage between "the wharf and the waterfall" came a new Boston aristocracy whose members Oliver Wendell Holmes labeled as the "Brahmins," and who could be identified by their "houses by Bulfinch, their monopoly of Beacon Hill, their ancestral portraits and Chinese porcelains, humanitarianism, Unitarian faith in the march of the mind, Yankee shrewdness, and New England exclusiveness." Like the Brahmin caste of the ancient Hindus, who performed the sacred rites and set the moral standards, the new leaders of Boston society emerged as the self-styled Brahmins of a modern caste system in which they were clearly and indisputably the superior force. By diversifying their investments and buying into all kinds of new enterprises, many of the Boston Associates had found that manufacturing offered a much more secure and stable way of life than anticipating the uncertainties of trade, thus affording them a greater amount of leisure time to patronize the arts and engage in philanthropic and humanitarian activities. They were able not only to furnish generous sums of money to such institutions as the Boston Athenaeum, the Massachusetts Historical Society, King's Chapel, and Massachusetts General Hospital, but also to serve personally and actively as trustees and directors for colleges, boarding schools, hospitals, asylums, libraries, museums, and other cultural institutions.

One practical result of this revival and diversification of Boston's fortunes —and especially the influx of new young blood into old Yankee veins—was a renewed sense of obligation on the part of older families to preserve the welfare and safeguard the interests of "their" town, and a renewed determination to participate actively once again in local political affairs. Just because the rest of the nation had lost its bearings and lowered its standards was no reason that Boston could not be saved. All it would require would be for members of "the more fortunate class" to take over their hereditary responsibilities and regain positions of social and political leadership in the community. Coming to the realization that the end of Congregationalism did not necessarily mean the end of moral principles or ethical standards, many families accepted the more liberal theology of Unitarianism as a happy medium between the old hell-fire-and-brimstone approach of Calvinism and the more science-oriented views of deists who saw no need of an organized religion at all. After a short time, Unitarianism was regarded as the best of two worlds—a religion that accepted the lessons of scientific reason, while still acknowledging the traditions of Boston's Puritan religious heritage. On Sundays, members of the Lawrence family would join with Nathan Hale, nephew of the famous Revolutionary spy, Harrison Gray Otis, and various members of the Perkins family, walk down Beacon Hill, make their way around the Congregational church at the junction of Park and Tremont Streets, and arrive at the Unitarian church at Brattle Street. There they could settle back in their pews and absorb what they deemed a more reasonable and intellectual approach to the Christian spirit—a theology that Ralph Waldo Emerson later caustically described as "the best diagonal line that can be drawn between Jesus Christ and Abbott Lawrence."

In similar fashion, once they had survived the initial shock of the Jeffersonian revolution, with its radical ideas about curbing industry and promoting popular democracy, a younger generation of Federalists still saw opportunities for political influence. At first glance, the refusal of New England to support the Madison administration in fighting the War of 1812, and especially the machinations of the Essex Junto, a group of Massachusetts extremists who considered seceding from the Union and forming a separate Northern confederacy, seemed to have destroyed the old Federalist party as an effective political organization. The changing character of national politics, however, offered new possibilities for advancement. The postwar spirit of nationalism was enhanced by the fact that there was now only one political party—increasingly referred to as the National Republican Party—that dramatized the new sense of national unity and harmony, causing the immediate postwar decade to go down in history as the Era of Good Feelings. With the growth of national pride and a heightened sense of national security, Jefferson's old states'-rights, agrarian, hard-money party, was quickly transformed into a much more modern and federalized organization that advocated central banking, higher tariffs, manufacturing, and strong national security.

The new National Republican Party, however, was far from being as unified and harmonious as it appeared on the surface. It was actually made up of such a variety of conflicting conservative and democratic factions within the different states that it proved unable to survive the fierce political rivalries that followed the end of James Madison's second term as president in 1824. From several states came a number of "favorite sons" eager to fill the political vacuum created by departure of the last member of the original generation of Founding Fathers. John C. Calhoun of South Carolina represented the plantation South; Henry Clay of Kentucky spoke for the interests of the West; William H. Crawford was a seasoned politician from Georgia; and Andrew Jackson of Tennessee, the hero of New Orleans, made his venture into national politics. For the voters of Massachusetts, however, the candidate who stood out above all others was John Quincy Adams. Not only was he the son of a former president, but he had considerable experience in both government administration, having served eight years as Madison's Secretary of State, and in foreign affairs, was reputed to have been the real author of the Monroe Doctrine. The election of Adams would not only provide the nation with a statesman of background, education, and experience, but would also restore the influence of Massachusetts in the highest councils of the land.

Although Andrew Jackson actually received the highest number of electoral votes (99) in the election of 1824, with Adams polling 84 votes, Crawford 41, and Clay 37, Jackson did not acquire the majority of votes necessary for election. The contest, therefore, was sent into the House of Representatives, where Clay eventually persuaded his supporters to give his 37 votes to Adams—making the Massachusetts candidate the sixth President of the United States. When Adams subsequently appointed Henry Clay his Secretary of State, however, disgruntled Jackson supporters immediately raised the cry of "Corrupt Bargain," charging that Adams had paid off Clay with an office that virtually assured his future accession to the presidency. Proclaiming Clay to be the "Judas of the West," the Jackson people claimed that it was impossible for any Western candidate to win against the entrenched power of the Eastern political interests until a new party—a truly "democratic" party—was organized, a party in which the representatives of the common people would receive fair and equal treatment. The Jackson supporters split away from the National Republican Party, organized the Democratic Party, and began preparing for the next election.

For the moment, however, New Englanders could ignore the clamor of mean-spirited political rivals, in the comfortable assurance that John Quincy Adams was in the White House and would surely turn things around. The news of Adams's election in 1824 was greeted with great celebrations in Boston by citizens who rejoiced that the country was in the capable hands of a president who would restore to the government in Washington those moral values and political principles so greatly admired by conservative New England. And these hopes and dreams seemed more than realized when President Adams, in his first message to Congress the following year, laid out an impressive blueprint for national development. The central government, he announced, would not only promote internal improvements, reform the patents laws, create a Department of the Interior, and pass laws to promote agriculture, commerce, and industry, but would also be responsible for establishing a national university, financing scientific expeditions, and establishing astronomical observatories he called "lighthouses of the skies." Convinced that the arts and the sciences were essential to the Republic's well-being, he called upon the government to encourage the mechanical and the "elegant" arts, to advance the cause of literature, and to oversee the progress of the sciences, both "ornamental and profound." It was, to be sure, a remarkable vision of federal activism, but one so grandiose in scope and elaborate in design that it was doomed from the very start, especially since Adams himself lacked the common touch and the political deftness to carry it through successfully. To his critics, including the elderly Thomas Jefferson, Adam's sweeping proposals to enhance the powers of the federal government, neglect the role of the states, and ignore the sovereignty of the people, proved that the Massachusetts statesman was out to establish a "splendid government of an aristocracy" along the same lines as Alexander Hamilton's old Federalist system. It would not do. As Adams went into the final years of office, it became painfully clear that his conservative New England precepts and policies were rejected by a nation that was moving in a different and more democratic direction.

Final proof that New England would be unable to influence the course of national history through political means came with the results of the election of 1828. Down to the last minute, old Federalists and new National Republicans never wavered in their support for John Quincy Adams and

JOHN QUINCY ADAMS

Son of the second President of the United States, John Quincy Adams came to the presidency himself in 1824 with a distinguished family heritage, a reputation for learning and erudition, and a political background that included extensive foreign travel as well as nearly eight years as President Monroe's Secretary of State. Adams's defeat by Democratic candidate Andrew Jackson in 1828 dashed the hopes of many New Englanders that Boston would set the cultural standards for the nation's future. (Courtesy, Bostonian Society/Old State House) clung to their conviction that American voters would reject the outrageous pretensions of a brawler, a duelist, and an adulterer like Andrew Jackson. On election day, November 3, 1828, the *Bunker Hill Aurora* assured its readers that Adams would sweep the New England states and win a sufficient number of the Middle Atlantic states to ensure victory. The *Boston Courier*, too, promised a solid conservative vote for the Bay State candidate. "Politically speaking," wrote editor and publisher Joseph T. Buckingham, "we are Federalists to the backbone, Hartford Convention to the core!" When the Boston votes were totaled, the *Boston Daily Advertiser* announced that John Quincy Adams had easily trounced Jackson by a one-sided vote of 3,112 to 838; ten days later the paper reported happily that Adams had carried all of Massachusetts. When the votes finally came in from all the states, however, the conservatives of Massachusetts could hardly believe that John Quincy Adams had been defeated, and that Andrew Jackson had been elected President of the United States by an electoral vote of 178 to 83. Adams had taken all of New England, it was true (except for one of Maine's 9 electoral votes), 16 of the 36 votes from New York, and 6 of the 11 Maryland votes. All the rest, however, had gone to the man from Tennessee.

The defeat of John Quincy Adams came as a crushing blow to all New England, with a clear realization that the new populism that had been ushered in with the election of Thomas Jefferson in 1800 had not been a temporary aberration but, as reaffirmed by the election of Andrew Jackson, a permanent part of the future political direction of the nation. Already distraught at the swift and unexpected collapse of the old Congregational orthodoxy and the rejection of those clear moral imperatives that Calvinism had always proclaimed, Boston's conservative Federalist establishment could hardly conceive of living under a political culture in which the qualities of birth, family, education, culture, and social status would no longer determine the standards of the nation's future leaders and statesmen. Under these circumstances, how could Boston continue to proclaim itself as a City Upon a Hill in the midst of secular views and mediocre accomplishments? Indeed, what was the future of Boston itself when it appeared obvious that its moral standards and social values were no longer regarded by the rest of the country as worthy of respect or emulation?

CHAPTER 2 } FROM TOWN TO CITY

"In choosing Old Hickory over John Quincy Adams in the election of 1828," observes Harlow Sheidley in her 1998 study *Sectional Nationalism*, "the nation rejected the political ethos of New England conservatives in favor of an expansive, individualistic, and competitive political order." Realizing that Jackson's election had put an end to any hopes they had of influencing the nation's future by political means, members of New England's conservative leadership concluded that it would be necessary for them to "mobilize culture where politics failed," and set out to establish Boston as the cultural standard by which national progress would henceforth be measured.

The first step toward this objective would be to firmly reestablish the traditional political leadership of their class in the public affairs of their town. In the past, Federalist leaders really did not need the mechanism of a political party as such, because they were so well known, and exuded such great personal authority, simply as a result of being patricians of wealth, talent, and respectability. Members of a younger generation of conservatives, however, men like Harrison Gray Otis, a successful merchant who had been active in local politics, and Josiah Quincy, a former U.S. congressman recently appointed to a seat on the Boston municipal bench, decided to adopt a more realistic attitude and appeal to the newly enfranchised mass electorate in a new and more "democratic" fashion. Although there is little doubt that these members of old Boston families still believed in the leadership of "the wise, the well-born, and the good," they had come to accept the idea of an enlarged electorate as regrettable but inevitable. They concentrated their efforts, therefore, on trying to reach out to the lower- and middle-class voters—the small businessmen, merchants, tradesmen, shopkeepers, innkeepers, chandlers, artisans, and craftsmen whose numbers had increased during the years of postrevolutionary prosperity. Their challenge was to convince these working people that the members of the town's upper classes, with their education, their high ideals, their exalted virtues, and their substantial incomes, could contribute far more to the social and economic well-being of the working people of the town than the Johnny-come-lately Jeffersonian Republicans who were only seeking political power and financial profit. In contrast to their elders, many of whom still refused to engage in the distasteful give-and-take of political campaigning (a proper Boston gentleman usually did not "run" for public office—he "offered himself" for the post), the younger breed of Federalists showed an appreciation of the importance of party politics, the power of the popular vote, and the influence of public opinion.

Pitching their appeals to the members of Boston's rising working class, often referred to as the "Middling Interest," the young Federalists emphasized the responsibility of the "happy and respectable classes" to watch over those laws that affected "the less prosperous portions of the community." Their obvious desire for political control of Boston carried with it a sense of responsibility for the prosperity of the town as a whole, and the welfare of its less fortunate inhabitants—a sort of moral stewardship, a form of noblesse oblige—that would continue to be an integral part of Boston's conservative political heritage well into the twentieth century. This arrangement would not only help the upper classes establish themselves permanently in positions of power, but would also condition the lower classes to emulate the moral, social, and political values of the Brahmin themselves, and thus became an unconscious part of that tradition. Conservative Bostonians might not be capable any longer of controlling national politics and saving people in the rest of the country from the "democratic" claptrap of Thomas Jefferson and the egalitarian nonsense of Andrew Jackson and his followers, but they could still use their talents and resources to keep Boston a model of the kind of moral superiority and intellectual excellence originally envisioned by John Winthrop in his celebrated "City Upon a Hill."

As part of their new efforts to position themselves at the head of local government, the young conservatives threw their support and encouragement behind what had been, for many years since independence, an on-and-off movement to transform Boston from a town to a city. To many politically conscious residents, it had become increasingly obvious that with an expanding economic structure and a rising population, the old town-meeting system was simply incapable of dealing effectively with the demands of what was clearly no longer a colonial seaport town, but a growing and more complex urban center. Dilapidated buildings needed to be razed and new ones erected; the lighting and paving of streets required immediate municipal attention; a fresh-water supply was a matter of serious concern, as was a more effective system for cleaning the streets and disposing of garbage. Even more important, the recent growth in the town's population pointed up the critical lack of adequate police and fire protection for the general public. Efforts to come up with a new form of city government to relieve these problems, however, met with the inertia of town leaders who were dedicated to the old way of doing things, the opposition of board members who were determined to spend as little tax money as possible, and the suspicions of working-class interests who feared that a strong executive system would result in the loss of their rights and liberties. And the character of the town meetings themselves provided little opportunity for serious discussion or civil debate. Attendance at the meetings was sporadic at best, and chaotic at worst. Either a mere handful of concerned citizens would show up at meetings when the agenda was fairly routine or, in cases where the agenda contained controversial items, the room would be so crowded, and the noise would become so great, that it was impossible to get any work accomplished or any issues resolved. Young members of the town's conservative leadership, conscious of the rapidly changing patterns of party politics, could readily see that a modernized form of city government would not only provide a more effective mechanism for dealing with the issues that required immediate attention, but would also provide a more centralized structure of management better suited to their own sense of political control.

When the question of a new charter of incorporation was raised again in 1821, it became the subject of heated debate in a series of packed meetings at Faneuil Hall that continued for three days. Despite prolonged and passionate arguments against changing the name of the "Towne of Boston," which had produced "our glorious revolution," and which had seen its narrow streets "died with blood," this time the vote in favor of incorporation was accepted by the populace on January 7, 1822. The state legislature passed the new charter, and a month later Governor John Brooks officially approved "an act establishing the City of Boston." This act provided that the administration of all the "fiscal, prudential, and municipal concerns" of the city would be vested in "one principal officer" called the Mayor, a committee of eight persons called the Board of Aldermen, and a council of forty-eight persons called the Common Council. An official city seal, designed by John Penniman, showed a view of the city from South Boston point, and incorporated a motto from the Book of Kings: "*Sit Deus nobiscum sicut fuit cum patribus nobis.*" Adapted for the city seal, the motto reads: "*Sicut Patribus, Sit Deus Nobis*"—"As God was to our Fathers, so may He be to us."

With the formalities out of the way, the city turned to the task of electing its first mayor. At this point, the political interest and influence of the conservatives in the creation of a new city government became immediately evident. One branch of the Federalist leadership put up fifty-seven-year-old Harrison Gray Otis as its candidate, while the so-called Middling Interest of the town favored the more activist Josiah Quincy as their nominee. When neither side could claim the required majority, the voters settled on John Phillips, a graduate of Harvard College and a member of an old Boston mercantile family. Phillips was not in particularly good health, however, and after completing his one-year term of office, he retired from public service, leaving the field to Josiah Quincy, who was elected the second mayor of Boston in 1823 and went on to seize the reins of government with such vigor and determination that he eventually became known as the "Great Mayor." Born in the town of Braintree to a distinguished colonial family, Quincy graduated from Harvard College in 1790, and served as a Federalist member of the U.S. Congress from 1805 to 1813, where he railed against the War of 1812. Returning to Boston from Washington, he served in the Massachusetts Senate from 1813 to 1820, and then took a seat as Justice of the Suffolk Municipal Court until his election as mayor of Boston in 1823. Serving six consecutive one-year terms from 1823 to 1828, Josiah Quincy established a program of urban planning and city development that few mayors have been able to duplicate.

In Josiah Quincy's day, Boston was still an impressive city to look at from a distance—especially to anyone coming into the harbor by ship. "Boston, rising up as it were, out of the water, makes a fine display whatever point it is approached," wrote Mrs. Anne Royall of Maryland, in the course of an extensive tour of the United States during the mid-1820s. The great wharves that stretched far out into the water were surrounded by large four-story brick storehouses. All were uniform in height, with streets on either side for unloading the commercial cargoes that came into town from all parts of the world. The visitor's eyes would be immediately attracted to the lofty dome of the new State House in the background, high atop Beacon Hill, and then be drawn to the irregular cluster of domes and spires that rose above the pointed gables and jutting chimney tops of the dwellings. The spire of the Old North Church, the cupola of Faneuil Hall, and the peaks of a dozen other public buildings, together with the graceful white spires of the numerous churches and meetinghouses scattered throughout the city, gave the low-lying seaport town the appearance of height and spaciousness.

Once ashore, however, closer inspection would reveal that the passage of time had taken a heavy toll on this venerable town, now more than two hundred years old. There were, to be sure, many charming reminders of the colonial times—along the tree-lined avenues of Pearl Street, High Street, and Summer Street, there were still handsome residences of prominent Bostonians, landscaped with colorful bushes, lovely orchards, and well-tended gardens. With the reclaiming of the farmland around the new Bulfinch State House, blocks of elegant mansions had gone up on the north side of Beacon Street, and along Tremont Street the attractive town houses of Colonnade Row provided attractive quarters from which more of the town's well-to-do merchants and businessmen could look across to the peaceful fields of the Boston Common.

Within the heart of the old town, however, especially along the crowded waterfront district and the congested area of the Town Dock, where John Winthrop's little band of Puritans had first settled some two hundred years earlier, things had deteriorated badly over the years. With a total population of nearly 43,000 people—already 25,000 more than in 1790—Boston's limited confines were showing the strains. Its meandering streets had always been notoriously crooked and narrow, but now they were hedged in by four- and five-story buildings that blocked out the sunlight and obscured the view. Pedestrians making their way into this part of town were in constant danger of being knocked down by stagecoaches, or bowled over by droves of pigs being hustled along the narrow streets on their way to the central market. On what were called "high market days," the congested Faneuil Hall Market district was a compressed, discordant mass of people, with butchers cutting their meat along the first floor of the building itself, vendors of fruits and vegetables lined up under wooden sheds along the outside walls, and fishmongers stationed behind long wooden benches with large tubs filled with all kinds of seafood.

What was new about this market scene—an integral part of Boston's downtown life for generations—was the abominable stench that now rose above it all. Not only the oily smells from the docks along the waterfront, the briny tang of saltwater, and the sickening odor of the mudflats at low tide wafted there, but also the repulsive reek of uncollected street refuse and untended garbage. To make matters worse, the town's sewerage system emptied out into the Town Dock, which was located directly behind the Faneuil Hall Market. This body of water became the stagnant receptacle for every sort of filth, rubbish, and waste. "The Mill Pond is a nuisance, full of putrid fish and dead dogs and cats," complained one Boston constable in his logbook for April 1805. By this time, the stench of the town was no longer confined to the immediate vicinity of the Town Dock or the Faneuil Hall Market district. All through the inner town, the obvious lack of any effective system for cleaning the streets on a regular basis had produced piles of rubbish, "house dirt," and "street dirt" that went uncollected for long periods of time. Open privies, contaminated wells, and pools of rancid water created such dreadful conditions that many of the more prosperous residents had given up on any possibility of saving the old part of town; they were already moving into the West End where young Bulfinch provided them with new houses, or across Tremont Street into the new Beacon Hill area, where a fashionable residential district provided welcome relief from the fetid congestion of the waterfront.

Almost as soon as Josiah Quincy was sworn into office as Boston's second mayor, he announced his determination to take things in hand and proceed against this "generated pestilence." Rich people, he observed in his inaugural address, could always move out of town during the hot summer months and seek refuge in "purer atmospheres." Poor people, on the other hand, were forced to remain in the city and inhale what he called the "noxious effluvia." In a dramatic demonstration of how an upper-class Federalist mayor could work for the welfare of the "less prosperous" classes of the city, Quincy set to work rescuing the oldest part of the city from decay and ruin. Although he ran into stubborn opposition from members of the newly formed Common Council who were alarmed that the new man's "crazy schemes" and grandiose renewal plans would raise the city debt to astronomical heights, Mayor Quincy moved fearlessly ahead, grabbing whatever municipal powers he needed to accomplish his purposes. By appointing himself chairman ex officio of all executive committees, for example, he assumed a controlling voice in all municipal activities and decisions. By appointing professional administrators who reported to him personally, he established a system of direct accountability for what he wanted to accomplish. On June 16, 1823, less than two weeks after taking office, Quincy appointed Benjamin Pollard,

JOSIAH QUINCY

*Elected in 1823 as second Mayor of Boston under the terms of the new City Charter,
Josiah Quincy became known as the "Great Mayor." He set a dramatic example
of how an upper-class Federalist official could work for the welfare of the "less
prosperous" classes of the city by rescuing the oldest part of the city from ruin and
decay. During his six consecutive terms of office, Quincy established a program of
urban planning and city development that few mayors were ever able to duplicate.
(Courtesy, Bostonian Society/Old State House)*

a Harvard graduate and a practicing attorney, Marshal of the City. In that capacity, Pollard was given wide-ranging powers not only to enforce the city's various by-laws and ordinances, but also to supervise the care of the streets, the condition of sewers, and whatever else affected "the health, security, and comfort of the city."

Despite his executive appointments, however, Mayor Quincy made it abundantly evident that he was personally in charge of things. Every morning he was up before daybreak and, after a bracing cold bath and a hearty breakfast, he was out of the house by five o'clock to gallop through the streets of the city on his daily inspection, making sure that his orders were being carried out as he wished. In a remarkably short time, the new mayor was having the streets cleaned by teams of sweepers, had the refuse collected on a regular basis, and brought the sewers under public control. By the end of his first year in office, he could boast of having collected six thousand tons of street dirt (he had it weighed!), making Boston reputedly one of the cleanest, healthiest, and safest cities in the United States. By filling up the Mill Creek, draining the polluted Town Dock, extending the sewer outlets to the mudflats, setting up a new series of seawalls, bringing in landfill, and getting the city to buy up as much dilapidated private property as possible, he was able to cut down on pollution, knock down old houses, and create a new expanse of usable land on which to lay out new streets and widen old ones.

In taking over the management of a city whose population had increased remarkably, and whose buildings had multiplied proportionately, Mayor Quincy was greatly disturbed by the fact that Boston's police and fire protection was woefully out of date and totally inadequate to meet the demands of a modern urban community. During the early 1800s, Boston had a total of 24 Constables who served as "Captains of the Watch" and supervised the activities of the town's watchmen. It was the civic obligation of all males over eighteen years of age to serve as watchmen to patrol the streets from ten o'clock at night until morning sunrise, to keep an eye out for fires, and to see that good order was maintained. Under the direction of the Constables, thirty-six watchmen worked each night in two shifts of eighteen men each, operating out of four watch stations located in different parts of the town. Although the system looked good on paper, in actual practice it left much to be desired. Most of the watchmen were young men from the lower classes who needed part-time jobs. Armed only with a wooden rattle for summoning help and a long hook that was practically useless for collaring troublemakers, they did not go out of their way to look for danger on a job that paid only fifty cents a night. Even with improved lighting, the watchmen generally avoided the narrow, crooked streets along the notorious waterfront, where sailors on leave were often drunk and disorderly, where petty theft was common, and where prostitutes plied a busy trade. The responsibility of the watchman was simply to report infractions of the law—certainly not to look for trouble, detect crime, or seek out violent situations. It was a totally unprofessional and ineffective system that obviously did not provide either security for private property or protection for personal safety.

Provisions for adequate fire prevention in Boston were not much better. Despite all the laws passed to diminish the causes of fire in a town where most of the houses were built of wood—such as regulations forbidding homeowners to construct their roofs of straw or thatch—the danger of a major conflagration was a constant menace in a town as small and as congested as Boston. After a particularly disastrous fire in 1711, the Boston Fire Society was organized in 1717, the first volunteer firefighting company in the Colonies. Boston was subsequently divided into several fire districts, administered by officers called Firewards, who were given special badges and a five-foot-long red staff topped with a brass spire. These men headed up groups of several hundred young residents who enrolled in volunteer fire companies, elected their own officers, designed their own colorful uniforms, held an elaborate annual supper, and became a powerful political force in town. In addition to performing their civic duty, many volunteers were also motivated by cash prizes regularly awarded to the first company to appear at a fire, as well as by the opportunities for slipping into burning buildings and walking off with valuable loot. Not only were these popular volunteer companies highly inefficient, but they were also likely to turn the scene of a fire into an occasion for a bloody brawl with members of rival volunteer companies who rushed to the same fire. Clearly steps would have to be taken to change these haphazard arrangements as soon as possible.

Despite his deep and continued concern with crime and safety in Boston, however, Mayor Quincy was unable to make any substantive changes in the entrenched ranks of either the police or the fire systems that were in place. Although he found it impossible to increase the overall number of constables or watchmen during his years in office, he did manage to increase their efficiency, and his earlier appointment of Benjamin Pollard as the new City Marshal provided a measure of professional leadership that had not existed before. In addition, Quincy himself took a personal and highly public role in dramatizing the importance of fighting crime and establishing law and order. There was a particularly troublesome district near the waterfront that for years had defied the efforts of town authorities to bring it under control. Robberies, beatings, and even murders took place fairly regularly; loud singing and fiddling went on at all hours of the night; houses of ill-repute did a thriving business. When Quincy complained to the head of the old town police about these goings-on, the officer could only shake his head in helpless frustration, admit that it was too much for the local constable to handle, and told the new mayor that it would take nothing less than a full-fledged military force to quell the nuisance. Mayor Quincy regarded this as nonsense. Acting in his technical capacity as Justice of the Peace, he issued a warrant for the arrest of the fiddlers whom he charged with inspiring the "orgies of the dance-houses," and then he revoked the licenses of all the "tippling shops" and barrooms in the area. When the disturbances still continued, on the night of July 22, 1825, Mayor Quincy placed himself at the head of a vigilante group of burly truckmen, marched into the area in force, broke up the noisy parties, frightened off the "nymphs of Ann Street," and sent the troublemakers "about their business."

Although the new mayor was able to bring some degree of efficiency into the city's police system, he ran into considerable resistance when he tried to bring similar changes and improvements into the town's existing volunteer fire companies. Quincy achieved some satisfaction by introducing the use of hoses to fight fires in place of the bucket-brigade system of passing buckets of water from hand to hand, and he also took steps to make sure that cisterns and small reservoirs were placed at strategic locations throughout the city so that adequate supplies of water would be available to fight fires. But well-connected members of the volunteer fire departments were successful in using their considerable political influence to oppose any further attempts to modernize and professionalize the fire-fighting system, and thereby undermine what they regarded as an old and cherished private volunteer tradition.

Among his more successful achievements in modernizing the city was Mayor Quincy's decision to construct an expansive new market district on filled land located directly behind Faneuil Hall. In 1826, he commissioned Alexander Parris, now one of Boston's leading architects, to design the new marketplace consisting of a central market house where residents would come to shop, flanked by two large granite warehouses that would store the cargo that was coming into Boston from all parts of the world. Parris's design for the central market house, a structure more than 500 feet long, featured a copper-sheathed eliptical dome that capped the center of the pavilion, while each end of the building was in the Greek Revival style, with four mono-lithic granite columns supporting a triangular pedimented gable. Visitors like Mrs. Royall, who came into Boston Harbor by ship, would now see be-fore them on the waterfront of the peninsula, an impressive kind of archi-tecture that resembled the ancient Parthenon in Athens.

The warehouses were opened in the spring of 1826, but technical prob-lems delayed the opening of the market house for several months. On Au-gust 7, 1826, after the Common Council had voted that the new structure would be officially known as "Faneuil Hall Market," the market was offi-cially opened for business. The new central market (that most Bostonians insisted on calling "Quincy Market") was an instant success, and most res-idents seemed to agree with the local correspondent who declared it to be "an ornament to the city."

Although Mayor Josiah Quincy had taken the position that it was the role of the mayor and the members of the municipal administration to assume primary responsibility for the physical maintenance of the city, he also be-lieved that the city had a similar responsibility for assuming more direct supervision of and direction for the needs of those members of the city's "unfortunate classes" who were poor, sick, unemployed, and homeless. In adopting this position, however, Quincy made it clear that any such pub-lic assistance programs should be more sensible, hard-headed, and profes-sionally administered than the traditional methods he obviously regarded as well-meaning and humane, but essentially haphazard and inefficient.

During colonial times, most community leaders had little sympathy for those unfortunate people who were poor, destitute, and homeless, voicing a general Calvinist conviction that such people had undoubtedly brought misfortune upon themselves, and that the very existence of poverty itself constituted a "crime and disgrace." The Reverend Cotton Mather, for ex-ample, complained that the streets of Boston were disfigured with beggars, whom "our Lord Jesus Christ himself hath expressly forbidden us to counte-nance." For a long time, each community dealt with the problems of poverty and homelessness in its own way, usually sending those who were described as members of the "worthy poor" to the local almshouse, where they would be fed and clothed, and assigning the "unworthy poor" to some sort of crude

QUINCY MARKET

Perhaps the most memorable enterprise undertaken by Boston mayor Josiah Quincy was the construction of a new market district near the Town Dock. In 1826, he had Alexander Parris design a new granite market house directly behind Faneuil Hall. Two stories high, and more than 500 feet long, it had a classical portico at each end in the Greek Revival fashion, with a copper-sheathed dome gracing the center. Two matching granite warehouses flanked the central market building to house products that came into the port of Boston from all over the world. (Courtesy, Bostonian Society/Old State House) workhouse where they would perform hard labor, and driving out of town anyone who was not an original member of that particular community. In 1753, the town of Boston created a twelve-member independent agency called the Overseers of the Poor to disburse whatever funds were available and to supervise the management of the care and treatment of the poor. Composed of prominent Yankees with names like Coolidge, May, Perkins, Phillips, and Webster, the members of the board agreed that care for the poor should continue to remain a local form of private charity, as distinct from a system of public charity they generally regarded as wasteful and inefficient. The Overseers continued the traditional practice of placing the "deserving poor" (widows, orphans, and the disabled) in the Almshouse and supplying them with direct assistance in the forms of money, food, and clothing. Those men and women who were assigned to the Workhouse, however, were expected to engage in hard labor, not only to repay their expenses but also to eventually escape poverty and "evil influences."

By the 1820s, however, Boston was changing, not only in its new Bulfinch environment, its expanding mercantile economy, and the general growth of its population, but also in the increasing and unaccustomed diversity of that population in a community whose distinctly white, Anglo-Saxon, and decidedly Protestant culture had changed very little over the course of two hundred years. For one thing, workers and their families who had abandoned the town during the period of British occupation had moved back after the establishment of independence to find new jobs and new financial opportunities. And after the War of 1812, New Englanders from the North Shore, as well as residents from the western counties also migrated to Boston to take advantage of the new opportunities that the innovative textile industry had brought to the urban economy.

Then, too, once the recent war with Great Britain had ended in 1816, there was a marked increase in the number of foreign-born newcomers from the Caribbean and various parts of South America, who came to Boston and augmented the small but cohesive African American community that had originally settled along the waterfront area in what was called the North End. Here, during the colonial period, a mixture of free blacks and slaves had formed a settlement of their own, close to Copp's Hill, which was often called "New Guinea" after that part of the west coast of Africa from which many of them had come. Many were free men who had settled near the docks and made a living from the various trades and services relating to the commercial activities there. But slavery was also a fact of life in colonial Boston, and some of its most respected white citizens ordered slaves from the West Indies to serve as household servants, domestics, laborers, and craftsmen. After the Revolution, when the new Massachusetts constitution had outlawed slavery, the town's black population grew larger as the local residents were joined by former slaves who had moved north to gain their freedom. The combination of increasing numbers and intensified competition from newly arrived white immigrants for the limited number of unskilled waterfront jobs, caused African Americans to move inland, away from the extreme tip of the North End, toward what became known as the West End. They settled on the north side of Beacon Hill, in a section north of Pinckney Street, running from Joy Street down to the Charles River. Here, in 1809, they founded their first all-black church, called the African Meeting House, which drew even more black families to this section of town. The end of the War of 1812 brought a further increase of persons of color into Boston, some arriving during the 1820s as various Latin American nations gained their freedom, others escaping political persecution in countries like Haiti, Brazil, and Venezuela, and still others who had been freed in 1834 by the abolition of slavery throughout the British Empire. By 1840, the size of Boston's African American community had grown to nearly two thousand persons, a sizeable number in a relatively small town.

When the members of Boston's African American community moved from their original location in the North End to the north side of Beacon Hill during the late 1700s, they set up a small school for their children in a private house. In 1808, they were able to construct a small school with a legacy from a wealthy merchant named Abiel Smith, that came under the jurisdiction of the Boston Primary School Committee, which established it as a primary school exclusively for colored children. As the African American community expanded in size, and as the number of school-age children grew larger during the 1840s, black families began petitioning the school board to remove the racial designation of the Smith School so that black children would be able to enroll in other schools nearer to their homes. Consistently, however, the members of the school board voted against the wishes of the black petitioners, insisting that it was the board's legal and moral responsibility to keep apart the two races "the All-Wise Creator had seen fit to establish." Despite these rebuffs, the black citizens, along with their white Abolitionist supporters, kept up their fight for desegregation through community organization, public petitions, and legal activities.

During this same period of time, when Boston's African American residents were establishing themselves as a permanent part of the city's community, the city also saw a dramatic rise in the size of its relatively small Irish population. Large numbers of impoverished Irish farmers fled to America to escape the oppressive results of English land-enclosure policies after the War of 1812. Many of the newcomers were still Protestants from the northern counties of Ireland (often referred to as "Scotch-Irish") who had come to New England in considerable numbers throughout the colonial period, and who had become generally assimilated into the Puritan community as a result of their Protestant religious beliefs (mostly Presbyterian), their sober attitudes, and their commendable work habits.

After 1815, however, the immigrants from Ireland also included a surprising number of families from the southern counties who professed the Roman Catholic religion and who lacked many of the occupational skills of the earlier arrivals. From only a handful of these so-called Papists who had formed their first official congregation in Boston shortly after Independence, their numbers rose to some two thousand by 1820, to more than five thousand by 1825, and to about seven thousand by 1830—more than enough to cause anxiety and unrest among the native Protestant majority who traditionally regarded the Irish from the southern counties as especially "wild" and unmanageable, and who viewed their Catholic religion as blasphemous and heretical. During the 1820s, signs of growing tension would be seen with the sporadic outbreaks of violence that took place along Ann Street, Broad Street, and other sections near the waterfront area where the Irish had settled. Throughout the summer months of July and August 1825, the *Boston Advertiser* reported that "disgraceful riots" took place almost every night, caused by local hoodlums who invaded the neighborhood, broke windows, damaged property, and destroyed "several small houses." Mayor Josiah Quincy and the aldermen finally assigned six constables to patrol the Irish district from 10 o'clock at night until morning in an attempt to keep the peace. Undoubtedly, Irish immigrants were among those noisy fiddlers and rowdy revelers whose late-night parties brought Mayor Quincy and his posse of burly truckmen into the Irish neighborhood on the night of July 22 to shut down the taverns, clear the streets, and drive out the troublemakers.

During the 1820s and 1830s, therefore, Boston faced a dramatic increase in the number of foreign-born newcomers who had few skills, no money, and little marketability, and who now joined with local transients and displaced itinerants who were also seeking some form of public relief. Boston's Overseers of the Poor were overwhelmed by the waves of unemployed and homeless men and women who confronted their overtaxed agency. Members of the Overseers complained bitterly about the failure of the Commonwealth of Massachusetts to regulate and control the influx of impoverished newcomers who were found begging on Boston Common, locked away in filthy jails, or filling up the almshouses that no longer had adequate funds and resources to care for them properly.

The growing problem of poverty and homelessness in Boston was something in which Mayor Josiah Quincy had already taken a serious and personal interest. "Poverty, vice, and crime," he once remarked, were "little else than modifications of each other." In 1821, two years before he became mayor of Boston, Quincy had resigned his post as Speaker of the Massachusetts House of Representatives to take a place on the Boston municipal bench; a short time later he was asked to serve as chairman of the Committee to Superintend and Aid the Overseers of the Poor. This appointment gave him the opportunity to study the situation at firsthand and formulate his own ideas regarding the current problems and the appropriate ways of dealing with them—ideas that did not always coincide with the views of the Overseers themselves. From the outset, Quincy made it clear that he felt that responsibilities for the poor and the homeless should now be in the hands of the newly established city government, and should not continue as an essentially private charitable agency with no effective system of public accountability. He took particular issue with the way in which the Board of Overseers operated the city's Almshouse and Workhouse, criticized their accounting methods, and made no secret of the fact that he viewed their approach as generally inefficient and unprofessional. Quincy felt that because of their well-meaning Christian charity, the Overseers of the Poor had often been duped by lazy and shiftless paupers—immigrants, transients, vagrants, drunkards—who had become unwelcome and permanent burdens on the resources of the Boston community. As far as the current system's effects upon poor people themselves, Quincy announced in his typical forthright fashion that the current system was "most wasteful, most expensive, and most injurious to their morals, and destructive of their industrial habits."

Although he said he was still willing to use the Almshouse to dispense municipal charity to those whom he labeled the "impotent poor"—the aged, the sick, the disabled—he urged that a significant number of the "laboring and respectable poor" be taken out of the Almshouse and reassigned to a new Workhouse where they would be engaged in hard labor. Despite the strong and angry objections of the members of the Board of Overseers to what they considered a blatant and unwarranted interference with their powers, Judge Quincy forged ahead with his plans, and early in 1823 the newly constituted Common Council approved his recommendation to construct a new and larger Workhouse—to be called, symbolically enough, the House of Industry—that would be located on the nearby peninsula of South Boston. A short time later, the Common Council informed the Board members that, while they could still "oversee" conditions in the new House of Industry, the Common Council itself would actually manage and "superintend" the new operation.

Any hopes that the Board of Overseers might organize their opposition and overturn the Common Council's new plan were dampened late in 1823 when Josiah Quincy was elected by the voters of the city as second Mayor of Boston. In addition to moving ahead with his extensive program of renovation in the old waterfront area of the city, Quincy also proceeded to implement his ideas regarding the establishment of new and more rigorous criteria for the treatment of the poor and started out by ordering the transfer of a large number of paupers from the old Workhouse to the new House of Industry in South Boston—apparently with satisfactory results. "I never saw more happiness, ease, and comfort than exist in the poor house in Boston," wrote Mrs. Anne Royall after she visited the new institution during her tour of America.

Clearly the new city administration, under the vigorous direction of its "Great Mayor," had begun to institutionalize and professionalize the care of the city's poor and homeless. Some measure of the speed with which Mayor Quincy put his plans into operation can be seen in the documentary record: From a total of 2,114 Almshouse residents listed in 1820, the number had plummeted to a mere 474 in 1825—920 men down to 228; 1,194 women down to 246—a reduction of over 1,600 residents in less than five years. Henceforth, admission to the Almshouse was carefully restricted to members of the "wretched poor." All others needing assistance were assigned to the new House of Industry, where they would pay their way and earn their keep.

In this way, the Christian obligation of charity and compassion could be reconciled with the sensible methodology of a rational mind.

Uncomfortable with Josiah Quincy's extraordinary display of executive power, alarmed by the size of his municipal expenditures, and uneasy about where his wide-ranging ambitions would next lead him, the voters of Boston turned out in favor of Harrison Gray Otis in the election of 1828, and put an end to Quincy's six consecutive one-year terms as mayor of Boston. The *Boston Patriot* later credited the "laboring class" vote with contributing to Quincy's defeat and criticized him for his "haughty anti-republican manners." Never one to remain idle, in January 1829, Josiah Quincy succeeded John T. Kirkland as the fifteenth president of Harvard College, where he proceeded to set about reforming the law school, while he still found time to write several books, including *The History of Harvard College*. As mayor of Boston, however, "The Great Mayor" had left behind him a pattern for political activism and social commitment that would greatly influence the members of the city's elite establishment for many years to come.

CHAPTER 3 } ʀESHAPING A COMMUNITY

Considering the extraordinary energy and vigorous determination of Mayor Josiah Quincy, it is easy enough to ascribe the extensive physical changes, the material improvements, and the professional bureaucracy, which arose in Boston during the mid-1820s, to the leadership qualities of a single individual. In many ways, however, this desire for reform, this striving for improvement, was symptomatic of a much deeper commitment to social and civic improvement on the part of an impressive number of Quincy's well-placed colleagues and wealthy associates who made up a significant part of the city's traditional elite establishment,

By this time, the original group of colonial mercantile leaders who had moved into power after the Revolution to fill the void created by the Tory exodus had expanded their numbers to include not only the members of what Peter Dobkin Hall, in his historical analysis of American elites, calls their own "not-yet-successful sons, cousins, and in-laws," but also enterprising young men from different backgrounds and different parts of the Commonwealth. The inclusion of such families as the Cabots of Salem, the Lowells of Newburyport, the Peabodys of Essex County, and the Lawrence brothers of Middlesex County not only provided a healthy degree of vitality and diversity, but also ensured that the profits originally derived from mercantile commerce would be substantially augmented after the War of 1812 by the income from textile mills, railroad companies, banks, and brokerage firms. Now settled in compact neighborhoods, safely isolated from the dangerous and unsettling ideas that had been generated by the election of Thomas Jefferson, they could meet with one another, dine together, carry on business, and carefully guide the consciousness of their children through such educational and socializing institutions as the Boston Latin School and Harvard College. In addition to promoting in their young people the ideal of "character," not only as a means of developing future citizens who would be dependable, predictable, disciplined, and self-controlled—traits that, according to Peter Hall, were the functional equivalent of old-time "piety"—

the members of Boston's commercial elite also believed, despite their loss of political power, that they were still entrusted with serious public responsibilities. As persons of wealth, learning, and respectability, they felt constrained to vindicate their exalted position in Boston society by using that wealth and influence for the benefit of the community as a whole.

Among the Boston Associates there had always been considerable philanthropic support for what were considered good and noble causes, such as Harvard College, the Massachusetts General Hospital, and the construction of the Bunker Hill Monument. For the most part, however, these philanthropic gestures were directed toward projects with which the prosperous classes themselves were personally involved and directly concerned. What was striking about events that took place during the late 1820s and early 1830s, however, was that members of Boston's commercial elite now extended their charitable activities to include humanitarian concerns for the less fortunate members of the community. Leading members of Boston's "happy and respectable" class obviously saw themselves as well-educated, high-minded, and responsible stewards of a truly special community. Members of old Boston families, such as John Phillips, Harrison Gray Otis, and Josiah Quincy, had already indicated that they were intent on using their powers of political leadership to refashion and renew the urban community in which they made their homes and raised their families. They were assuming this responsibility not only out of concern for their own comfort and convenience, however, but also for the benefit of those members of the "less fortunate classes" who had voted them into power, and who now had the right to expect a better life in a better city. Using the same kind of rational analysis, scientific categorization, and personal dynamism that had already characterized Josiah Quincy's approach to municipal reform, members of that same leadership elite undertook to make further changes and improvements in the life of the citizens whose welfare they had chosen to safeguard and improve.

The continued growth of poverty and homelessness during the 1820s, for example, was something that greatly disturbed many prominent Bostonians, not only because of the political and economic burdens they placed upon the municipal government, as Mayor Quincy had pointed out, but also because of the terrible sufferings they brought to individuals and their families. A number of the town's religious leaders were visibly concerned about the lack of facilities to respond adequately to the rapid increase in the number

OLIVER WENDELL HOLMES

A truly Renaissance man, Oliver Wendell Holmes was an eminent physician who was famous for his lectures on anatomy and other medical subjects at the Harvard Medical School. At the same time, however, he was a talented writer who achieved early popularity with his poem "Old Ironsides," but who gained later fame with "The Autocrat of the Breakfast Table" and other witty essays. Extremely proud of his city, he proclaimed Boston to be nothing less than "The Hub of the Solar System." (Courtesy, Bostonian Society/Old State House) of paupers and began forming their own private relief agencies to help deal with the problem. In 1826, for example, the Reverend Joseph Tuckerman, a local Unitarian minister, undertook an experimental "ministry-at-large" program in an effort to reach and rescue paupers, not only those who were languishing in the Almshouse and the Workhouse, but also those who were sleeping in the alleyways and roaming the streets without any kind of care or supervision at all. The Reverend William Ellery Channing added his influential voice in support of those who ministered to the poor, and a short time later a group called the Benevolent Fraternity of Churches was formed to provide even wider support for the various ministries at large.

The needs of the poor and the suffering of the homeless also attracted the interest and sympathy of many Boston women who involved themselves in charitable work designed especially to help females who were poor, widowed, and homeless. These were activities that further increased the gradual and often subtle progressions that brought women out from their accepted place of hearth and home into the world beyond. Once the Revolution had ended, the realities of independence were negligible as far as American women were concerned. There were no legal codes for females, no right to vote, no changes in property ownership except for those women still engaged in small family enterprises or home-based earnings. Then, too, with the steady movement toward industrialization after the War of 1812, and especially with the development of mechanical techniques such as the power loom and the spinning jenny, the manufacture of goods was moved out of homes and into factories, with the result that traditional gender relations were changed significantly. While the income-earning husbands now left the home to work at a factory, a store, an office, or a courthouse, the middle-class wife remained at home, extending her influence over a separate and independent realm of her own. Once manufacturing shifted from the confines of the home to factory and workplace, women were left to exercise their authority over the "domestic sphere," where they assumed primary responsibility for housekeeping, child rearing, the care of their husbands, and the direction of the moral and religious life of the family. "Domestic life," writes historian Nancy Woloch, "was now under female control." Whatever charitable or voluntary activities women engaged in outside the home were usually associated with their church and had a distinctly moral or religious purpose that usually made their efforts acceptable to the general community.

EDWARD EVERETT

Edward Everett was a remarkable example of Boston's ideal scholar-statesman. After being named professor of Greek at Harvard College, he served in the U.S. Congress for ten years, became Governor of Massachusetts in 1836, and was later appointed Minister to Great Britain. Everett then served as president of Harvard College until called to Washington to become Secretary of State. In November 1863, Edward Everett was the principal orator at the dedication of the Gettysburg cemetery, where President Lincoln had been asked also to make "a few appropriate remarks." (Courtesy, Bostonian Society/Old State House)

There were, of course, women, chiefly in the lower- and lower-middle classes who were forced by economic necessity to work outside the home for pay. But even in these categories, nineteenth-century society tolerated only a reasonable number of exceptions. During her extended visit to the United States during the mid-1830s, the English writer Harriet Martineau listed only four major occupations she found open to women: factory work, domestic service, manufacturing hats and clothing, and teaching school. Although teaching was not yet regarded as a formal profession, local widows or impoverished wives would set up small grammar schools, often called "dame schools," where girls as well as boys could learn the rudiments of reading and writing. For the most part, however, respectable Boston women who were not required by circumstances to acquire an outside income to maintain their families were expected to remain at home. According to Catharine Beecher in an 1842 tract, persons who had wealth and education were called "ladies," while those who did not have an education and who had to labor for their support, were called "women." A "lady," according to Beecher, would feel offended if she were called a "woman," since that term was used to denote "persons whom she regards as below herself."

Outside the confines of the home, and beyond the responsibilities of the family, religion was one of the few activities in which middle-class "ladies" could feel free to participate without abandoning their "proper" domestic sphere or compromising their modesty and respectability. Many women, therefore, were caught up in the passionate revivalism of the Second Great Awakening in the early 1800s, and soon formed the bulk of the membership of the new religious congregations. These activities not only provided a measure of self-fulfillment and self-esteem for themselves, but also created the base for an expanding network of voluntary religious societies in which women could associate with one another without causing scandal. Along with their active participation as "auxiliaries" in such organizations as Bible and tract societies, missionary societies, and Sunday School associations, local women also banded together in the Boston Female Society for Missionary Purposes, where they made clothing and knitted goods for all kinds of religious causes. By the 1830s, a number of Boston women had begun to move beyond the bounds of exclusively religious groups to form associations for pious and benevolent purposes, and from there to even broader charitable and humanitarian causes. In their efforts to participate in early reform activities dealing with issues ordinarily related to men, such as intemperate

WILLIAM ELLERY CHANNING

Originally ordained to the Congregational ministry, William Ellery Channing gradually rejected the old Calvinist-Puritan beliefs in an angry God, a debased humanity, and a concept of predestination that limited salvation only to members of the elect. In preaching a loving God, the perfectibility of human beings, and the ability of all souls to attain salvation, Channing established a more liberal and rational approach to Christianity that became known as Unitarianism. (Courtesy, Bostonian Society/Old State House) drinking and imprisonment for crime, women found that such movements were dominated by men in general, and by the clergy in particular. In such movements, women were purely "auxiliaries," and although they were active at meetings and carried out many of the administrative and organizational details, they were not allowed to attend conventions or to run for office.

Participation in religious and missionary societies, female-reform associations, and prison-reform societies, the creation of orphanages, and the support of charitable institutions not only strengthened the middle-class women's sense of sisterhood and common purpose, but also provided them with essential administrative talents and political skills. When women applied these organizational talents to activities more directed at uniquely female problems and needs, they were much more successful. During the 1830s, for example, a group of prominent Boston women, including Mrs. Samuel Appleton, Mrs. William Ellery Channing, Mrs. Joseph Coolidge, and Mrs. Samuel Eliot, formed a new agency, called the Society for Employing the Female Poor, in an effort to assist poor widows, abandoned wives, impoverished mothers, and other women who did not have any visible means of support. The organizers of this society maintained a shelter on High Street, where poor women could apply for work as seamstresses or laundresses, and where instruction was also provided to teach marketable skills to poor women as well as to their daughters. In 1835, a group of seventy women formed the Boston Female Moral Reform Society, which gradually expanded into an influential national organization. A number of "respectable women" of the city organized the Boston Society for Widows and Orphans, and other Boston women formed a variety of charitable programs designed to rescue prostitutes and lift up "fallen women" by establishing such agencies as a Home for Unprotected Girls, a Refuge for Migrant Women, and an Asylum for the Repentant. These women also set up organizations to help rehabilitated women find gainful employment, and also created day nurseries where employed mothers could leave their children during working hours. Sarah Hale, a successful female publisher, formed the Seaman's Aid Society specifically to help the wives, widows, and orphans of Boston sailors who had gone to sea and never returned. Hale and her supporters also provided boarding houses, reading rooms, savings banks, and facilities of religious services for sailors when they were in port. The emergence of a group of prominent women as an active force in providing both moral support and practical assistance to the poor and the homeless—

activities by this time well out of the range of home and church—signaled a subtle but interesting change in the status of females in a traditional male society.

In an increasingly urbanized community, the problems of poverty and homelessness were closely associated with the problem of crime, as well as the subsequent treatment of criminals, issues that were of serious concern not only to Mayor Quincy himself, but also to many other members of the city's Beacon Hill establishment. During the eighteenth century, American law codes tended to be somewhat more humane than the laws that were in effect in England at that time. Although the Massachusetts Body of Liberties listed twelve crimes that were punishable by death, the death penalty was rarely invoked, except for murder or piracy, when the executions were generally conducted as gala events, carried out in public and attended by all classes and ages of citizens. In the old days, prisons were generally ramshackle affairs, cold, damp, and unclean, designed to hold lawbreakers for only short periods of time until the appropriate punishment could be applied. The only group of prisoners who might look forward to lengthy jail sentences were debtors—primarily to prevent them from leaving town without paying their debts. Burglary, robbery, and other crimes against property—many of which were still punishable by death in England—were considered much less serious in the American Colonies. Usually offenders were expected to make restitution, and subjected to some form of public humiliation—branding, whipping, mutilation, confinement in stocks—to punish the culprit himself, as well as to deter spectators from committing similar crimes.

Slowly the barbarities of early physical punishments disappeared, and in the postrevolutionary period a number of states rewrote their criminal codes and began doing away with what were considered to be "cruel and unusual" punishments. After a revolutionary struggle based on the idea that all men were created equal, and with the emergence of a more progressive theology that held out the possibility of salvation for everyone, there was a growing insistence that punishment should no longer be cruel or vindictive, but that it should also hold out the opportunity for individual reformation. One of the results of the reduction in the use of the death penalty, and the disappearance of such earlier practices as flogging and branding, was an increase in the use of the jail and the prison as the principal means of punishment rather than a place of brief and temporary confinement.

Now that a much greater number of men, women, and juvenile offenders were being given prison sentences for longer periods of time, community leaders began expressing concern not only about the deplorable physical conditions of the prisons, but also about the health, welfare, and moral circumstances of the prisoners themselves. In various localities, many clergymen saw prison conditions as a serious moral issue and took the lead in establishing what were called prison discipline societies, whose main purpose was to foster the religious life and spiritual regeneration of prisoners. In the process, however, the members of these societies also concerned themselves with improving and reforming the terrible physical conditions they found in the prisons that worked against the development of any kind of religious faith or spiritual conviction. Most jails were more overcrowded than ever, with little furniture, wretched food, inadequate clothing, and no facilities for either exercising the body or enlightening the mind. To make matters worse, there was usually no separation of the sexes, nor was there any segregation of youthful first-offenders from older, hardened criminals. Members of Louis Dwight's Boston Prison Discipline Society took the lead in raising the public consciousness about the state of local prisons by denouncing the deplorable conditions they found in the old state prison across the Charles River in Charlestown and used their findings to try to persuade the Massachusetts state legislature to appropriate funds with which to make necessary improvements. Prisons should be places for reforming criminals, Dwight insisted, and should not be used merely for punishing or detaining them. After all, he argued, criminals were also "creatures of the same glorious Creator with ourselves." They, too, had immortal souls, and were "objects of regard to Christ." Mayor Quincy was in accord with the objectives of the Boston Prison Discipline Society, especially after he had occasion to visit the county jail at Leverett Street, and found nearly four hundred prisoners crammed into thirty-two rooms. This was a situation that offended both his sense of charity and his commitment to progressive reform.

By the late 1790s and early 1800s, humanitarians and reformers in several East Coast cities were calling for drastic changes in the appalling state of American prisons. The lead in prison reform in the United States was taken by the Pennsylvania Quakers, who worked constantly to reduce the severity of punishments and to make much-needed improvements in the prison system. Largely through their determined efforts, various states began to experiment with the creation of what became known as penitentiaries. One of the most significant steps was taken in 1829, with the introduction of the "Pennsylvania System," in which each prisoner was separated from contact with all other criminals and placed in an individual cell that was comparatively large, with a small outdoor courtyard attached for fresh air and a certain amount of physical exercise. Although they were permitted to work and to read—especially the Bible, religious tracts, and works of spiritual inspiration—prisoners were provided with their meals three times a day and kept in solitude throughout their terms of imprisonment so that, in Quaker fashion, they would be better able to receive the "inner light." At just about the same time, other experiments in penal reform were begun in upstate New York that eventually produced what was known as the "Auburn System"—first used at Auburn, then at Sing Sing, and eventually employed in most large penitentiaries throughout the United States. Prisoners were isolated at night in small cells arranged in tiers, but during the day were marched in close-order formation to dining halls, workshops, and recreation areas. Although this allowed for some measure of contact with other prisoners, as well as the possibility for some kind of vocational training, the men were strictly monitored and forced to keep absolute silence at all times. Although each of these two systems left much to be desired (some criticized the solitary confinement of the Pennsylvania System; others deplored the harsh discipline of the Auburn System), they were nevertheless a vast improvement over the old methods of confinement and served as a starting point for more enlightened prison reforms to come.

Progressive results in the treatment of prisoners in Boston institutions came about largely as the result of the efforts of Louis Dwight, a former agent of the American Bible Society, and a group of upper-class men and women who made up the membership of the Society, and who kept in close touch with programs and experiments being conducted in other parts of the country. In 1825, as a result of their persistent efforts, as well as the influence of Mayor Quincy, the Massachusetts state legislature finally agreed to authorize the construction of a new state prison in Charlestown, in a form that incorporated some of the more humane innovations recently introduced by New York's so-called Auburn System. Later, Dwight collaborated with the well-known Boston architect, Gridley J. Fox Bryant, on the design of a new Suffolk County Jail at Leverett Street, known generally as the Charles Street Jail, whose cruciform shape demonstrated the new and more progressive attitudes toward the incarceration of prisoners. Individual cells now separated first offenders from hardened criminals, and provisions were made for inmates to engage in recreational activities and to learn new occupations, which would, it was hoped, make it possible for them to return to society without resorting to crime. "This is the best prison, and the best kept, of any in the U. States, at least, that I have seen," commented Anne Royall during her visit to Boston. "The wardens and keepers are gentlemen of education, and discharge their trust with great humanity."

In exploring others ways in which the old prison system could be substantially upgraded, and criminals might be provided with means of reform and rehabilitation, officials agreed that from now on the treatment of juvenile offenders would take place at a different location from hardened criminals. Although fully convinced that society had the obligation to punish young people for criminal offenses, Mayor Josiah Quincy also felt that society had no right to confine young people to a "moral pest house, out of which nothing good can ever issue." In 1828, therefore, following his strong urgings, a new House of Reformation was constructed across the Fort Point Channel on the nearby South Boston peninsula. Here, at what would later generations would call the Reform School, juvenile offenders were not only separated from older and more hardened criminals, but they were also provided with a program of instruction in reading, writing, and arithmetic based on the plan of the city's common schools. In addition, there was limited occupational training in a variety of crafts that would help develop the kinds of mental discipline and manual dexterity that would be useful when the young people were later contracted out ("bound out") as inexpensive labor to the tradesmen and merchants of the city.

Although there was growing concern about the long-range effects of crime and the appropriate treatment of criminals, the effective treatment of crime itself had considerably diminished. Unfortunately, the time and attension that Josiah Quincy had expended on upgrading the efficiency of the police and fire services in the city during his six years as mayor were not followed up by those who succeeded him in 1829. Perhaps the few improvements he had made in the police and fire departments—and especially his numerous and highly publicized accomplishments in so many other areas— had created the overall impression that the city was now safe and secure so that no further reforms were needed. His immediate successor, Harrison Gray Otis, for example, showed much less interest in the more mundane aspects of city services such as sweeping streets, collecting garbage, and cleaning sewers, and more in those enterprises such as building courthouses and constructing railroads, that seemed of greater importance to members of the city's upper classes. Believing that the operations of the City Marshal were being carried to what he called a "needless and pernicious extreme," he reduced Benjamin Pollard's salary from one thousand to eight hundred dollars, and made similar cuts in the incomes of the constables and the watchmen, despite the fact that the city's population had grown from 49,000 to about 65,000 in the ten years between 1822 and 1832. When Otis retired from office in 1831, he was succeeded by Charles Wells, a master carpenter, who reflected the resentment of working-class voters against what they perceived as the "magnificent" and high-handed ways in which patricians like Quincy and Otis had spent public money and managed city affairs for the benefit of the upper classes.

Although he was committed to a policy of retrenchment, however, Wells did respond to complaints of his middle-class constituents about a rising level of violence in the city by restoring the City Marshal's salary and appointing more constables to help suppress "riots, routs, and tumultuous assemblies," especially those that were reported as still taking place around Ann Street and Broad Street where many of the Irish immigrants made their homes. Beyond this, however, few steps were taken to reorganize the constabulary any further, or to take more aggressive action in searching out the causes of the frequent "brawls" and fights that were causing disturbances in various parts of the city. After Wells had served two one-year terms in office, he was succeeded in December 1833 by Theodore Lyman, an old-time Federalist, a Harvard graduate, and the son of a successful merchant. It was during the Lyman administration that Boston was confronted with the harsh realities of large-scale mob violence that made the need for better organized and more effective police protection painfully evident. The first episode occurred on the night of August 11, 1834, when an angry mob of disgruntled truckmen and local brickworkers attacked a Catholic convent on Mount Benedict in Charlestown, where an order of Ursuline nuns conducted a rather fashionable school for girls. The continued growth in the number of Irish Catholics in the city during the 1820s and 1830s had raised the level of fear and hostility among native Protestants, especially among working-class laborers and workmen who feared losing their jobs to lower-class immigrants. Aroused even further by bizarre rumors of nuns being locked away in underground cells and of Protestant girls being forced to become Catholics, the men smashed their way into the building, forced the nuns and the girls to flee into the night, and then burned the convent to the ground as hundreds of local residents stood around and cheered. This scandalous outrage came as a great shock to most members of Boston's upper classes, who responded immediately to show their displeasure. On the very next day, August 12, Mayor Lyman organized an indignation meeting at Faneuil Hall, where former mayors Josiah Quincy and Harrison Gray Otis joined Lyman in denouncing this "base and cowardly blot" on their city's name and reputation. Despite such protests, however, none of the arsonists was ever found guilty, nor was any restitution made to the nuns for the destruction of their property.

It was only a year later when another riot broke out, this time in downtown Boston itself. On the afternoon of October 21, 1835, a mob smashed its way into a meeting of the Female Anti-Slavery Society on Washington Street, and caught hold of William Lloyd Garrison, leader of a new protest group called the Abolition movement that called for the total and immediate emancipation of slaves, and dragged him at the end of a rope through the city to Boston Common. Although Garrison was finally rescued by the police, Mayor Lyman quickly sent him out of town before any further harm could befall him. There were obviously many members of the city's financial establishment who were sympathetic to the attack on Garrison and his female supporters, but there were others, however, who lamented that an incompetent police response had allowed the confrontation to get completely out of hand. It was just one more disruptive event that caused authorities to take more serious consideration of the state of safety and security in the city.

The year 1836 was a period of relative quiet, during the administration of a local printer named Samuel T. Armstrong, who was succeeded by Samuel Atkins Eliot, a member of a distinguished Boston family, another graduate of Harvard College, and a public-spirited citizens who worked with the Boston Prison Discipline Society as well as with several other reform movements of the period. Eliot was in office only six months when, on June 11, 1837, rioting broke out—once again in the very heart of the city. A company of Yankee firemen, returning from a call, clashed with members of an Irish funeral procession traveling along the same street. In moments, what started out as a fistfight had mushroomed into a full-scale riot, at one point reportedly involving some fifteen thousand persons, as residents from both sides spilled out of their homes, or rushed in from their fire stations, to take part in the bloody brawl. What became known as the "Broad Street Riot" was obviously too much for the local constabulary to put down, and the struggle raged on until Mayor Eliot, at the head of eight hundred horsemen with sabers drawn, brought in the state militia for the first time in its history to disperse the rioters and restore order to the city.

Genuinely concerned at the prospect of even more serious outbreaks of violence—after all, this was the third major riot in only three years—Mayor Eliot pressured the city government to turn to the task of providing the city with a stronger and more professional police force. On September 18, he delivered a strongly worded address to the Common Council, describing a frightening "spirit of violence abroad" that, he said, was increasing at a faster rate than the population itself. To combat this spirit of violence, much stronger measures would have to be taken that would adapt to circumstances far different from those of "a half a century ago." Since citizens could not protect themselves in a large urban setting, and since the use of the armed militia could be a dangerous expedient when large numbers of innocent civilians were concerned, he called for a study committee to come up with a plan for a modern system of crime prevention that would be supported by public tax money. In its subsequent report, the committee recommended a system based on the London model, with the city divided into four districts, each patrolled by eight officers supervised by a captain who, in turn, would be responsible to the city marshal. These new officers would be full-time professionals who would work a full day, be paid a regular salary ($2 a day), and serve as a "preventive" force, to search out crime in advance and not just wait for it to happen. The report also proposed an increase of thirty watchmen, a move that would provide additional reserves in case of future riots. The watchmen already on staff would be kept on, would continue to serve only at night, watch for fires and fights in a "non-preventive" manner, and pay for themselves through fees and other concessions.

Having taken steps to improve police security for the city, Mayor Eliot next made a similar effort to reorganize and essentially professionalize the volunteer fire companies that, by this time, were becoming an embarrassment to the city, not only because of their greedy pursuit of money at fires, but also because of their increasing inclination to engage in public brawls, such as their recent involvement in the Broad Street Riot. The mayor's efforts in this respect, however, only served to provoke an angry response from many of the volunteer firemen. Over the years, members of the fire companies had come to regard themselves as public-spirited volunteers who were "doing the city a favor," according to historian Roger Lane, and who, therefore, assumed that they should not be subject to official discipline or control. During the summer of 1837, however, at the strong urging of Mayor Eliot, the Common Council decided to professionalize the fire-control system, bring it under municipal supervision, reduce the number of members, and pay the remaining firemen an annual salary ranging upwards of $65. Although members of the volunteer companies complained loudly about the insulting way in which they were being treated, city authorities were forced to continue using volunteer fire patrols for many years, until the new professional companies could be properly recruited and organized.

The first source of trouble between Mayor Eliot's strengthened police force and the general public grew out of an important shift of emphasis concerning public drinking. The creation of a new corps of officers in 1838 was followed by the passage of the Fifteen-Gallon Law, the first modern piece of legislation intended to restrict seriously the private consumption of alcohol. Chapter 157 of the Acts of 1838 limited the sale of spirits to quantities of fifteen gallons or more, in large measure to make it much too expensive for the poor, the improvident, and the immigrant in the city to purchase liquor. In dealing with such complex issues as police protection, fire safety, public riots, serious crime, poverty, and homelessness, in an old town that was rapidly becoming a modern city, it was almost inevitable that the problems of intoxication and public drunkenness should be addressed by the leaders of the community who were anxious to eliminate social deficiencies that they were convinced harmed the quality of life in Boston and tarnished its idealistic image as the "City Upon a Hill."

Certainly there was nothing new about intemperate drinking in the American Colonies, and nothing particularly surprising about the widespread use of intoxicating beverages in New England during the colonial period. All kinds of beverages, made with barley, wheat, rye, and corn were produced and consumed in the average household, and the brewing of ale and beer also became as much a household enterprise as a profitable industry. The triangular trade that carried slaves in Yankee ships from Africa to the West Indies brought cargoes of molasses back to New England, where it was promptly converted into rum. The distilling of rum quickly became a large-scale commercial enterprise, with more than 150 distilleries located throughout New England by the end of the colonial period. By that time, about 4 million gallons of molasses were being imported from the West Indies, with each gallon of molasses converted into a gallon of rum, much of which was consumed, not only in American homes and inns, but also in the dormitories of Harvard College. "Probably at no other period in the history of the Cambridge institution," wrote historian Herbert Allen in his biography of John Hancock, "had so much liquor been consumed per capita as during the second half of the 18th century." In the days when Hancock was a student, rum was the favorite drink, sometimes taken straight, but usually mixed with beer, ale, cider, or whatever else happened to be available. The capacious pewter mugs, tankards, and beakers still preserved in Robinson Hall testify to the vast volumes of spirits consumed by rollicking Harvard students.

And during the revolutionary period, it was almost impossible to find political gatherings, arguments, and debates that did not take place in one of the town's well-known taverns. On the south side of King Street was The Bunch of Grapes, frequented by the more prosperous members of the local Patriot faction, while The Green Dragon, on Union Street near Faneuil Hall, and The Salvation, in the North End, were the taverns where the less well-to-do members of the local opposition met to present their views and air their grievances. Like the young political organizer Samuel Adams, whose father owned a brewery that he bequeathed to his son, many men dropped into several of these popular taverns in the course of a single day and night, participating in the discussions and carrying the various arguments from one group to another as the liquor flowed freely all the while. In 1761, John Adams observed that these well-attended taverns had become the "nurseries of our legislators" and speculated that all a clever man had to do to get votes in those days would be to multiply the number of taverns and dramshops in the town.

Not that public drunkenness was either encouraged or condoned by the civil authorities, who recognized that abuse in the use of liquor in public places could not only produce disturbances of the peace, but also lead to the neglect of work and a breakdown in family life. Colonial courts routinely sent local drunkards to the stocks or made them stand in a public place with the letter "D" on a placard around their necks. Colonial legislatures, too, passed laws following the old English custom of limiting the right to sell liquor by the glass to certified taverners who were supposed to provide the full range of room, board, and stabling. The purpose was to ensure that the sale of intoxicating beverages would be kept in the hands of "responsible and respectable people." After the Revolution, under the new state constitution of 1786, the General Court reinforced an old license law that forbade the sale of liquor, without a license, in quantities less than 28 gallons. Licenses were granted, for one year only, upon the recommendation of the selectmen who certified the number that were "necessary for the public good." The law also required that "all public houses shall be on or near the high streets and places of great resort," allowed no credit above 6 shillings, and denied sales to servants, minors, and "reputed drunkards."

Despite all these laws and restrictions, however, over the years many of the old statutory regulations were gradually relaxed, drinking continued, and public intoxication fast became a serious social problem in a town whose leaders were anxious to preserve its image as a moral, sober, God-fearing community. Habits that might have been acceptable, or at least endurable, in rural communities where populations were relatively small, and houses a considerable distance apart, or even in small seaport towns like Boston whose residents were long established and well acquainted with one another, could no longer be tolerated in a growing urban center with a large and congested population increasingly composed of newcomers, transients, foreigners, and immigrants. To someone like Mayor Josiah Quincy, vitally concerned with the health and welfare of his city, the evil effects of intemperate drinking were becoming more obvious every day, constituting not only a moral evil for the individuals themselves, but also a serious social menace to the peace and security of the entire city. His work with the Overseers of the Poor, his own investigations of the conditions of the poor and the homeless, his visits to the Almshouse and the Workhouse, his involvement in prison reform and juvenile delinquency, impressed upon him the close and insidious relationship between intemperate drinking and the terrible conditions of those victimized by poverty and crime. Clearly, he believed that a substantial reduction in intoxication and drunkenness would invariably result in a corresponding reduction in crime and pauperism among members of the "unfortunate classes."

The damaging effects of distilled beverages, on both the body and the mind, had already been noted as early as 1784 by the respected physician Dr. Benjamin Rush, professor of medicine at the University of Pennsylvania, who wrote a treatise, *Inquiry into the Effects of Ardent Spirits*, in which he urged doctors and pharmacists to become more active in curbing the use of alcohol among their patients. With the election of Dr. John Collins Warren of Boston as president of the Massachusetts Society for the Suppression of Intemperance in 1823, a number of local physicians worked closely with Mayor Quincy and the aldermen to prohibit the sale of alcoholic beverages in all theaters and public buildings in Boston. Dr. Warren also persuaded many of his friends and colleagues in the Massachusetts Medical Society to adopt resolutions urging all physicians to refrain from prescribing alcoholic medications whenever possible.

A growing number of city leaders also pointed out the increasing dangers of intoxication in a time of a rapidly changing economic system that had emerged from the War of 1812. In the earlier days of an agrarian economy, most men were independent farmers, half the houses were little more than log cabins, profitable cash crops were extremely rare. And an effective system of transportation was virtually nonexistent. Time was measured in terms of the seasons of the year, and the average workday went from sunrise to sunset. Most plows were still made of wood, and the plowing of an acre of land with a team of oxen was usually more than a day's work. With low levels of production in a subsistence economy, there was no need to hurry; it made just as much sense to spend time at the local tavern "tippling" with friends and neighbors. In the new industrial economy, however, time was of the essence. Factories now operated by the clock, railroad trains and steam engines moved on strict schedules, and new forms of industrial machinery required an increased measure of alertness and dexterity to avoid a crippling blow or the loss of a limb.

Apart from the negative effects intoxication might have on the future of the Bay State economy, humanitarians and reformers in Boston, as well as in many other states, also emphasized the moral evil of intemperate drinking and dramatized the many ways in which intoxication brought untold anguish and suffering to abandoned wives and innocent children in so many homes of America. Perhaps the most powerful force that took up the cause of temperance was that of organized religion. It was really only during the days of the early Republic that a widespread institutional concern about promoting the virtues of temperance began to emerge, sponsored in some cases by the Quakers of Pennsylvania, and in other cases by the Baptists and Methodists, whose circuit-riding preachers spoke out regularly against the moral dangers of drinking intoxicating beverages. One of the most vigorous temperance advocates in the New England region during the 1820s was

Reverend Lyman Beecher, pastor of the Congregational church in Litchfield, Connecticut, and a leader of the orthodox resurgence against the liberal views of Unitarianism. In the fall of 1825, Beecher emphasized the moral evils of intemperance in a series of six lengthy sermons, which were printed and reprinted for many years to come, and established his reputation as a major spokesman for the movement. Moved by Beecher's declaration that intemperance had become "the sin of our land," and that with our "boundless prosperity" it was coming in upon us "like a flood," the General Association of Presbyterian Churches officially deplored the prevalence of the "sin of drunkenness." Largely in response to these powerful pressures from leading religious organizations, a state convention was held in Boston in 1813 that resulted in the creation of the Massachusetts Society for the Suppression of Intemperance. In a short time, similar societies were established in other places throughout the country and, following Boston's precedent, committees of correspondence were appointed to maintain contacts between the various groups. By this time, the battle cry was no longer simply moderation or temperance in the use of alcohol, but *total* abstinence—a goal to be achieved by effective organization, constant propaganda, and personal pledges.

From these beginnings came the temperance crusade that had attracted more than a million dedicated members by the time Josiah Quincy had become mayor of Boston. Reverend Lyman Beecher, now a well-known advocate of a return to the strict Calvinist forms of Protestantism, had come to Boston in 1826 as pastor of the Hanover Street Church, where he not only lashed out regularly at the new rationalism of Unitarianism and the threatening resurgence of "Popery," but also spoke out forcefully in an effort to awaken the public conscience to the dangerous implications of intemperate drinking. With increasing church support and moral encouragement, many of those opposed to alcoholic beverages in any form became even more militant in their approach and began urging "total abstinence" in their efforts to conquer the satanic temptations of "Demon Rum." In 1833, various elements of the crusade for "teetotalism" came together in what became known as the Massachusetts Temperance Society. According to historian Allen Krout, it was after the religious groups became involved that the temperance reform movement took on many of the attributes of a "great revival." Temperance workers became evangelicals preaching a new gospel, and they stated its dogma in what Krout calls the "pulpit phraseology of the day," a reference to the emotional evangelical camp meetings of the Baptists and the Methodists that were sweeping through the Southwest during this same period of time. The highly charged appeals of reformed drinkers, and the heart-rending "testimony" offered by those who had already taken the pledge, were strongly suggestive of the methods being used by various evangelical sects. It is significant that persons who responded to the powerful appeals of impassioned speakers and who afterward came forward and signed the pledge, were known as "converts." "The Holy Spirit will not visit, much less will He dwell with him who is under the polluting, debasing effects of the intoxicating drink," declared the *Temperance Manual* of 1836.

Despite the fervor and commitment of those who advocated temperance, by the late 1830s, there were many indications that, although their programs were achieving some significant and often dramatic results, all too often these results were temporary and short-lived, as well-meaning men would take the solemn pledge and later slip back into their old habits. As a result, some reformers began to feel that an individual's willpower, especially in the case of the reformed drinker, would never be strong enough to overcome the insidious influence of Demon Drink. As a result, many reformers started to advocate a process called "prohibition"—putting pressure upon the various states to enact legislation that would actually prohibit the manufacture and sale of alcoholic beverages. In this way, they could remove temptation entirely, and thus make it possible for the drinker to overcome his addiction and honor his solemn pledge.

True temperance advocates, however, reacted strongly against this idea of resorting to the police authority of the government to forbid the manufacture of alcoholic liquors or to prohibit their purchase by private citizens. As believers in the better nature of human beings, and the ability of the rational mind to analyze alternatives and make the proper decisions where their own lives were concerned, they preferred to rely upon intelligence and common sense to make individuals realize the dangers of intemperate drinking and to use their own free will to improve their lives. One development that reinforced the idea of moderate temperance and slowed down the more radical movement toward prohibition, came one night in April 1840, when a group of men met at Chase's Tavern in Baltimore, Maryland. Members of a "mechanics drinking club," in a spirit of fun they sent several of their fellow drinkers to a nearby church where a temperance meeting was taking place. When the men returned to the tavern, they all talked about temperance, and then decided to sign a pledge promising never again to drink "any spirituous or malt liquors, wine or cider." These six "reformer drunkards," as they called themselves, formed what came to be known as the Washingtonian Society that soon had thousands of converts attending meetings in Baltimore, which consisted mainly of personal testimonies. The movement grew rapidly, the meetings overflowed churches and halls, and teams of speakers traveled to other cities and towns to spread the word. When an agent named John H. W. Hawkins came to Boston to speak, local newspapers reported that the Odeon Theater was filled to its "utmost capacity" with local residents who had come to hear the "Reformed Drunkard" speak in "bang-up style," and "work up" his audience—sometimes bringing them to laughter and applause; at other times, reducing them to moans and to tears. After further emotional presentations, hundreds would come up onto the stage and sign the pledge. With the apparent success of these pledge-taking performances, temperance advocates were encouraged in their determination to hold out against any prohibition programs by state authorities. It was obvious that foes of liquor still wanted what historian Gilbert Seldes called "the morality of the church, and not the menace of the law," in order to persuade individuals to adopt temperance.

In this regard, Protestant temperance advocates in the Boston area found an unexpected and somewhat surprising ally in the Roman Catholic Church, whose leaders were seriously concerned about the extent of drinking among their Irish parishioners, anxious about the way in which this particular weakness was being used by critics as further proof of the instability of members of the Irish race and as a serious obstacle to their eventual assimilation into the American culture. *The Pilot*, the Irish–Catholic weekly in Boston, frequently warned its readers about the dangers of intemperate drinking, and on one occasion gave a vivid description of the disgraceful effects of alcohol at some Irish wakes, where crowds of people stood around "drinking and smoking as they would in a common barroom." During the 1830s, therefore, a number of local Catholics took up the temperance movement from Irish pride and patriotism, as well as for moral reasons, and, in April 1840, Bishop Benedict Fenwick, a Jesuit from Maryland who had been named the second Bishop of Boston in 1825, attended an early meeting at the downtown cathedral on Franklin Street for the purpose of forming a separate Catholic temperance association. Once begun, the movement spread quickly throughout the diocese, supported by a number of priests such as

Fr. James McDermott, pastor of St. Patrick's Church in Lowell; Rev. Thomas O'Flaherty, Vicar-General in Boston; and Fr. Terrence Fitzsimmons, pastor of SS Peter and Paul Church in South Boston, who made energetic efforts to warn their parishioners about the dangers of the "fruit of the bewitching glass," and to rescue them from the "premature grave of intemperance." By 1845, according to one Protestant observer, there were almost fifteen thousand Catholic total abstainers in Boston, adding: "It is but justice to say that none, who sign the pledge, regard it more sacredly, or keep it more faithfully."

A few years later, after Boston-born John Bernard Fitzpatrick had succeeded Fenwick as the third bishop of the diocese, Dr. John Collins Warren and a number of prominent Bostonians, invited the famous Irish temperance priest, Fr. Theobald Mathew, to preach a crusade for total abstinence. This Capuchin friar had traveled the length and breadth of Ireland, persuading thousands of his countrymen to take the solemn pledge of total abstinence, and it was obvious that local temperance advocates hoped that he would have a similar effect upon his immigrant countrymen in America. Although Fitzpatrick admitted to having personal reservations about seeing a Catholic priest appearing on the same public platform with a group of "sectarian fanatcics, Calvinist preachers, idolaters, and other such," he made no particular effort to interfere with the priest's work or to prevent his association with Protestant groups. Indeed, he still agreed in principle with the goals of the temperance people in using the power of free will to combat alcoholism, and in opposing the intervention of government into what they regarded as the private affairs of the individual. The true remedy to the problem, said Bishop Fitzpatrick, was in either individual moderation or in total abstinence—but not in government regulation or prohibition. As long as the use of alcohol was not an evil per se, he argued philosophically, then Catholics should have the opportunity of using their free will and exercising "individual conscience," without the interposition of the government—and, in the process, gaining spiritual grace by overcoming what could be considered a moral evil.

At this point, most of the humanitarian reforms movements in New England continued to remain essentially nonpolitical in nature, relying more on the self-reliant character of the individual than the police power of the state to achieve their well-meaning purposes. Members of the city's social

BISHOP BENEDICT FENWICK

A descendent of one of Maryland's oldest families, Benedict Fenwick was a Jesuit priest who served as pastor of churches in New York and Charleston, before becoming president of Georgetown College. In 1825, he was assigned as the second Bishop of Boston. At a time when opposition to the growing number of Catholics in the city produced such violent responses as the burning of the Ursuline Convent and the outbreak of the Broad Street Riot, Fenwick sought ways in which to explain the truths of the Catholic religion while trying to protect the lives and property of his parishioners. (Courtesy, Archdiocese of Boston) and financial conservative elite still preferred to give their time, their efforts, and their money to voluntary associations, whose largely well-to-do members served without pay or benefits, and who used a combination of moral suasion and rational discourse to raise the cultural and intellectual level of their community.

CHAPTER 4 } *An End to Pain & Suffering*

Mayor Josiah Quincy could take great pride that his extensive program of urban renewal and restoration had transformed Boston, he boasted, into one of the cleanest and healthiest cities in the United States. Members of the city's elite establishment had undertaken successful efforts to lessen crime, reduce poverty, improve conditions for the homeless, modernize the prisons, and make inroads against the debilitating effects of public drinking. But it was in the improvement of medical care and health services for the residents of the city that Boston made a significant contribution to urban development and enhanced its reputation as a progressive city during the early nineteenth century.

During colonial times, American physicians had little formal education, and the science of medicine itself was even more backward in the New World than it was in Europe. Most aspiring physicians were not trained in colleges or in hospitals; they usually apprenticed themselves to some established physician for four or five years, until it was time to hang out their shingles and set up practices of their own. Diagnoses were often inaccurate and confused, and many disease patterns were not clearly identified. Even large outbreaks of illnesses were not always recorded, although the dramatic onslaughts of diseases like smallpox and yellow fever never failed to leave their devastating effects behind them in towns and villages throughout the land. To add to this problem, new colonists coming in from Europe were extremely susceptible to dysentery and malaria, as well as influenza, pleurisy, and pneumonia. In treating their patients, colonial doctors often relied upon older forms of treatments such as bleeding and purging, and in North America many borrowed some herbs and remedies from Native American medicine men. The use of the local cinchona bark in the Colony of Virginia, for example, proved remarkably effective in reducing mortality from malaria there.

During the course of the eighteenth century, conditions in the medical profession saw a distinct improvement, although in 1721, of the ten physicians practicing in Boston only one actually held a medical degree, and it has been estimated that, as late as the time of the Revolution, only 400 of the 3,500 practitioners in America held medical degrees. Even then, however, most efforts to deal with medical problems centered around quarantining vessels and visitors, regulating the butchering of animals, seeing to the cleaning of streets, yards, and privies, and administering inoculations during periods of epidemics of yellow fever and smallpox. In the course of the century, however, there was an increase in the number of American physicians who were wealthy enough to travel to England or Scotland for a medical education, and by the end of the colonial period two medical schools had been established in America—the Medical School of Philadelphia, founded in 1765 and affiliated with the University of Pennsylvania, and the medical department of King's College (now Columbia University) in New York, established in 1767.

Two institutions were clearly not sufficient to supply formal medical training in New England, however, and so, in September 1782, corrective measures were taken, thanks in great measure to the influence of John Collins Warren, a colonial physician, son of Dr., Joseph Warren, and brother of the late Revolutionary hero, Dr. Joseph Warren, who had fallen at the Battle of Bunker Hill. Under young Warren's direction, plans were adopted for the creation of a medical school at Harvard College, with the original faculty consisting of three young Bostonians: John Collins Warren himself (age twenty-nine), who would head up the program as Professor of Anatomy and Surgery; Benjamin Waterhouse (age twenty-nine), originally from Newport, Rhode Island, who had studied at London and Edinburg before joining the Harvard faculty, who would serve as Professor of the Theory and Practice of Physics; and Aaron Dexter (age thirty-three), who was appointed Professor of Chemistry and *Materia Medica*, and who also served as the first librarian for the Massachusetts Medical Society. The first classes of the new school of medicine were held in the basement of Harvard Hall in Cambridge, before being moved to Holden Chapel, also located on the main campus. Since most of the physicians still lived in Boston, however, in 1810 the Harvard Medical School was moved across the Charles River, and for six years classes were held in rented rooms above an apothecary shop on Marlborough Street (now Washington Street), before moving, in 1816, to Mason Street, in a building that bore the rather impressive name: "Massachusetts Medical College."

Dr, Warren might have been very happy with his success in helping launch what would become the Harvard Medical School, where young men could be properly trained, but he obviously deplored the fact that New England was still without a proper hospital where new physicians would have an opportunity to apply their learning and develop their professional skills. The closest things to such a facility were a quarantine station on nearby Rainsforth Island; a public dispensary created by the Boston Chamber of Commerce to provide outpatient care for the poor, which operated out of Bartlett's apothecary shop on Corn Hill and was later moved to Ash Street; and a small marine hospital for the treatment of seamen on Castle Island that was moved in 1803 to Charlestown. In an effort to rectify this situation, Rev. John Bartlett, chaplain of the Boston Almshouse, issued a call for a public meeting of the town's residents on March 8, 1810, to point out the need for a hospital for the physically and mentally ill. Dr. John Collins Warren and his friend Dr. James Jackson, who had come down from Newburyport to practice medicine in Boston, responded to this call, and on August 20, they began circulating letters among the town's wealthy residents, outlining the need for a hospital to care for "lunatics and other sick persons" and soliciting charitable contributions for such a community enterprise. Playing effectively on the pride that most leading citizens of Boston took in considering themselves "treasurers of God's bounty," the young doctors emphasized how necessary it was for members of their class, particularly, to see the propriety, "and even the obligation," of visiting and healing the sick. The fund-raising program inaugurated by these two young and enthusiastic physicians proved to be a great success, and within six months, on February 25, 1811, the state legislature granted a formal charter for the establishment of the Massachusetts General Hospital, with a condition that the supporters of the project raise an additional $100,000 of private money within a five-year period. Prominent Bostonians not only made substantial individual contributions, but also helped to organize vigorous door-to-door campaigns in all parts of the community to raise the necessary funds.

On July 4, 1818, the governor of the commonwealth and the members of his council joined with "a great concourse of citizens" to witness the laying of the cornerstone of the new hospital. After the selection of Prince's Pasture on the banks of the Charles River in Boston's West End as the site, Charles Bulfinch was chosen to design the main building of the new hospital on Allen Street. This was actually Bulfinch's last architectural commission in Boston, before he moved to Washington, D.C., at the request of President James Madison, to rebuild the national's Capitol and restore other public buildings the British had burned or otherwise damaged during the War of 1812. He turned over supervision of the construction work to his young friend, Alexander Parris, who had come down from Maine to work in Boston, and who would later design the new Faneuil Hall Market area. The handsome hospital of Chelmsford granite, designed in the Greek Revival style, with a pedimented portico of massive Ionic columns, was topped by a shallow saucerlike dome. Intended as a truly "general" institution, the Massachusetts General Hospital was designed for the "whole family of man," not just for Bostonians, and it was to be open to everyone, rich and poor alike.

For many years, wealthy members of the Boston Associates and their families continued to take a strong personal interest in the MGH. Dr. John Collins Warren's friend, Dr. James Jackson, was the brother of Patrick Tracy Jackson, a well-known merchant and financier. Francis Cabot Lowell, the textile manufacturer, was elected to the hospital's first board of trustees. Twenty-seven members of the Boston Associates served as hospital trustees, and many more continued to make substantial personal contributions to the institution on a regular basis. In January 1844, the trustees voted to add two new wings to the Allen Street buildings, in response to the needs of a growing population. Once again the general public responded generously to a fund drive that was organized and directed by such well-known figures as Thomas Handasyd Perkins, a prominent merchant and philanthropist, and Abbott Lawrence, a leading textile magnate and prominent Whig politian. Under the general direction and supervision of these managers and administrators, procedures at the hospital were carried out with great care and businesslike precision. According to Mrs. Anne Royall, every surgical operation was performed in the presence of several individuals; every medication was prepared by prescription and entered into a written record; every patient was visited at least once a week by a visiting committee; every change in food or medication was recorded in a book that was made available to members of the visiting committee. Here was another impressive example of how the spirit of humanitarianism, combined with the rational principles of modern science and directed by men of education and influence, could promote the welfare of the entire community.

A spectacular event occurred on October 16, 1846, that provided the first entirely American contribution to medicine and further enhanced the

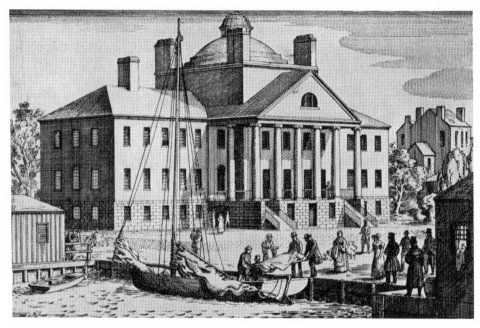

MASSACHUSETTS GENERAL HOSPITAL

On July 4, 1818, the Governor of Massachusetts joined with "a great concourse of citizens" along the banks of the Charles River in Boston's West End to witness the laying of the cornerstone of the Massachusetts General Hospital. Charles Bulfinch had originally been chosen to design the main building but was called to Washington to rebuild the nation's Capitol. The task was taken over by Alexander Parris, who constructed a granite structure, designed in the Greek Revival style, with a portico of Ionic columns and topped by a low saucerlike dome. (Courtesy, Bostonian Society/ Old State House) professional reputation of the Massachusetts General Hospital. On that day, Dr. William T. G. Morton successfully administered ether to a patient of Dr. John Collins Warren in the amphitheater of the Bulfinch building. Born near Worcester in 1819, Morton was forced to leave school at an early age, worked for a while in a publishing house, and then decided to become a dentist. Traveling to Baltimore for his studies, he became acutely aware of the dreadful pain and suffering to which patients were subjected in the process of surgery. Some patients were given brandy, laudanum, and even opium to dull their senses; others were simply pinned down on the table by sheer force while the surgeon went about his gruesome business.

Realizing the relief that the application of ether or some other form of gaseous sedation could bring to dentistry, as well as to medical surgery in general, Morton gave up a lucrative practice manufacturing artificial teeth and devoted all his time at MGH to the study of various forms of gases. Discovering the use of ether as an effective and safe means of rendering a person unconscious, Morton used the gas successfully in extracting a tooth from a patient at his Boston office at 10 Tremont Row. He then asked Dr. Warren, senior surgeon at MGH, for permission to administer ether to a patient at the hospital. Dr. Warren allowed Morton to enter the operating room and administer ether to one of his patients who was suffering from a tumor of the jaw. After rendering the patient insensible, Morton turned the man over to Dr. Warren, who proceeded to remove the tumor from under the man's jaw. Afterward, when the patient acknowledged that he had experienced no pain during the operation, Dr. Warren is reported to have remarked to his colleagues: "Gentlemen, this is no humbug." Dr. Oliver Wendell Holmes, reflecting on what had taken place, agreed that "a new era has opened on the operating surgeon." As a result of this new invention, he mused, "the fierce extremity of suffering has been steeped in the waters of forgetfulness, and the deepest furrow in the knotted brow of agony has been smoothed forever."

One local physician who was as excited as the rest of Boston medical community about the news of Dr. Morton's successful use of an anesthetic was Dr. Walter Channing, the town's leading specialist in obstetrics, who could see its obvious application for female patients. In their concern for the creation of a general hospital and more professional training for physicians, leading Bostonians had also felt that there was need for more specialized medical care for women in labor—not only for women who were respectable members of the community, but also for those who were without adequate resources. Those who were poor, but not "respectable," it was agreed, would have to be treated at the House of Industry. On May 28, 1832, the Massachusetts Charitable Fire Society voted a grant of $5,000 toward the establishment of a hospital for the care of poor women in labor. The Massachusetts Humane Society contributed an additional grant of $5,000 to the project, and the idea of the Boston Lying-In Hospital was conceived. A board of trustees was appointed, including two merchants, two lawyers, a teacher, a wharf-owner, a surgeon from Massachusetts General Hospital, and a Unitarian minister. Members of the board purchased a small brick house at 718 Washington Street in Boston, where two attending physicians were in residence—Dr. Enoch Hale Jr., a well-known local practitioner, and Dr. Walter Channing, the town's leading obstetrician.

Walter Channing was the brother of Boston's eminent Unitarian preacher Rev. William Ellery Channing. Although he had been dismissed from Harvard College for participating in a minor student rebellion, he decided to became a physician by resorting to the traditional method of apprenticeship. After a year of studying with Dr. James Jackson, he went to the Pennsylvania Medical School, from which he received his M.D. degree in 1809, and later traveled to England, Scotland, and France to learn new skills and techniques for successful midwifery. Returning to Boston in 1811, he hung up his shingle, and with his reputation as an obstetrician, along with his family connections, he soon developed a thriving medical practice. Awarded an M.D. degree from Harvard in 1812, Channing was appointed a lecturer in midwifery at the Harvard Medical School and three years later was promoted to the rank of professor, thus guaranteeing that the medical curriculum would henceforth include adequate instruction in the procedures of childbirth.

In the course of his practice, according to his biographer, Amalie M. Kass, Dr. Walter Channing traveled regularly to the homes of expectant mothers, from the very wealthy to the very poor, working with skill and compassion to ease their suffering and make their deliveries as painless as possible. He was supportive of the Boston Lying-In Hospital for its improved care of women and served as one of the two attending physicians. But it was the significance of Dr. Morton's use of ether that excited his interest in visualizing how an anesthetic could help free women from the fear, anxiety, and pain that usually accompanied the ordeal of childbirth in those days. He had little patience with critics who used passages from the Scriptures to support their objection to the use of anesthesia to make the process less painful. The Creator, he argued, with that sense of rationalism that pervaded his brother's Unitarian faith and that characterized so many of the reforms of that period, had endowed human beings with the intellectual capacity to improve their lives, including their health. He carefully recorded his experimental procedures, published a *Treatise on Etherization in Childbirth*, based on a series of actual case studies, and became the first American physician to use anesthesia in an instrumental delivery. "Channing's advocacy of anesthesia is his most important contribution to the practice of obstetrics," concluded Amalie Kass in her biography of this progressive Boston physician.

While Boston was taking steps to educate future doctors, professionalize hospitals, and mitigate the pains of surgery, provisions to safeguard public health in general still lagged behind. The gradual adoption of vaccination put an end to the scourge of smallpox as a major killer in North America; by 1830 the discovery of quinine had significantly reduced the number of deaths from malaria in tropical climates; and the annual ravages of yellow fever had virtually disappeared from most northern states by the early nineteenth century. Nevertheless, there were other plagues and diseases that posed serious health problems for the general public. Tuberculosis, for example, was probably the nation's biggest single killer in the years before the Civil War, taking a particularly heavy toll among younger people between the ages of fifteen and twenty-five. Although it reportedly took a great many lives among destitute young women living in the most congested sections of town, the "White Plague," as it was called, was also capable of striking at members of the upper levels of Boston society as well. Dr. Walter Channing's young wife, Barbara Higginson Perkins, died of consumption in 1822, and the terrible disease wiped out the whole family of Ralph Waldo Emerson's first wife, Ellen Tucker, for another example, killing her father and brother, then her, and finally taking her mother and her sister. Henry Sumner, the younger brother of Charles Sumner, the future senator from Massachusetts, succumbed to tuberculosis in 1843, and a year later his twenty-year-old sister Mary also died of the disease. Sumner himself was diagnosed with consumption at about the same time, and he was considered so gravely ill, according to his biographer David Donald, that at one point his friends filed solemnly into his home to pay their final respects. Although it was later determined that the medical diagnosis was incorrect, it took some time for the young lawyer to recover fully from his debilitating illness.

Tuberculosis continued to claim its victims at a steady and deadly pace, with few effective measures taken by public health authorities to bring it under control, but it was a sudden and frightening outbreak of an epidemic, called Asiatic Cholera, that produced paralyzing fear and consternation in several major American cities during the first half of the nineteenth century. Spreading westward from Europe during the fall and winter of 1831–32, outbreaks of cholera were reported in Montreal and Quebec early in June 1832, and then moved southward into the Atlantic seaboard states during the summer months. It was the "spectacular symptoms" of cholera that struck terror within the hearts of the public, according to Charles E. Rosenberg in *The Cholera Years*, although such diseases as tuberculosis and malaria actually caused a much greater loss of life over a longer period of time. The abrupt onset of the disease—the blue face, the darkened skin, acute diarrhea, violent vomiting, painful cramps—and then the sudden death that wiped out entire families, made it the kind of dreaded epidemic that Americans would confront with the periodic outbreaks of poliomyelitis a century later. New York City was hard hit during July, despite last-minute measures taken to clean streets, collect garbage, and build special hospital facilities. Although many families loaded up their personal belongings and headed for the country as quickly as possible, by September the five newly constructed hospitals had already treated more than 2,000 patients, with an additional 555 cases cared for at the Bellevue Almshouse. Cities such as Newark, Philadelphia, and Baltimore suffered significant numbers of deaths. But as the disease moved into the deep south, it was New Orleans that was the hardest hit, with the loss of some 5,000 lives.

To prepare for the possibility of a similar outbreak of the disease, in June 1832 Boston created a special Board of Health, as well as an agency called the Boston Relief Association to direct the efforts of thirteen separate ward committees. At the same time, many neighboring towns set up special health measures and formed volunteer associations to care for the sick, distribute food and clothing, and care for widows and orphans in the event of a full-scale epidemic. Massachusetts General Hospital was advised to expect an overflow of patients from municipal facilities that had been especially created for the emergency. Fortunately, however, Boston escaped the most serious effects of the first cholera epidemic, in 1832, and did not have to resort to such emergency measures. Some observers, like Dr. John Collins Warren, felt that Boston was saved as a result of the vigorous sweeping and cleaning programs that had been instituted by Mayor Josiah Quincy some six years earlier. Others suggested that the city was protected by a heavy layer of chlorine of lime that had been laid on the streets. Still others, however, believed that God himself had played a significant role in safeguarding the good citizens of Boston. In his historical study of the phenomenon, Charles Rosenberg has noted that many, if not most, Americans believed that cholera was not really a contagious disease at all, but a pestilence that targeted poor and ignorant people, "drunkards and filthy wicked people of all description." They tended to view the epidemic as a sort of punishment from God—like the biblical plague of locusts—designed to drain off the "filth and scum" of human society. Since Bostonians regarded their cherished City Upon a Hill as one of the cleanest cities in America, as well as one of the most virtuous, and looked upon their citizens as models of morality, they assumed that this explained why most of their citizens escaped the worst ravages of the fearful epidemic.

Boston was not so fortunate, however, when a second cholera epidemic broke out in 1849. Once again, as had happened seventeen years earlier, a major cholera epidemic swept out of India, moved through western Europe, and crossed the Atlantic during the winter of 1848–49. In anticipation of an outbreak in America, East coast cities began reviving their boards of health and launching half-hearted sanitation programs in an effort to clean up decades of accumulated dirt and filth that covered city streets. Although Josiah Quincy's vigorous street-cleaning projects had been largely neglected in recent years, most Bostonians were still convinced that any outbreak of cholera would be confined to the poor, the ignorant, and the wicked, living in small, congested districts apart from the general population. Freezing winter temperatures held down the number of cases in the North, while the disease spread quickly from New Orleans, through Arkansas and Tennessee, and up into the Mississippi Valley.

Once the weather turned warm, however, the cholera broke out in full force throughout the Northeast, with New York City losing at least twice as many victims as it had back in 1832. But this time, New York was not alone. Boston, which had failed to keep up Mayor Quincy's program of sweeping the streets, collecting the filth, emptying the drains, and cleaning the cesspools, did not escape the effects of the cholera epidemic that swept through congested areas of the city. Many of the districts hardest hit were the enclaves where the Irish lived, and in much greater numbers in 1849 than in 1832, as a result of the heavy immigration that followed the Great Famine of the mid-1840s. The listings of 611 fatal cases and 96 deaths from other unidentifiable causes, according to Oscar Handlin's statistics, were reported in the district from Broad Street to Fort Hill—in locations described as "the least perfect in drainage, the worst ventilated, and the most crowded." Just across the harbor, in East Boston, in immigrant neighborhoods such as Liverpool Street, more than 500 of the 700 fatalities were Irish immigrants, or the children of Irish families. The death rate, "boosted by dirt and overcrowding in the Irish district," writes historian Roger Lane in *Policing the City*, averaged 29.4 per thousand in the five-year period before 1850—a record for the century.

In the absence of an effective municipal response, the disease continued to run its deadly course. The Board of Health proved largely ineffective in dealing with the crisis; public meetings and town meetings lacked the power to organize resources or to enforce emergency measures; taxpayers steadfastly refused to have their taxes increased; the Common Council was unable to establish new sanitation policies. Since most physicians agreed that cholera may have been "portable," but definitely not contagious (it was supposed to have "atmospheric origins"), they refused to support any provisions for an enforceable quarantine. Undoubtedly, the fact that the greatest number of fatalities occurred in the congested Irish neighborhoods gave additional support to the traditional belief that a plague like cholera was probably a form of divine retribution visited upon poor and ignorant people, with their "dissolute" lifestyles, who insisted on living in poverty, misery, and vice, and who were not, therefore, deserving of organized forms of municipal assistance. The most immediate and effective response to the epidemic came from a variety of private and voluntary associations throughout the Boston area. Charitable individuals volunteered to work in hospitals or to tend the afflicted in their homes; committees of "Christian gentlemen" raised money for food and clothing; churches of all denominations held special collections for the benefit of the sick and the poor; groups of Catholic nuns cared for homeless orphans who had no one to take care of them. "I believe that if anybody goes to Heaven from Boston," Richard Henry Dana wrote to his sister, "it will be the Sisters of Charity and the Roman Catholic clergy." In the absence of a determined, energetic, and charismatic public figure such as Josiah Quincy, Boston's "Great Mayor," who showed that he could override public lethargy and general apathy, it seemed that Boston, as well as most other urban centers at the time, lacked both the will and the desire to marshal the public forces of the community to respond effectively to major public emergencies.

As for more specific reforms, however, especially those affecting the mental and physical welfare of individuals, Bostonians responded with much greater seriousness and compassion. The irrepressible optimism of the age, the absolute conviction that people were innately good and capable of improvement, and the belief that rational science and modern technology could provide the solution to most human problems brought major changes in the care and treatment of those individuals who were handicapped, deformed, or disabled. In the atmosphere of reform that characterized the 1830s and 1840s, society would tolerate "neither poverty nor suffering; it would condemn no condemned classes or deprived citizens, no criminals or forgotten men," observed historian John L. Thomas. Members of the Boston leadership elite could take pride in the fact that they had already brought hope to those oppressed by poverty, addicted to crime, enslaved to alcohol, or wracked by physical pain. There were other forms of pain from which many Americans suffered, however, perhaps more subtle and complex ones that were nonetheless more devastating and debilitating, usually marginalizing those who were afflicted far beyond the ordinary boundaries of normal society.

Blindness, for example, was an affliction that denied many Americans an equal opportunity to share in the benefits of an enlightened and progressive society and to enjoy the spirit of perfection that was energizing much of Boston. It was in keeping with this ideal of improving the status of every citizen that Dr. Samuel Gridley Howe became internationally renowned for his imaginative work, not only with the blind, but also with persons who were mentally retarded and physically disabled. Born in Boston in 1801, Howe graduated from Harvard Medical School in 1824 and then, at the age of twenty-three, went off to Greece, where he spent seven years as a surgeon in the army of the Greek rebels fighting for their independence from the Ottoman Empire. After the Greeks had driven the Turks from their country, Howe returned to Boston, a charistmatic local celebrity—but one without an immediate outlet for his irrepressible reformist tendencies, until he was asked to accept the directorship of a newly created asylum for the

SAMUEL GRIDLEY HOWE

Physician, humanitarian, and reformer, Samuel Gridley Howe graduated from the Harvard Medical School and then went off to Greece to fight in the struggle for Greek independence. After his return to Boston, he accepted the directorship of what became the Perkins Institution for the Blind. There, he experimented with the use of musical instruments, raised alphabets, and other innovative techniques that could be employed in educating young blind persons so that they could go out into the world and "earn a livelihood by honest work." (Courtesy, Bostonian Society/Old State House) blind. Howe immediately accepted the challenge to command this new enterprise, and set sail for Europe to find out more about the latest innovations in the field.

In the course of his travels through the British Isles and France, according to Harold Schwartz's recent biographical study, Dr. Howe visited several institutions that were modeled on the National Institution for Young Blind Children, founded in Paris in 1784 by Valentin de Hauy, designed to provide both academic and vocational training for blind young people. Howe returned to America, however, impressed by what he had observed, but convinced that he himself could do a much better job—not only by using more effective teaching techniques, but also by developing an educational system that would encourage blind persons to become less dependent on restrictive institutional settings and more determined to go out into the world to "gain their own livelihood." Society had a "sacred and fundamental" responsibility to help those who could not provide for themselves, said Howe, who also believed that those who were "afflicted" had a responsibility, too, to escape dependence, and become self-reliant citizens through the application of their own talents.

After his return to Boston, Dr. Howe set up his first school for the blind in his own house at 140 Pleasant Street, where he worked with six pupils. His experiments attracted the attention of Colonel Thomas Handasyd Perkins, a wealthy merchant, who offered the school his spacious house in downtown Boston at 17 Pearl Street, if the citizens could match his gift with the sum of $50,000. The women of Boston held one of the first great municipal fairs at Faneuil Hall and, within a matter of weeks, had raised the entire amount needed to found what would become the Perkins Institution for the Blind. Early in 1839, the Mount Washington Hotel, constructed only a few years earlier as a resort hotel on the corner of Broadway and H Street in South Boston, was offered to the trustees of the Perkins Institution in exchange for the property in downtown Boston. The trade was agreed upon, and during the month of May the clients were transferred to the new site, with the moving expenses paid by the private contributions of Samuel Appleton and several other wealthy Boston gentlemen.

The selection of South Boston as the site for the Perkins Institution was just one more indication of the way in which the peninsula district across the channel from downtown Boston, still a sparsely populated rural area of grazing lands and fruitful orchards, was quickly becoming a favorite place in which to locate a number of the city's public institutions. Indeed, as far back as 1792, town authorities had already seen the advantages of the peninsula's fresh salt air, open beaches, and broad expanses of green pastures when they established a special hospital there to isolate smallpox patients, as well as those who had submitted to the controversial procedure of inoculation. Civic leaders continued to show an interest in the physical attractions of the district, and in the years that followed they used it for public health purposes. When Mayor Josiah Quincy established his new House of Industry, for example, he located it in South Boston because of its easy accessibility to downtown Boston—only two and a half miles from the center of the city by land, and only one and a half miles by water. After his reelection in 1823 to a second term as mayor, Quincy proceeded to sell off the old almshouse on Leverett Street, near the Charles River, and by 1825 he had moved the entire population of poor and unfortunate inmates to the new House of Industry now open in South Boston. Obviously looking forward to similar municipal decisions, city leaders purchased a tract of 53 acres of land in the easternmost part of the "City Point" section, running from the corner of L and Fourth Streets to the corner of O and Fourth, which subsequently became known as the City Lands. This area eventually became the site of a cluster of large brick institutional buildings that included the House of Industry, a new poorhouse, a lunatic asylum, a house of correction for adults found guilty of misdemeanors, and a separate house of reformation for juvenile offenders.

It was in this area, therefore, that the new Perkins Institution for the Blind became a well-known feature of the South Boston landscape. During his bachelor years, Dr. Samuel Gridley Howe lived at the institution until 1843, when he married Julia Ward of New York and brought his young bride to live in an old colonial house in South Boston, not far from the institution. Julia raised five children, played the piano, wrote plays, produced recitals, and greeted a procession of visitors who came to visit her famous husband and witness his work with the blind at firsthand. During the 1840s, most visitors to Boston from Europe and from all parts of the United States arrived with a list of things they were determined to see. These included not only Faneuil Hall, the Bulfinch State House, the Boston Common, the Boston Latin School, and the new observatory at Harvard College, but also the Perkins Institution for the Blind, where they could observe the new mechanical devices and experimental techniques Dr. Howe was using to educate and rehabilitate young blind persons. With the aid of the American

Bible Society, for example, he had already produced a vast amount of printing in raised type in order to bring the Scriptures within the reach of the blind. Ferenc Pulszky, who followed the Hungarian patriot Louis Kossuth into exile in America after the failure of their liberal uprising, was among those who visited the Perkins Institution and marveled at what was being accomplished. "He [Dr. Howe] is the regenerator of many a child who, without him," he later wrote, "would not only be lost to the world without, but would likewise remain blind to the light within."

But visitors came, also, to observe the fascinating work being done by Dr. Howe in educating a pupil named Laura Bridgman, a young women who was deaf as well as blind. Born in 1829 near Hanover, New Hampshire, Laura was stricken with scarlet fever at the age of two and was left without sight or hearing. Several years later, after reading a newspaper account of Laura Bridgman, Dr. Howe arranged with her parents to have the eight-year-old girl brought to the Perkins Institution. In establishing initial contact with Laura, Howe taught her the alphabet by labeling common objects such as pins, knives, spoons, and cups with raised lettering. After several weeks of frustrating experimentation, in a sudden flash of understanding, Laura discovered the relationship between the objects and the letters. The young girl subsequently learned the entire alphabet, and was then taught to communicate by tapping the alphabet in manual form into the hands of others. As Ernest Freeberg describes it in his recent study of Laura Bridgman, the process was slow and tedious, but over the years she learned not only to read, but also to write by using specially grooved paper. On special exhibition days, visitors to the Perkin's would stand behind a barrier and watch the young woman at work, neatly dressed, sitting erect, knitting, sewing, braiding, a green ribbon covering her sightless eyes. Davy Crockett, celebrated frontier hero, went to the Perkins Institution during his visit to Boston in 1834, two years before he was killed at the Alamo, and was "astonished" to watch Laura Bridgman using raised letters to read, playing the piano, and making "pretty little baskets." Eight years later, Charles Dickens traveled to the Institution on his 1842 visit to Boston and marveled at Laura's abilities, and he included an account of her achievements in his *American Notes*, published in England the following year. Since Dr. Howe himself was away at the time, the British author and his wife were escorted to the Perkins school by Charles Sumner, a young Boston lawyer and a friend of the Howe family. After meeting and speaking with Laura Bridgman, Dickens, the young woman's teacher reported, "could hardly believe the evidence of his senses, and was much more surprised than people generally are," and even suggested that, along with Niagara Falls, Laura Bridgman might also be considered one of the wonders of the New World.

In allowing members of the public to watch Laura Bridgman at work, observed Ernest Freeberg, Samuel Gridley Howe was not only promoting his own professional career, but he was also trying to arouse the sympathy of the general public by bringing blind people out of their "social invisibility" into open view, where they could demonstrate their accomplishments, and visitors could marvel at the "miraculous" power of the human spirit to overcome all kinds of adversity. Whether putting Laura on display at the Institution, or taking her along on his numerous traveling exhibitions, Howe also used these occasions to promote his theories about discipline—a form of "moral discipline"—instead of the old-fashioned practices of verbal threats and physical punishment so often used in most institutions of the period. In this respect, Howe, as a firm supporter of the principles of liberal Unitarianism, felt that he had an opportunity to discredit the old Calvinist theology by providing rational explanations of the causes of blindness, as well as scientific techniques for treating it. Claiming that Calvinism was "the greatest obstacle to all kinds of human progress," he rejected the long-standing superstition that God had caused people to suffer blindness because of some sin they had committed.

Although best known for his work with the blind, Samuel Gridley Howe was also concerned about the plight of other young people with serious mental and physical infirmities. The Massachusetts state legislature decided to consider the plight of "idiots," a term generally used to describe what later generations would classify as retarded or emotionally disturbed persons, as compared with the term "lunatick," used to categorize persons who were insane or "furiously mad." Dr. Howe, assigned to the investigative commission, visited sixty-three towns in various parts of the Commonwealth, and examined nearly six hundred unfortunate children. In his 1846 report to the legislature, he requested state funding in order to improve the condition of these handicapped persons and offered to assist in their special training and education. In 1848, work was begun at the Perkins Institution with a state appropriation of $2,500 a year. At the end of this period, the appropriation was increased, and additional funds were provided for a separate building to be constructed in the so-called City Lands section of South Boston.

Howe himself was named superintendent of what was then called the Massachusetts School for Idiots, a residential facility designed to accommodate some fifty retarded and emotionally disturbed young people ranging from seven to fifteen years of age. "Dr. Howe now bestows his care on idiots, likewise," wrote Ferenc Pulszky admiringly during his Boston visit, "to arouse in them the divine spark, buried in their defective physical constitution." Under Howe's direction, the clients followed a carefully regimented program, rising at 5:30 each morning, eating breakfast at 6:30, dinner at noon, and supper at 5:30, with a period set aside every day for physical exercise in a gymnasium located in a separate building. In between, the clients attended classes for a total of six hours a day. Those who were judged to be educable were taught the basics of reading, writing, and speech; those with more limited abilities were instructed in "form, color, and size." The girls were also given instruction in such manual skills as sewing and needlework.

Because of his work with Laura Bridgman, who lacked both sight and hearing, Dr. Howe also became interested in working with deaf mutes, inspired by the pioneering work of Rev. Thomas Hopkins Gallaudet of Connecticut. A graduate of the Andover Theological Seminary near Boston, Gallaudet found the ministry less fulfilling than working with young deaf persons, and providing them with the social skills and manual dexterity that would allow them to make a living in the larger community. After a visit to Europe in 1813, where he studied educational methods in London and Paris, he returned to find that his home state of Connecticut had established an asylum for the education of deaf and dumb persons that became known as the American Asylum. Gallaudet's small experimental school soon attracted widespread attention, especially after he began taking his pupils on exhibition tours that soon stimulated other states to follow his example. In Boston, meanwhile, Samuel Gridley Howe experimented with new techniques of his own in the treatment of the deaf, especially in developing a different method of instruction that would teach children to form words and use speech, rather than resorting to the use of the manual sign language that was the preferred method of Thomas Gallaudet.

If many Bostonians were aroused by the difficulties faced by those who were blind, deaf, retarded, and disabled, others were appalled by the shameful neglect and callous brutality visited upon those persons who were afflicted by mental illness. A tentative approach in dealing with this problem in the Boston area had been made in the early nineteenth century, when the founders of Massachusetts General Hospital declared that the institution should be equally concerned with the mentally ill as with the physically impaired. While the main hospital was under construction in the city's West End, the proposed asylum for the insane had already been established on a spit of land overlooking the harbor in nearby Charlestown. The comparative speed with which this took place was due not only to the ability of Dr. Warren and Dr. Jackson to raise more money for the asylum than for the hospital, but also to the fact that a fortuitous real estate opportunity gave them a head start. Back in the mid-eighteenth century, a wealthy businessman named Joseph Barrell had built a handsome three-story, English-style country house on an expensive eighteen-acre estate in Charlestown, in great part to enjoy his enthusiasm for gardening. In 1804, Barrell died, burdened by business failures, and as a result of his indebtedness, the hospital trustees were able to purchase his estate and its adjoining properties at a very low price. After the purchase, the trustees commissioned Charles Bulfinch to add three-story wings to each side of the central brick manor house. With Dr. Rufus Wyman serving as the first superintendent, the new asylum opened its doors in 1818, with facilities available for six hundred mentally ill patients. Rejecting the older, inhumane, and often brutal practices so often employed in dealing with those who were mentally ill, Wyman adopted a much more sensitive and enlightened approach, boasting that "chains or straight jackets have never been used or provided in this asylum." In an 1830 address to the members of the Massachusetts Medical Society, he insisted that in dealing with people who were insane, a "judicial moral judgment" was much more successful than mere medical treatments, and that patients should be directed to engage in "agreeable occupations." He encouraged his own patients, many of them members of Boston's best families, to exercise, read, dance, develop their manual skills, and attend religious services, thereby setting the stage for the hospital's later pioneering efforts in psychiatric treatments. "Moral treatment is indispensable," he insisted, "even in cases arising from organic diseases."

For several years, the asylum at Charlestown (sometimes called the Somerville Asylum, when the area later incorporated itself as Somerville) was the only mental hospital in Boston, and during its early years it attracted a fairly diverse patient population. Wanting to make sure that their institution was not perceived as "a merely pauper establishment," the trustees insisted that patients pay at least something for their treatment so that they would appreciate the value of the services they were receiving. The directors charged admittance fees on a sliding scale and resisted the demands of the state legislature to admit charity patients free of charge. By the end of 1821, only four years after opening its doors, a total of 126 patients had entered the asylum, causing the trustees to have Bulfinch design additional wings to accommodate a hundred more patients. Under Wyman's successor, Luther Bell, the idea of providing leisure and comfort for the patients was expanded even further. With the use of Appleton family money, he provided carpeting, wallpaper, mirrors, fireplaces, and elegant furniture to grace the halls, and even allowed some of the wealthier patients to provide separate lodgings for their personal servants. According to Alex Beam in his 2001 study, *Gracefully Insane*, some of the "boarders" were permitted to come and go as they pleased. Many took walks, attended Sunday services, went rowing on the Charles, and one gentleman was observed to be a frequent visitor at the reading room of the Boston Athenaeum. The names of the older houses at the Charlestown Asylum—Appleton, Codman, Higginson, and Bowditch—are illustrative of those wealthy sea captains and successful merchants of the town who continued to form the basis for the financial support of this humanitarian undertaking.

The success of the asylum, the number of patients, and the additional construction work, however, had put the hospital some $20,000 in debt, and raised serious questions as to how long it could continue to operate. Fortunately, a wealthy merchant named John McLean came to the rescue. A series of business reverses had forced McLean into bankruptcy court, when one of his vessels, long presumed lost at sea, suddenly showed up in Boston harbor in 1823 laden with precious cargo. Not only did the grateful merchant pay off all his debts, but he also decided to leave a legacy of $120,000 to the Charlestown Asylum. In return for this unexpected largesse, the trustees promptly renamed the institution the McLean Asylum, in honor of their unexpected benefactor. Increasingly, the revived institution began to attract what superintendent Bell referred to as "an improved class of sufferers." McLean was well on its way to becoming an upper-class institution, and by the middle of the nineteenth century, according to historian Silvia Sutton, "pauper patients became the exception at McLean."

The distressing lack of proper care for the state's impoverished mentally ill population was an issue raised in 1830 by Horace Mann, a member of the state legislature, who especially criticized an existing law that said that any person characterized as "furiously mad" would be incarcerated in prison. Not until 1827 was that law changed so that such persons were assigned to lunatic asylums rather than jails. This was still not satisfactory for Mann, who passionately argued that "the insane are the wards of the state," and for four years he worked on a survey of Massachusetts prisons, almshouses, and houses of corrections, determining that more than 150 insane persons languished in poorhouses, houses of industry, jails, and houses of corrections, while a similar number went completely unrecorded and untreated. As a result of Mann's constant prodding, the legislature finally agreed to appropriate $30,000 for the construction of a state hospital in Worcester, which was calculated to draw off most of those unfortunates still languishing in jails and prisons. Seven years later, through the efforts of Mayor Samuel Eliot and members of the Boston Prison Discipline Society, the Boston Lunatic Asylum was established to accommodate many insane persons in the local Boston area who were found to be inmates of the House of Industry.

With the rapid growth of the population in the Greater Boston area during the 1830s and 1840s, however, it was impossible for the small number of asylums to keep pace with the increased demand for human custodial care. In 1840, for example, the city's total population was listed at 93,383; in 1845, it rose to 114,366; by 1850, it reached 136,881, an increase of almost 50 percent in the course of only ten years. Although nearly 90,000 of the residents in 1850 had been born in the United States, over 35,000 had been born in Ireland—a clear indication of the effects of immigration on the city's population. It was obvious that there was a large number of people with serious mental illnesses who were no longer receiving appropriate care and treatment. In the rural areas of the state, the feebleminded and the insane were usually allowed to roam through the villages, the butt of cruel jokes and painful pranks. If they became violent, either to themselves or with others, they were usually thrown into a locked cellar, an empty stable, or a vacant garret, often chained to a wall, flung a few crumbs and a dirty blanket, and left to be forgotten. Although some relatives of well-to-do families in urban areas might be taken care of in private homes by sympathetic relatives or by paid attendants, most were usually assigned to poorhouses or prisons where they were at the mercy of derelicts and criminals. Very often, unfortunate victims of hallucinations, strange voices, or epileptic seizures were further regarded as "possessed"—filled with an evil, Satanic spirit—and regarded as little more than dangerous beasts.

DOROTHEA LYNDE DIX

A native of Hamden, Maine, Dorothea Lynde Dix moved to Boston as a young woman, taught school, and encountered the terrible condition of insane persons when asked to instruct a Sunday-school class at the East Cambridge House of Correction. After conducting a two-year investigation of jails and almshouses throughout Massachusetts, in 1843 she made a powerful presentation of her findings to the state legislature in a Memorial *that succeeded in producing an increased appropriation for the care and treatment of the insane. (Courtesy, Bostonian Society/Old State House)*

No real and substantial changes were made in this situation until the restless energy and untiring efforts of Dorothea Lynde Dix created a whole new dynamic that would change both attitudes and policies with regard to the treatment of the mentally ill. A native of Hampden, Maine, Dorothea Dix had come to Boston at the age of thirteen to live with her grandmother, and she found comfort in the compassionate teachings of the Unitarian faith. Quiet, gentle, and somewhat withdrawn, she taught in a school for young girls and also involved herself in the Boston Female Asylum and other benevolent activities. In 1841, Miss Dix was asked to give religious instruction to a Sunday School class at the East Cambridge House of Correction, where she was appalled by the conditions of the insane persons she found there, abused, neglected, huddled together without blankets or warm clothing on a cold March morning. Shocked beyond words, she found similar conditions in various jails and asylums in other parts of the city and, then, after consulting with Rev. William Ellery Channing, Dr. Samuel Gridley Howe, and later with Horace Mann, she started out on what would become a two-year journey throughout the state of Massachusetts investigating jails, prisons, and almshouses. With painstaking precision, she recorded in her notebooks every locality she visited, every institution she explored, and every inhuman abuse inflicted upon the helpless insane men and women she discovered in the course of her relentless visitations. Through summer heat and winter snows, she traveled to places like Dedham, Newton, Groton ("a young man, an iron collar around his neck, with a strong heavy chain"), Granville, Pepperell, Sandisfield ("young woman kept in a cage and chained and beaten"), Plymton, Concord, Ipswich, Danvers ("young woman . . . caged . . . half-naked and disheveled . . . tearing off her skin, inch by inch"). There was little that escaped the woman's tireless search and exhaustive inquiries.

After competing her survey, Dorothea Dix incorporated her findings in a classic *Memorial* that, in 1843, she presented to the members of the Massachusetts state legislature, calling their attention to "the *present* state of insane persons confined within the Commonwealth in *cages, closets, cellars, pens! Chained, naked, beaten with rods,* and *lashed* into obedience!" "If my pictures are displeasing, coarse, and severe," wrote the frail woman almost apologetically to the all-male members of the Great and General Court, "my subjects, it must be recollected, offer no tranquil, refining, or composing features. The condition of human beings reduced to the extremist state of degradation and misery cannot be exhibited in softened language, or adorn a polished page." At the end of her heartrending litany of callous neglect and inhuman brutality, Dix formally petitioned the Massachusetts legislature to take action and supply state funds for the sympathetic care of the mentally ill. Once again appealing directly to the vaunted manhood of her listeners, she cried out: "Men of Massachusetts, I beg, I implore, I demand, pity and protection for those of my suffering outraged sex. Fathers, husbands, brothers, I would supplicate you for this boon."

Many members of the legislature exploded in indignation at the "impossible" charges raised by this female troublemaker, making a spectacle of herself in public, and appearing to have no appreciation of the "propriety of one of her sex." Directors and supervisors of the various institutions she visited angrily dismissed her charges as "slanderous" and "sensational," while local townspeople denied even hearing about such "awful things" going on in their communities. Even the influential Boston *Courier*, which had earlier been sympathetic to her activities, now raised doubts about the accuracy of her findings. But Dix had her defenders, too. Dr. Samuel Gridley Howe strongly supported the accuracy of the details in her *Memorial*, drawing upon his own observations in the field, and insisting that many of the abuses were the result of unprofessional and poorly trained personnel. Horace Mann also came to her defense, as did Luther Bell, the humane superintendent of the McLean Asylum, who cited similar instances of neglect and abusive treatment from his own records and experience. And the female crusader found a new ally in the person of thirty-two-year-old Charles Sumner, an impressive young Harvard lawyer, who had only recently returned from Europe and begun involving himself in the city's various reform activities. Sumner came out strongly in support of Dorothea Dix, explaining that he himself had also visited several of the almshouses cited in her *Memorial* and insisting that what he had seen confirmed everything she had written.

Gradually the opposition died down, as members of the legislature, as well as members of the general public, began to realize that Dorothea Dix's charges were well founded and carefully documented—not simply the wild fantasies of a deranged female imagination. The legislative committee to which her *Memorial* had been assigned, endorsed her petition for immediate action and recommended that additional buildings be constructed at the Worcester Hospital in order to provide accommodations for at least two hundred more patients. Now more acutely aware of the true dimensions of the problem, the members of the legislature passed the so-called hospital bill by a substantial majority—much to the delight of Miss Dix and her supporters.

As Dorothea Lynde Dix now carried her fight into other states, investigating public institutions, deluging state legislatures with "memorials," appealing for more funds and more institutions to care for the mentally ill, the leaders of Boston could take great pride in a city that had appeared to keep faith with John Winthrop's admonition that in achieving their status as citizens of a City Upon a Hill, his Puritan followers should treat each other with "brotherly affection," and be willing to "abridge ourselves of our superfluities for the supply of others' necessities." Even as Boston was transformed from a town to a city, it had proceeded to care for its poor, treat its sick, and provide for those who could not provide for themselves. But was it enough? Was it enough in this new and changing century to guarantee that Boston would assume a position among the cities of the United States that would be so elevated, so distinctive, and so preeminent that it would ensure, in Winthrop's words, that "the eyes of all people are upon us."

CHAPTER 5 } THE GRECIAN MODEL

It was a matter of enormous pride, but also of soul-searching concern, to be a direct descendant of a member of that great generation of Americans, known collectively as the Founding Fathers, who had led Boston through the precarious years of rebellion and revolution against the powerful domination of Great Britain, who had won their independence against overwhelming odds, and who had then gone on to formulate the Constitution for a new and democratic republic.

By the close of the eighteenth century, a new generation of Bostonians had inherited an independent, orderly, and well-mannered community that seemed to incorporate the finest characteristics of John Winthrop's fabled City Upon a Hill. They now faced the obvious question: What should they do with it? In what ways could they develop its ideas and shape its institutions so as to face the challenges of a new and rapidly changing century? And what could they themselves do to match the accomplishments of their forebears whose leadership and energies had given Boston such an inordinately suasive role throughout the colonial era as the model for religious orthodoxy, academic excellence, and political democracy?

Boston, it is true, had already come far and had accomplished a great deal since the dismal days of British occupation during the Revolutionary War. Once independence had been achieved in 1783, the town had steadily restored its maritime prosperity, invested in textile manufacturing, and diversified its economy by engaging in railroads and banking. It had changed its political structure from that of a town to that of a city, stabilized its urban political structure under the stewardship of an informed leadership elite, and proceeded to modernize the life of the new city with a series of far-reaching humanitarian reforms designed to cure long-standing social ills and moral problems.

But was all this enough to ensure Boston the distinctive image it wanted to present to the larger world beyond the heights of Beacon Hill? After all, New York, Philadelphia, Baltimore, and several other American cities were at work concurrently on similar urban reforms and humanitarian projects. What was it about Boston, particularly, that would make it rank as a rising star in nineteenth-century America? Bostonians were acutely aware that they were at the start, not merely of a new century, but of a truly new age, with all sorts of remarkable changes that were bound to have a significant impact on their life and society. Already new technologies were powering their textile mills out at Lowell and Lawrence, while old forms of transportation were being revolutionized by steam engines that made it possible for trains and steamboats to achieve speed and distances never before imagined. Members of this new generation of Bostonians were clearly looking for ideas and models that would help them establish a theme for the new century that would dramatize Boston's role as the nation's leading city.

In the past, Bostonians had often turned to the writings of classical antiquity for insights into the ways in which they could serve as examples for the kind of moral and social ideals necessary for formulating important political decisions. As long as the young republic was still in its formative stages, the principles of the old Roman Republic seemed especially appropriate to the circumstances they faced. Out of their readings of such influential writers as Cicero, Sallust, and Tacitus, many Americans created a conception of an ideal republican society filled, as John Adams wrote, with "all great, manly, and warlike virtues," convinced that excess and luxury would inevitably be followed by decadence and decline. Integrity, statesmanship, and devotion to the public good were regarded as essential factors of good order and stability.

Once independence had been achieved and the new American Republic settled on a firm and stable basis, however, there was an end to what historian Harlow Sheidley called "an age of certainty," an essentially conservative and orderly period where there had been fixed principles, behavior, and events. There was no doubt that Bostonians now had secured their "City Upon a Hill," but in trying to establish what that city would look like and how it would function in the new republic, many prominent citizens tended to find new inspiration in the ideals of Athenian democracy with its exalted sense of art and literature, philosophy and citizenship. At the Boston Latin School and later, at Harvard College, young Bostonians had learned all about the glories of Athens in their ancient-history textbooks. It was not too difficult for them to come up with a highly idealized version of that famous Greek city that closely resembled the mental picture most of them had of their own city of Boston. Certainly there was little difficulty in reconciling the ancient society of kings and aristocrats, members of the landed ruling elite, with the members of their own leadership elite who shaped the moral values and cultural standards of their own day, and whose self-assertiveness and defensive attitudes helped establish for Boston the kind of preeminence Athens had assumed among the other city-states. And the fact, of course, that Athens was universally hailed as the Cradle of Civilization was hardly lost on Bostonians who had always believed that the true democratic spirit had originated in the town-meeting system in the local Puritan republic, and who had always referred to their own Faneuil Hall as the Cradle of Liberty. "The Greeks invented politics," states the eminent British historian J. M. Roberts, who describes the political process as "running collective concerns by discussion of possible choices in a public setting." That was certainly the way most Bostonians conceived of their own historical ventures into public debate and democratic solutions. Conscious that they were moving into a new and different age, Bostonians also found themselves intrigued with the Athenians' love of inquiry, their spirit of invention. "There was nothing the ancient Greeks did not poke their noses into, no experience they shunned, no problems they did not attempt to solve," writes Thomas Cahill, in *Why the Greeks Mattered.* And it was precisely this sense of intellectual curiosity that fascinated Bostonians and led them to concern themselves less about the foundations of their government and more about the decorative nature of their culture and institutions.

Actually, evidences of this idealized Greek influence began to appear very early in Boston's postrevolutionary history. As early as 1788, Thomas Bland Hollis, the last of a noted English liberal family who saw America as the "rising star of the West," wrote to Samuel Langdon, president of Harvard College, suggesting that the ancient Olympic games be revived in America. "All her friends wish it and saw they are capable of it," he wrote. "Having acted upon Greek principles," he concluded, "you should have the Greek exercises." The city of Boston, it was said in some quarters, according to Jane Holtz Kay, perfectly suited Plato's ideal of urban life, since it was small enough to hear the voice of a single orator. And there were early signs of the Greek Revival style of architecture as it began to be assimilated into the Federal red-brick structures that were going up in the recently developed Beacon Hill residential district, as Douglass Shand-Tucci has observed in his work *Built in Boston.* The white bowfront of the Sears House at 42 Beacon

E 6427 CUSTOM HOUSE, BOSTON, MASS.

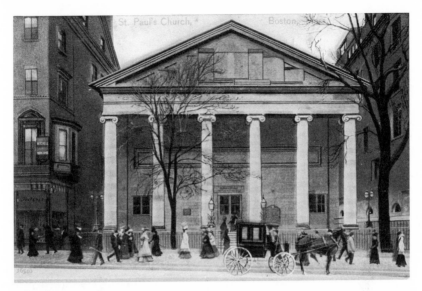

(*above*) ST. PAUL'S CHURCH

Constructed in 1820 on Tremont Street near the Park Street Church, St. Paul's Episcopal Church provides an opportunity to contrast the old Federal style of architecture with the new Greek Revival style. Designed by Alexander Parris, it features a colonnade and a massive pediment. The great columns were made in sections, as were those of the ancient Greek temples, and the Ionic capitals were carved by Solomon Willard. (Courtesy, Bostonian Society/Old State House)

(*opposite top*) MERCHANT EXCHANGE

The Boston Exchange Company Building was designed in 1841 by Isaiah Rogers, and constructed at 48–57 State Street in downtown Boston. A magnificent Greek Revival structure, the Merchant Exchange was strong enough to withstand the fury of the Great Fire in 1872 and prevented the destructive flames from going down State Street. The Exchange was demolished in 1891. (Courtesy, Bostonian Society/Old State House)

(*opposite bottom*) CUSTOM HOUSE

In 1837, when construction began on the Custom House, the new granite buildings going up in Boston were in stark contrast to the old red-brick Federal-style buildings. With the Greek Revival style of architecture becoming fashionable during the 1830s, Ammi B. Young supplied Boston with one of its finest neoclassical structures. Each one of its massive Doric columns was a single shaft of granite weighting some forty-two tons. (Courtesy, Bostonian Society/Old State House)

Street; the columned doorways in the adjoining houses at 39 and 40 Beacon Street belonging to Nathan Appleton and his colleague Daniel Parker; the Greek Revival post-and-lintel doorway at 59 Mount Vernon Street, all designed by Alexander Parris in 1819, were clear indications of the new trend. When he designed the main building for the Massachusetts General Hospital in the West End, Parris had provided a classical portico with a series of Ionic columns, but perhaps even more dramatic evidence of the Greek influence was his design, the same year, of St. Paul's Episcopal Church on Tremont Street, across from Boston Common, with its full-scale monumental Greek temple front. Parris's design of the new Quincy Market some five years later, furnished the new city with perhaps its finest example of Greek Revival architecture, featuring porticoes at either end of the central building, with four massive columns with Doric capitals supporting a simple pediment. Perhaps the most ambitious production of the Greek influence was produced by Ammi Burnham Young with his Custom House close to the Boston waterfront, at India and State Streets. Built as a Greek temple, and arranged in the form of a Greek Cross, around its exterior stand thirty-two fluted Doric columns, with a Roman dome surmounting the central portion of the building. The Greek Revival influence proved extremely popular and flourished for many more years in Boston, with the design by Isaiah Rogers of the luxurious Tremont Hotel in 1828, featuring a stately front of four large Doric columns, and with the construction by Solomon Willard, designer of the Bunker Hill Monument, of the handsome Suffolk County Court House in 1836, displaying a fine classical Greek Revival style carried out in American granite.

This appetite for Grecian themes had been further stimulated by the sympathetic response of many Americans to the outbreak of fighting by Greek nationalists against the rule of the Ottoman Turks. Throughout many parts of the United States, statesmen and citizens expressed sentiments of friendship and sympathy for the patriots of Greece whom they viewed as fighting for the same principles of freedom that had inspired Americans in their struggle against Great Britain. "The mention of Greece fills the mind with the most exalted sentiments, and arouses in our bosoms the best feelings of which our nature is susceptible," announced President James Monroe in his annual message of 1822. Shortly after graduating from the Harvard Medical School in 1824, twenty-three-year-old Samuel Gridley Howe of Boston sailed off to join in the fight for Greek independence, while back home classic colonnades were being added to government buildings, modest private residences, and elegant plantation houses as expressions of support for the struggle for Greek independence and the ideals of Athenian democracy.

Porticoes and pediments, posts and lintels, colonnades and domes, Ionic columns and Doric capitals—all proclaimed the fact that the ideal of ancient Athens provided a stimulating and sophisticated model for how Boston could make up in intellectual significance what it was losing in national political influence. As the "Athens of America"—a city of statesmen and philosophers, artists and writers—Boston might well be able to control the destiny of the American Republic through the influence of its cultural institutions and the high-minded virtue of its citizenry. Convinced that learning, knowledge, inquiry, and education were the keys to success in every endeavor, and absolutely essential to the character of a truly civilized society, local intellectuals set out to create a distinctive national culture that would express the hopes and dreams of America and that would respond in positive fashion to the snide remark of the English literary critic who inquired in 1820: "In the four quarters of the Globe, whoever reads an American book?"

This might have seemed to be an unusual and highly unlikely question, considering the fact that the citizens of a town like Boston were fully convinced that they had already established a reputation for themselves as members of a highly civilized and decidedly learned community. They had created the Boston Latin School and Harvard College within six years of the town's founding, they could boast of outstanding theologians such as Jonathan Edwards and William Ellery Channing, internationally recognized painters in John Singleton Copley and Gilbert Stuart, an excellent silversmith in Paul Revere, an accomplished architect in Charles Bulfinch, and an articulate political propagandist in Samuel Adams. These were some of the proudest boasts of early Boston that caused their citizens to see their own "City Upon a Hill" as a leader in American intellectual circles.

But in the more exalted spheres of speculative philosophy, as well as in the more theoretical areas of poetry and literature, Boston, like most other American cities at the time, still had produced little that would draw critics' attention to America as a cultivated civilization that could produce the kind of high-minded thinking necessary for truly great philosophy and literature. Americans, to be sure, had become known as quick, bright, and "sharp," capable of coming up with all sorts of mechanical gadgets, contraptions, and inventions, designed to reduce labor, increase productivity, and make a great deal of money. But almost always their emphasis was on the practical and applied aspects of life, seldom on the theoretical or speculative. As far as most Americans were concerned, the real importance of knowledge lay in its ability to improve a person's health, home, farm, or business. Local scientists such as Benjamin Silliman at Yale or Louis Aggasiz at Harvard, for example, specialized in such subjects as botany, mineralogy, geology, and chemistry, preferring to classify natural phenomena, work in mathematical astronomy, or develop new techniques relating to maritime affairs, rather than explore the more theoretical dimensions of what could be called "pure" science. Americans paid great attention to the purely practical part of science, observed the French traveler, Alexis de Tocqueville, in *Democracy in America*, published in 1835, "but scarcely anyone [devoted] himself to the essentially theoretical and abstract portion of human knowledge." And that seemed perfectly acceptable to most Americans. Dr. Benjamin Rush, a signer of the Declaration of Independence and an active social reformer who helped establish a number of schools and colleges, made it a point to reject the "ornamental" and "elitist" character of the English colleges he had encountered that catered to the wealthy and the privileged. The Pennsylvania physician insisted that American colleges should produce citizen-leaders who were not only well grounded in the traditional liberal arts, but who also had explored such "useful" subjects as history, geography, mathematics, politics, and the natural sciences. That was the way by which future Americans would be able to secure the "new and peculiar state of our country."

Although the United States had technically won its independence from Great Britain in 1783, the history of the new nation from that year until 1816 had been continually marked by the influences that developments in Europe had not only upon America's foreign policy and economic issues, but also upon its literature, its culture, and its taste. Such European events as the French Revolution, the rise of Napoleon, the Napoleonic Decrees, neutral rights, the embargo, impressments, the Orders in Council, had obvious effects not only on the course of American foreign policy, but also on the formation of political parties and the transition of local economies. Less obvious, perhaps, but nonetheless significant, were the many ways in which European influences shaped American cultural tastes and restricted American intellectual creativity. Long after 1783, Americans continued to insist on attending British plays, reading British novels, and patronizing British newspapers and magazines. In order to be accepted, and regarded as truly successful, talented American artists such as Benjamin West, John Single-ton Copley, and Gilbert Stuart felt it necessary to travel to London to study and make their name in the larger world of art. American architecture, too, was little more than a warmed-over version of the classical British styles then in vogue, as Bostonians witnessed with Charles Bulfinch's new State House, Asher Benjamin's Charles Street Meetinghouse, and Peter Banner's Park Street Church.

With the close of the War of 1812, however, the United States took a giant step in cutting itself off from the bonds that had connected it with Europe for so long. By this time, most Americans felt that the Old World had become so old, corrupt, priest-ridden, and decadent that it had little to offer the New World that had by now become confidently conscious of its own vigorous youth, its rugged vitality, and its free democratic spirit. Consciously and quite deliberately, the United States turned its back on Europe and looked inward. For a century—from the end of the War of 1812 in 1816 to the outbreak of the First World War—the United States would never again be seriously or significantly involved in the affairs of Europe. Historians are not wrong when they refer to the pathetic War of 1812 as America's "Second War for Independence," for it resulted in an enthusiastic wave of patriotic fervor and a proud spirit of nationalism that, in turn, prompted a fierce determination to cut loose from the rest of the world and set sail on an independent course that would be uniquely and distinctively "American."

It was certainly no coincidence that it was right after the War of 1812 that the first full-fledged American authors made their appearance, exploring recognizable American themes, and writing for a distinctively American audience. With moving verses like "Thanatopsis" and "To a Waterfowl" that no longer imitated British poetry, either in ideas or poetic method, William Cullen Bryant became the first American poet to stand comparison with the great poets of other countries. Establishing his reputation as a major poet when he was only eighteen or nineteen years of age, Bryant drew inspiration from the trees and flowers of his own New England countryside while reflecting upon the meaning of death and the healing power of nature. Washington Irving of New York was another early American writer, who first raised the short story to the dignity of literature with the publication of his *Sketch Book* in 1820. In stories like "Rip Van Winkle" and "The Legend of Sleepy Hollow" he often used a rollicking sense of humor to skillfully rework old folk legends and unforgettable personalities into a truly American romantic setting along the banks of the Hudson River valley. James Fenimore Cooper, too, established the historical romance of America with such classic works as *The Pioneers* (1823) and *The Last of the Mohicans* (1826). His series of five historical novels called *The Leatherstocking Tales*, followed the life of a distinctively American character named Natty Bumppo through the years of frontier warfare involving the English, the French, and the Indians in the untamed wilderness of northern New York and southern Canada, dramatizing the clash between primitive traditions and the values of civilized society. These were some of the early attempts by American writers to break away from the traditional guidelines and strictures of the Old World, and forge an entirely new and different literary tradition based on the rugged physical environment and solid moral values of the New World.

These inspiring themes that drew in a positive manner upon the youth, vigor, and vitality of the American experience, especially as compared with what many regarded as the age, the decadence, and the artificiality of the European system, were certainly an integral part of the new and unprecedented burst of literary imagination that turned the rugged terrain of New England's "stern and rockbound coast" into a veritable garden of delights. During what historian Van Wyck Brooks has aptly called *The Flowering of New England*, those who had complained that Americans had contributed virtually nothing to the world of letters now had more outstanding literary works than they ever could have imagined. Boston writers soon won international distinction with a flood of works that not only continued to emphasize the theme of "America," but also placed great store in the innate goodness of all people and their natural ability to rise to great heights, thus epitomizing the optimistic and progressive spirit of the day. Ironically, although most of writers were mainly nonpolitical and generally conservative, most of their works echoed precisely the same ideals that were found in the political rhetoric of Jacksonian Democracy during this very same period. A living symbol of the American frontier West, without benefit of family, wealth, or education, Andrew Jackson had earned a reputation as something of a backwoods lawyer before gaining national stature with his astonishing defeat of the British at the Battle of New Orleans. As one of the few successful war heroes to come out of the War of 1812, "Old Hickory" was elected President of the United States in 1828, and proceeded to make dramatic changes, not only in the office of the presidency, but also in the very nature of holding public office in a democratic government. Emphasizing the principles of liberty, equality, and opportunity, Jackson took issue with the established notion that public office should be restricted to members of a small, wealthy, educated class. The holding of public office, he insisted, was "so plain and simple" that any man of intelligence could readily qualify for any position, without the necessity of family background, higher education, or prior political experience. In stressing the importance of such homegrown moral values as honesty, integrity, and common sense in the cause of public service, Jackson's definition of the "common man" came remarkably close to the self-reliant "natural man" being so eloquently depicted by Ralph Waldo Emerson.

It was Emerson who had clearly become the best known and most charismatic spokesman for the new intellectual movement generated by a group of young scholars, writers, poets, and philosophers who sought to create a new metaphysics for America. After graduating from Harvard College, Emerson had entered its divinity school, was ordained to the ministry, and in 1829 took a position at the Second Church of Boston. In 1842, however, he professed that he could no longer find the kind of spiritual passion and creative vigor in what he referred to as the "corpse-cold Unitarianism of Brattle Street," and he left the ministry to devote himself to a life of philosophy, developing a theory of the "oversoul" in a mystical union with God. A journey to Italy, Scotland, and England allowed him to meet Coleridge, Wordsworth, Carlyle, Kant, Schiller, Goethe, and other leading European intellectuals, whose idealistic philosophies influenced his first essay called "Nature" (1836), in which he declared that nature was man's greatest teacher. After his return to America, Emerson took up a successful career as a lecturer. Tall, exceedingly thin, with piercing blue eyes and smiling curved lips, he spoke with a "tranquil authority" that captivated his listeners and influenced those aspiring writers and philosophers who followed his lead.

In 1837, Emerson got an opportunity to expand further upon some of his ideas when he was asked to give the annual Phi Beta Kappa address at his alma mater, Harvard College. It was on this occasion that Emerson delivered what Oliver Wendell Holmes aptly characterized as an American "intellectual Declaration of Independence," calling upon American scholars to stop imitating "the courtly muses of Europe" and strike out on their own. The spirit of the American freeman, said Emerson disparagingly, had become "timid, imitative, tame," with the result that the American scholar appears "decent, indolent, complaisant." He urged young writers to break with the

RALPH WALDO EMERSON

Ordained to the Unitarian ministry, Ralph Waldo Emerson left his post at Boston's Second Church in 1832, when he felt he could no longer find the kind of spiritual and creative vigor he needed in the "corpse-cold Unitarianism of Brattle Street." He devoted himself to a life of philosophy, developing a theory of the "oversoul" in a mystical union with God. At his home in Concord, a group of friends and disciples formed the Transcendental Club as a means of discussing philosophical ideas and literary trends. Through his writings and personal charisma, Emerson became one of the most influential figures of the antebellum era. (Courtesy, Bostonian Society/ Old State House) past, forget about dusty archives, exotic locations, and ancient sources, and derive their inspiration from the bright creativity of their own minds as well as the scenes of natural beauty right around them. "I embrace the common," he exclaimed in words that sound remarkably Jacksonian. "I explore and sit at the feet of the familiar, the low. Give me insight into today, and you may have the antique and future worlds. . . ." Emerson had already suggested, in his earlier essay, "Nature," that people must learn the lessons of the universe firsthand if they were ever to understand the complete workings of the world of eternal truth. In a later series of essays, he emphasized the virtues of individualism, self-reliance, and self-improvement, accentuating the optimism of the age and the unlimited opportunities available to the American people. A person should learn to trust himself by listening to the whisper of the voice within him. "Insist on yourself," he wrote; "never imitate."

One of Emerson's close friends was Henry David Thoreau—poet, writer, and incurable nonconformist. For two years, Thoreau lived in a small shack on Emerson's property beside Walden Pond, near Concord, without any of the then-modern conveniences. He eventually provided a memorable record of those two years in *Walden* (1854), in which he not only described the beauties of nature during the changing seasons of the year, but also philosophized about the importance of the individual and the desperate need for simplifying the innumerable details that complicate human life. "Simplify, simplify, simplify," he urged his readers. A rugged individualist himself, Thoreau spent a night in the local jail for refusing to pay his taxes that would go to support the war with Mexico, and then justified his position with his essay "Civil Disobedience" (1849), a thoughtful treatment of passive resistance and civil disobedience that was destined to have lasting influence throughout the world. In the twentieth century, Thoreau's ideas would inspire Mahatma Gandhi in his struggle against British colonialism in India, and Rev. Martin Luther King Jr., in his struggle for civil rights in the United States.

Almost every conceivable phase of the American experience was explored by a host of writers who were friends and acquaintances of Emerson, and who were greatly influenced by his philosophical writings. Nathaniel Hawthorne, a native of Salem and a descendant of a judge who conducted the witchcraft trials, reached back into the early New England past to write with biting and perceptive criticism about the dark natures of the old Puritans in his *Scarlet Letter* (1850) and *House of the Seven Gables* (1851). Certainly one of the most popular poets of the day was Henry Wadsworth Longfellow,

HENRY WADSWORTH LONGFELLOW

*Born in Portland, Maine, and a graduate of Bowdoin College, in 1835 Henry
Wadsworth Longfellow became a popular professor of modern languages at
Harvard College. After his marriage to Frances Elizabeth Appleton, daughter of
Nathan Appleton, Longfellow lived an idyllic life at Craigie House in Cambridge
with his wife and six children. As a poet, Longfellow gained a national reputation
with such epic works as* Evangeline, The Song of Hiawatha, *and* The Courtship of
Myles Standish, *which transformed the events of early American history into colorful
legends for future generations of American schoolchildren. (Courtesy, Bostonian
Society/Old State House)*

whose *Voices of the Night* (1839) ranked him as one of the leading American poets. His best-known works came later, however, as he delved into the American past and produced such memorable historical narratives as *Evangeline* (1847), *The Song of Hiawatha* (1855), and *The Courtship of Myles Standish* (1858). His "Midnight Ride of Paul Revere" (1860) became an instant popular classic and a permanent part of the romantic folklore he was in the process of creating for the American people. Descendant of a long line of Quakers, John Greenleaf Whittier, devoted himself for many years to the crusade against slavery, and first gained attention as a poet with his *Voices of Freedom* (1846), a volume of moving antislavery verse. Later, however, he won a much wider audience with such nostalgic poems as "The Barefoot Boy" (1856) and "Snow-Bound" (1866), tenderly reminiscent of his New England boyhood—a time of rustic simplicity that was already giving way to the harsher complexities of industrialization and urbanization. During this same period, Oliver Wendell Holmes, essayist and poet, as well as an eminent physician and authority on anatomy, achieved wide literary fame with his witty and urbane series of essays entitled "The Autocrat of the Breakfast Table," which would later appear in the pages of the *Atlantic Monthly*.

At a time when a spirit of unbridled optimism was in the air, citizens had little time or patience with works of literature that failed to convey that same sense of intellectual progress and human perfectibility. Edgar Allan Poe, for example, may have been later recognized as an original poet of haunting verse and the creator of the modern detective story, but in his own day he was largely ignored by the reading public. His Gothic horror stories, "The Tell-Tale Heart" and "The Pit and the Pendulum," as well as his gruesome mystery novels, such as *The Murders in the Rue Morgue*, seemed unnatural and unhealthy to early nineteenth-century Americans. Shunned as a disturbed eccentric, depressed and impoverished, Poe died an early and tragic death. Herman Melville was another writer of the period who suffered similar rejection in his own day. Born in New York, he worked in his brother's fur store before shipping out to sea as a cabin boy, and then later sailing to the Pacific aboard a whaling vessel. Melville attracted early favorable attention as a writer with a series of colorful adventure stories, such as *Typee* (1846) and *Omoo* (1847), which were based on his travels to Tahiti. His literary reputation went into decline, however, when his great masterpiece, *Moby-Dick* (1851), failed to attract a large and appreciative audience. The willingness of Captain Ahab to allow the destruction of his own vessel, and the death of everyone aboard, in order to satisfy his obsessive and vengeful search for the great white whale, was much too dark and depressing a story for most readers to accept. It would take a later generation to appreciate the deep and subtle meaning of the eternal struggle of the human caught between the competing forces of good and evil. Most Americans, at the time, had little interest in exploring such depressing and philosophical issues that were clearly not capable of clear and definite resolutions. They believed they were living at a time when a new millennium had arrived, and when a new utopia had come about. There was a feeling that there was no problem that could not be solved, no obstacle that could not be overcome, if only Americans would put their minds to it.

During the same period of time when scores of Boston writers were producing brilliant works of creative literature, other scholars were searching the American past to uncover the tangled roots of the democratic experience and explain the outstanding success of the American constitutional system. For a good two hundred years, Americans were so preoccupied in settling the New World, struggling to gain their independence, and trying to forge a new nation of their own, that they had little time or inclination to reflect upon their origins or compile the details of their own history. By the middle of the nineteenth century, however, a number of Boston scholars, most of them Unitarians and all of them graduates of Harvard College, began going through the original records, sources, and documents in order to piece together America's history. At a time when American colleges offered few elective courses and no graduate degree programs at all, these men were actually gentlemen of letters, products of a traditional classical undergraduate education, who developed their particular historical skills as a form of literary art. These were the early days of Unitarianism, historian David Levin reminds us, when it was "the Boston gentleman's duty to promote American letters." Men of comfortable means, they had the leisure to travel wherever they wanted in search of their subjects, and the wealth to purchase libraries of books and cartons of manuscripts with which to substantiate their findings and conclusions. Starting in 1834, George Bancroft (who also found time, as a Democrat, to serve as Secretary of the Navy in President James K. Polk's cabinet) devoted himself to the whole sweep of American history, and began producing what would eventually become a ten-volume *History of the United States*. Heavily nationalistic and profoundly Democratic ("Every page was a vote for Andrew Jackson," commented one reviewer), he traced the course of the nation's history as part of a grand providential design of human progress that led eventually—and inevitably—to the greatness of American freedom. For many years, Bancroft's histories continued to be extremely popular with American families who were only too happy to purchase his patriotic works for their children and for their homes.

Jared Sparks, a Unitarian minister and Harvard professor, was another prodigious worker who, in addition to editing the *North American Review*, also managed to publish the twelve-volume *Diplomatic Correspondence of the American Revolution* (1829–30) as well as equally long sets of *The Writings of George Washington* (1834–37) and *The Works of Benjamin Franklin* (1836–40). William Hickling Prescott, a charming and exuberant young scholar who suffered from partial blindness, interested himself in the history of Spain, especially where it concerned the colonial origins of the United States. In 1837 he published *A History of the Reign of Ferdinand and Isabella the Catholic*, followed by colorful and exciting studies entitled *The Conquest of Mexico* (1843) and *The Conquest of Peru* (1847), which are still regarded as models of exciting literary history. A colleague of Prescott, John Lothrop Motley, found that the heroic saga of Holland's fight for freedom against the armed might of imperial Spain offered a fascinating prelude to America's own struggle for independence against the power of Great Britain, and won fame with his work on *The Rise of the Dutch Republic* (1856). Superior to both Prescott and Motley, though most of his work would not appear until after the Civil War, was Francis Parkman. Overcoming disabilities of terrible health and virtual blindness, Parkman produced a series of historical works dealing with French exploration and colonization in North America over the course of a century and a half. With *Pioneers of France in the New World* (1865), *The Jesuits in North America* (1867), *The Conspiracy of Pontiac* (1851), and many other works, Parkman established a model of scholarly history and excellent literature for future American historians to admire and emulate.

The creative imagination that produced this remarkable American literary renaissance was further intensified by a new philosophical movement called Transcendentalism. Although the term was borrowed from the ideas of the German philosopher Immanuel Kant, who insisted that objective reality exists only in the mind, the American version corresponded only vaguely to its original German meaning. Indeed, historian Irving H. Bartlett, in *The American Mind in the Mid-Nineteenth Century*, has suggested that the new

philosophy was really much more in the tradition of such colonial theologians as Anne Hutchinson and Jonathan Edwards than in later European
models, and in that sense he sees American Transcendentalism bringing
back a form of the "old pietism" that had been excluded from Unitarianism.
Some of the most active adherents of this new philosophy were Ralph Waldo
Emerson and his literary friends who met regularly in his hometown of Concord and formed what they called the Transcendental Club, where they could
discuss their ideas, exchange views, and critique each other's work. From
1840 to 1844, the members even published a journal called *The Dial*, edited by
Margaret Fuller, a woman of extraordinary intelligence, in order to memo-
rialize their ideas and ensure that they would be circulated to a much larger
audience. At one time or another, membership in the group included Fuller,
Thoreau, William Ellery Channing, Theodore Parker, Bronson Alcott, and
Nathaniel Hawthorne. Like most Unitarians of the period, the Transcendentalists emphasized the divine goodness of human nature and the possibility
that all people could achieve salvation through their own efforts. But, unlike most other New England denominations, the Transcendentalists placed
less importance upon doctrinal creeds and scriptural revelation, emphasizing, instead, the intuitive power of the human mind to know truth, and the
willingness of people to apply religious principles to social needs. The highest truth, they claimed, could be known not so much by study, research,
observation, or deliberate reflection, but rather through inner, instinctive
faculties—by intuition. The Transcendentalists felt that the true Christian
spirit was to be found not in scriptural studies, in elaborate ritualism, or in
pious doctrines, but in the application of moral principles and eternal truths
to uplifting the human spirit and in caring for the needs of the oppressed
and the disadvantaged.

With this remarkable gathering of highly regarded philosopher, poets,
novelists, essayists, and historians, Bostonians could now boast of having an
intelligentsia of their own, one so well known and internationally celebrated
that they now felt that their city was, without question, deserving of the title
of the "Athens of America." Indeed, the fragrance of high culture seemed
to permeate the very atmosphere of Boston. Alexander Mackay, an English
barrister serving as a correspondent for the *London Morning Chronicle* during his visit to the United States in 1846, was suitably impressed by the outstanding work of the Boston writers, the quality of the medical work being
carried on in the city, and the general excellence of the local law libraries.

MARGARET FULLER

An admirer of Ralph Waldo Emerson and a member of the Transcendental Club, Margaret Fuller was a talented writer and poet who served as editor of The Dial, *and who later wrote literary criticism for the New York* Tribune. *Author of a notable work titled* Woman in the Nineteenth Century, *Fuller was an outspoken feminist who resented the prevailing opinion that a woman's mind was either different from, or inferior to, a man's. "I know all the people worth knowing in America," she once told a friend, "and I find no intellect comparable to my own." (Courtesy, Bostonian Society/Old State House)*

"The American brain," he remarked, "is as active as American hands are busy." And he was overwhelmed by the level of intellectual activity that was going on in all parts of the city. If one met a gentleman in the vicinity of Washington Street "with a decent coat and a clean shirt," he wrote, chances were that he was "either a lecturer, a Unitarian minister, or a poet; possibly the man might be all three at once." Beacon Hill was a favorite location, where many of the literati made their homes. George Ticknor, professor of romance languages at Harvard College, had moved into the old Amory House on the corner of Park and Beacon Streets; William Prescott worked on his histories of Mexico and Peru at 55 Beacon Street, where he could look out his window and see the Boston Common. The Parkman House stood just a little down from the new State House on Beacon Hill; Longfellow lived for a while on Cedar Street; Oliver Wendell Holmes came down to his break-fast table first on Bosworth Street, then on Charles Street; Julia Ward Howe and her reformer husband, Dr. Samuel Gridley Howe, lived for a while on Chestnut Street. It was customary for many of these writers to join their colleagues coming in from Cambridge and Concord, walk down the hill, cross Tremont Street at King's Chapel, and then gather at the Old Corner Book Store at the corner of Washington and School Streets, an intersection that became known as Parnassus Corner after the mountain in central Greece considered sacred to Apollo and the Muses. There, the writers would browse through the books on sale on the ground floor of the building managed by William Ticknor, a cousin of George Ticknor, and then wander over to the "curtained corner" to discuss their works in progress. Later in the afternoon, they would often dine at the home of Ticknor's partner, the jovial and heavily bearded James T. Fields, where they continued their literary conversations and occasionally enjoyed the company of a visiting British author, perhaps Charles Dickens, who spent some time in the city in 1842 during his visit to America.

Another favorite gathering place for the members of the Boston literati was the nearby Boston Athenaeum. Over the years, well-to-do Boston citizens had built up substantial private collections of books. The Athenaeum (named, appropriately enough, after a temple dedicated to the Greek goddess Athena, and frequented by poets and men of learning) was established in 1808 in order to bring these private collections together under one roof, along with family portraits, oil paintings, and a variety of historical artifacts, in a kind of institution—"a place of social intercourse"—where members could read and study in quiet and comfortable surroundings, reminiscent of a fashionable gentleman's club in London. "No one is permitted, not even the proprietors, to take a book so much as from one room to another," observed Mrs. Anne Royall during her visit to Boston. "No one is allowed to speak above their breath, lest they might interrupt the readers." At first, the Athenaeum was located in the large home of Thomas Handasyd Perkins on Pearl Street, but it was later moved to an impressive sandstone Renaissance-style building at 10½ Beacon Street, only a short distance from the State House. The Athenaeum was a proprietary library, owned by shareholders who provided its financial support as a private institution, but who also made its valuable resources available to reputable scholars.

Throughout history, almost all cultures and civilizations have had their intelligentsias, those tight circles of exalted members of the literati, who usually formed an exclusive inner society of their own. Cities such as London, Paris, and Vienna were celebrated for their royal courts and fashionable salons where clusters of creative artists would come to meet with each other, with their patrons, and with their many admirers. Snippets of the amusing dialogue, the scintillating gossip, and the cutting remarks that went back and forth during these soirees usually became the subjects of animated conversation the next day. When Alexis de Tocqueville and Gustave de Beaumont visited Boston in 1831 during their tour of the United States, they found that Bostonians resembled "almost completely" the upper classes of Europe. They discovered the manners of Bostonians to be "distinguished," their conversation "intellectual," and their libraries "altogether literary." Some twenty years later, in 1852, a Hungarian nobleman named Ferenc Pulszky visited Boston and also marveled at what had been accomplished by the city's leadership elite—hospitals, asylums, charitable institutions of every kind, philanthropies, lectures, athenaeums. "Boston is for America what the court of Weimar once was for Germany," he exclaimed, "the center of literature and science."

What Pulszky did not grasp, however, was that what he perceived as Boston's intelligentsia was different from that of Europe in at least two respects: First, its ranks were not confined to academic scholars, although certainly the great writers, poets, historians, and philosophers of the period —figures like Emerson, Holmes, and Ticknor—were a very important part of the group. But Boston's leadership elite also consisted of doctors, lawyers, ministers, bankers, merchants, businessmen, and men of affairs, who were intent on learning everything they could about all the new literary and scientific movements in progress. In 1846, for example, Dr. John Collins Warren, founder of the Massachusetts General Hospital, brought together a group of his friends, "congenial gentlemen," for the purpose of informally discussing "all matters pertaining to the physical sciences, to manufacture and to commerce, and all new plans which might be devised for the amelioration of the country." The first meeting of what became known as the Thursday Evening Club was held on October 27, 1846, at Dr. Warren's home on Park Street, and was attended by Francis C. Gray, a lawyer and benefactor of Harvard; Martin Brimmer, a German American merchant and Boston's first non-Yankee mayor; Abbott Lawrence, the textile magnate; George Darracott, a local business agent; Dr. Charles Jackson, Dr. Warren's medical colleague; and Dr. Augustus Gould, a physician and leading conchologist. Before the evening was over, it was agreed that Warren would extend invitations to Oliver Wendell Holmes, noted surgeon and popular essayist; William Appleton, a Whig congressman; Rev. Dr. A. H. Vinton, an Episcopal clergyman and physician; and Rev. John Bernard Fitzpatrick, Catholic bishop of Boston, a graduate of the Latin School, and a respected churchman. After dinner at their weekly Thursday evening meetings, these gentlemen would sit around and listen to presentations by various authorities on all sorts of topics. Dr. Jackson spoke about developments in the field of telegraphy; Louis Agassiz, who had recently arrived from his native Switzerland to lecture at the Lowell Institute, talked about his work in zoology; young Theophilus Parsons elaborated on various aspects of maritime law; and Joseph Wightman (later to become mayor of Boston) explained the workings of a new fire-alarm system operated by something called "electromagnetism." These were exciting times, when the American Association for the Advancement of Science was being founded, and the Harvard Astronomical Observatory had just been equipped with the world's largest refracting telescope. During the summer of 1848, Bishop Fitzpatrick arrived on the Harvard campus, escorting a visiting specialist in astronomy from Italy, Fr. Di Vico, along with Fr. Augustus Thebaud, president of New York's Fordham College, to see for themselves the impressive observatory. In the absence of regular faculty members during the summer recess, President Edward Everett himself insisted on taking the bishop and his guests on a personally conducted three-hour tour of the classrooms, the laboratories, and the grounds of the Cambridge campus.

AMOS A. LAWRENCE

Son of Amos Lawrence and nephew of Abbott Lawrence, entrepreneurs who had come down from Essex County to invest in textiles, young Amos Adams Lawrence was typical of the new generation of Boston Brahmins. Determined not to become a "plodding, narrow-minded merchant," he wanted to be man of the world, a literary man "in some measure," and a farmer, too, with a happy cottage in the countryside. As a member of the Thursday Evening Club, he joined with his friends to learn about the latest developments in the arts and the sciences. (Courtesy, Bostonian Society/Old State House)

Meeting together in groups to explore new literary ideas and learn about wide-ranging cultural matters, however, was not the exclusive domain of Boston men, for many women of the city also enjoyed opportunities to exchange views on matters of common interest. A leader in providing such an opportunity was Margaret Fuller, the oldest of nine children, whose father had provided her with a vigorous program of academic studies that set her educationally well above most other women of her age. As a teacher for a brief period at Bronson Alcott's Temple School in Boston, Fuller made lifelong friendships with Ralph Waldo Emerson and most of the other prominent intellectuals of the day. Her talents as a critic as well as a poet were recognized by the members of the Transcendental Club, who appointed her editor of their journal *The Dial*. At the invitation of Horace Greeley, she later became a literary critic for the *New York Tribune*, and five years later her book, *Woman in the Nineteenth Century*, called for the opening of every occupation and profession to women. Minds and souls, said Fuller, are neither masculine nor feminine: genius, she insisted, has no sex.

In 1839, Margaret Fuller started a series of "Conversations" with a group of women from cultivated Boston society, who met on Wednesday evenings at the Boston home of Elizabeth Peabody. Daughter of Salem parents who had developed her interests in languages, literature, theology, and philosophy, Peabody had also become acquainted with intellectuals like William Ellery Channing, Bronson Alcott, and Ralph Waldo Emerson. She opened a bookstore on Boston's West Street, which quickly became a headquarters for local Transcendentalists, and the place where Margaret Fuller held her weekly "Conversations." Peabody herself also published various books and pamphlets produced by her Transcendental friends, and for a brief period published *The Dial*, establishing herself as the first female publisher in Boston. These activities not only provided a measure of self-fulfillment and self-esteem for the women themselves, but also encouraged their activities beyond the traditional confines of their "proper domestic sphere" of home and family.

In addition to its remarkable diversity, however, there was a second difference in Boston's leadership elite in those days. Unlike many of their European counterparts, they had little interest in remaining apart from the general population as a separate caste. They were not satisfied with merely raising their own intellectual standards, or those of their own circle of upper-class, well-placed, and highly educated friends and colleagues. Firmly convinced that what they were doing was extremely important, they wanted everybody in America to know what they had to say about philosophy and religion, about the arts and the sciences, about what life and society should be like in the changing world of America. Bursting with new ideas, confident that they had found the way to a more happy, prosperous, and progressive future, Boston's intellectual leaders looked for whatever outlets would let them make their views known to as wide a general audience as possible.

Certainly, newspapers, magazines, and literary journals offered the most immediate opportunities for considerable circulation. Back in 1803, a small group of prominent Bostonians, devoted to literary interests, had formed a club they named the Anthology Society. Although they were not what might be called professional men of letters—Joseph Stevens Buckminster and William Ellery Channing were preachers; William Emerson was founder of the Philosophical Society; William Tudor (who is credited with making the first reference of Boston as the "Athens of America") was an enterprising merchant who soon became involved with his brother Frederic in the ice trade; John T. Kirkland was president of Harvard College—they enjoyed meeting one evening a week over dinner, when they discussed manuscripts for their small magazine, the *Monthly Anthology*. With Channing as the editor-in-chief, and young Richard Henry Dana as his assistant, the members of the club now inaugurated what would eventually become a famous Boston magazine called the *North American Review*, whose articles, essays, and works of poetry cut across a whole range of thinking in Boston literary and academic circles during the 1830s and 1840s. Noted Harvard professors such as Jared Sparks, Edward Everett, Charles Eliot Norton, and James Russell Lowell charted the direction of this influential publication for many years to come. Another local work was the Transcendentalist publication, *The Dial*, which appeared only from 1840 to 1844 but still provided another opportunity for many Boston writers to express their literary ideas and philosophical views well beyond Concord. In 1857, a number of the local literati decided to found an even more ambitious journal that would demonstrate to the English-speaking world the superior thoughts and ideas of American writers. Ralph Waldo Emerson worked with Oliver Wendell Holmes to found the *Atlantic Monthly* (named by Holmes) and managed to get contributions for their first issue from Motley, Longfellow, Whittier, Harriet Beecher Stowe, and Holmes himself, who published his popular column, "The Autocrat of the Breakfast Table," in the pages of the new journal that continued well into the twentieth century. Another magazine, but one of a slightly different nature, which appeared during the 1830s, was published by a woman named Sarah Hale. A widow with five children to support, she worked as a milliner, but turned to writing pieces for local magazine to supplement her income. Asked to become the editor of *Ladies' Magazine*, she turned it into a profitable venture—the first journal to be edited by a woman, and the first actually to publish its own material. Emphasizing the importance of education for women, Hale used her journal to help women develop their powers and abilities so that they could become moral exemplars within their "women's sphere." Eventually her *Ladies' Magazine* merged into the more successful and influential *Godey's Lady's Book* that set the standards for women's dress and fashion in the mid-nineteenth century.

The printed page alone, however, was not enough to satisfy the vigorous energies and exploding ambitions of Boston writers and thinkers. They missed few opportunities to take to the public lecture circuit whenever possible, not only to expound on their own particular fields of literary, artistic, or scientific expertise, but also to air their personal ideas and opinions on many of the controversial social and political issues of the day. And many of Boston's prominent citizens were eager to know more about the new ideas and movements that were circulating. Raised from childhood in the belief of the "infinite capacity of human nature," the leaders of Boston's cultural revival were not satisfied with merely raising the intellectual standards of their own narrow circle of upper-class, highly educated friends and colleagues. "Boston, all New England, respected learning," wrote Van Wyck Brooks in his historical account of the New England renaissance. "No New England boy was allowed to question that he was destined to succeed in life, provided that he knew enough; and Boston was determined that the boys and girls, and the blind and the lame as well, should have the opportunity to know enough." With this perfectionist attitude in mind, the members of the intelligentsia were seriously concerned that even those people who occupied the lowest rungs of Boston's socioeconomic ladder should have as much "useful knowledge" as possible in order to raise themselves up and improve the quality of their own lives, and the lives of their children.

This happened to be the time when Josiah Holbrook of Connecticut, a Yale graduate and an itinerant lecturer on scientific topics, was organizing various community groups into a system of town lyceums in order to promote what he called mutual improvements. The idea of lecture programs quickly caught the public's attention, and by 1839 the American Institute of Instruction and the American Lyceum Association had established almost a thousand local societies throughout New England to satisfy the growing thirst on the part of the general public for information regarding literature, the arts, the sciences, and all the new social and educational movements that had sprung up everywhere. Boston writers and academicians, too, picked up on this popular "lyceum system," and began using a variety of local clubs and institutions to establish a program of public lectures all over the city. Edward Everett of Harvard, now a Massachusetts congressman; Daniel Webster, only recently elected to the U.S. Senate; and Nathan Hale, editor of the *Boston Daily Advertiser* created what they called the Useful Knowledge Society in order to promote the diffusion of knowledge throughout the community; within a short time, other similar groups were established to promote speaking programs for their memberships. The Boston Lyceum, the Natural History Society, the Mercantile Library Association, and the Mechanics' Apprentices' Association, were among the best-known groups that emphasized the importance of self-education, and made the "lecture habit" a prominent feature of Boston society. In 1839, John Lowell Jr., son of the textile magnate Francis Cabot Lowell, founded the Lowell Institute, to which he left half his estate in trust in order to continue the sponsorship of free lectures "for the promotion of the moral and intellectual and physical instruction or education of the citizens of the said city of Boston." The Lowell lectures proved to be extremely popular in their day, with as many as eight to ten thousand people applying for tickets to a particular lecture by some of the best minds and the most prominent scholars in the country. Dr. Jacob Bigelow, a Harvard botanist, gave lectures on "The Elements of Technology," a word he did much to popularize; Benjamin Silliman of Yale spoke on science and chemistry, as did Professor John White Webster of Harvard, who was later hanged for the brutal murder of his Beacon Hill neighbor, Dr. George Parkman. Henry Ware of Harvard gave a popular course on Palestine; Edward Everett delivered lectures on Greek antiquities; James Russell Lowell discussed poetry and literature; Ralph Waldo Emerson gave a series of biographical lectures; and John Farrar, Hollis Professor of Mathematics at Harvard, discussed the implications of the steam engine. Edward Everett Hale, in his reminiscences of *A New England Boyhood*, recalled attending such lectures when he was a young man growing up in

Boston, and enjoying them as much as social occasions as intellectual experiences. He remembered meeting with his friends at the hall, listening to the lecture, walking home with a group afterward, and sometimes ending up at somebody's house where dishes of oysters, crackers, and cheese were usually available.

To ensure a truly literate public, however, some way would have to be found to provide all those people who were flocking so eagerly to the public lectures and seminars with the books and journals that would further satisfy what seemed to be their insatiable thirst for knowledge. The number of circulating libraries in the city had grown impressively, and there were also a number of literary reading rooms, stocked not only with all sorts of new books and pamphlets, but also with the leading British and American journals that were in great demand. But these facilities usually charged their subscribers an annual fee of five or ten dollars, far beyond the means of the working classes. The lack of a free library in Boston, therefore, became increasingly evident, as more and more citizens were caught up in the excitement of self-improvement and self-education. It was George Ticknor, Smith Professor of the French and Spanish Languages at Harvard College, who served as what historian Walter Muir Whitehill, in his delightful centennial history of *The Boston Public Library*, calls the "arch-agitator" in devoting himself to creating a circulating library that would be open to all citizens of the city without a fee. Ticknor's efforts were temporarily overshadowed, however, by the activities of a well-known French stage ventriloquist, Alexandre Vattemare, who became obsessed with the idea of forming great public libraries. When he arrived in Boston in the spring of 1841, in the course of a theatrical tour, Vattemare launched a campaign to create a public library in the city. After a meeting at the Masonic Temple on May 5, 1841, presided over by Mayor Jonathan Chapman, a committee sent out letters to fifteen Boston institutions, asking them to cooperate in combining their collections of books under a "single roof" where they would be accessible to the general public. Although several small private libraries responded positively, the Boston Athenaeum cited "insuperable objections" to having its facilities "thrown open" to the public, and other repositories, such as the American Academy of Arts and Sciences, the Massachusetts Historical Society, and the American Antiquarian Society did not even bother to reply.

Even though in most quarters the little French ventriloquist was dismissed as a charlatan and a humbug, Vattemare's well-publicized activities did get many Bostonians thinking about the possibility of a public library, and in 1847 the members of the Common Council appointed their own special committee to look into such a project. After former mayor Josiah Quincy, one of the committee members, made an anonymous cash gift of $5,000 for the establishment of a library, in November 1847 the Council ordered the committee to apply to the state legislature for authorization to "establish, regulate, and control a library for the free use of every citizen. . . ." On March 18, 1848, the legislature passed, and Governor George Briggs signed, the required legislation for the City of Boston to establish a public library. Founded in 1848 as the first large municipal library in America, the Boston Public Library originally shared space with the Massachusetts Historical Society in rooms above the archway of Charles Bulfinch's Tontine Crescent on Franklin Street. After a move to larger quarters on Boylston Street, just off Tremont, the library finally moved to its permanent location in Copley Square, to occupy an impressive Renaissance-style building designed by the firm of McKim, Mead, and White. Some years later, on a visit to Boston in the course of a lecture tour, Oxford poet and British educator, Matthew Arnold, observed a barefoot newsboy reading quietly in the public library, and he commented: "I do not think I have been so impressed with anything else I have seen since arriving in this country."

Creating an insatiable thirst for knowledge, promoting popular lecture programs, building a public library, and making sure that everybody in Boston "knew enough," inevitably meant that something would have to be done to reform and improve the educational system of the day, especially in a city that prided itself on being the "Athens of America." During the early years of the Republic, there were some excellent private schools and academies, many of them conducted by church-related denominations, available to those young people whose parents could afford the tuition. Many boys and girls from well-to-do families could also attend local "dame" schools, run by highly respected women who often taught several generations of the same family. Occasionally, especially during the new period of cultural activity, there appeared several schools that sought to introduce new educational ideas. In 1841, for example, George Ripley and his wife Sophia organized an experimental community called Brook Farm, in the rural suburb of West Roxbury, that was intended to create a cultured and harmonious environment for its members and attracted such writers and intellectuals as Emerson, Thoreau, Hawthorne, and Richard Henry Dana. In a small school building called "the Hive," they used progressive teaching methods and a form of discipline based on reason and explanation for their students who attended classes in the morning and did manual work in the afternoon. At the same time, in downtown Boston, an eccentric but idealistic educational innovator named Bronson Alcott conducted his short-lived Temple School based on trust and affection. In attractively arranged classrooms, he set up programs of amusement and recreation and adopted the Socratic method of posing questions and eliciting responses from his students, rather than using the traditional system of strict discipline and rote memory.

For members of the general public, however, anything like a satisfactory system of public education was much less available, and far less acceptable. As early as 1647, it is true, the General Court of Massachusetts had ordered all townships with more than a hundred families to establish grammar schools. In order to read and interpret the Scriptures, Puritanism demanded both an educated clergy and a literate congregation. And as a growing commercial center, Boston also needed men who could understand ledgers and calculate inventories. After the Revolution, a new comprehensive state law in 1789 confirmed the practice of requiring townships to establish primary and grammar schools that would be open to all children and be administered by a popularly elected School Committee.

Over time, however, the results of the new school system proved to be usually uneven, and generally unsatisfactory. Heavily burdened taxpayers begrudged money for buildings, books, and equipment; teachers were poorly paid, and often so inadequately prepared that they were little ahead of their pupils in the ability to read, write, and do arithmetic. At first, the teachers were mostly men, often young college men who did not regard teaching as a permanent career, but who worked in the classroom, either as a form of temporary employment while they were preparing for a career as a lawyer or a preacher, or as part-time work during seasonal breaks at the local college or during slack seasons on the farm. As the population grew, however, and as the number of schools rapidly increased, so did the number of women who entered the field as teachers. Even then, however, few women had any kind of professional preparation or formal training, but were selected either for their availability—widows, unmarried women, wives of preachers—or for what was considered to be their compassionate and sympathetic nature as females.

With the increase in white manhood suffrage during the Jacksonian period of the 1830s and 1840s, however, and with the nation looking forward to many more Americans taking part in the political process, it seemed absolutely necessary to extend educational benefits to as many people as possible. The haphazard and completely unprofessional educational system that existed seemed to be not only undemocratic, but actually dangerous to the interests of a republic whose future was based on the voting power of a literate and informed electorate. There were many who saw public education as a form of what historian Stanley Schultz, in his study *The Culture Factory*, has called "social insurance," a means of transforming poor, idle, and immigrant children into grown-ups who would become literate, responsible, and patriotic American citizens.

By the late 1830s and early 1840s, an even more immediate problem was the fact that the prevailing system of common schools that had developed in the rural environment of the "little red schoolhouse," with its single room and ungraded classes, was no longer suited to the social and economic conditions of a complex urban environment. In a city like Boston, whose general population would grow from 43,298 in 1820 to 177,840 in 1860, the number of school-age children was already outgrowing the limited number of schools available in their respective neighborhoods. In developing a more organized and systematic approach to the problem, as Schultz has described it, town leaders drew on the familiar elements of the region's factory system whereby the elected members of the School Committee served in a supervisory capacity as the Board of Trustees; where school administrators performed the executive functions of managers; and where the schoolchildren were, in effect, members of the workforce. The subsequent system of graded classes, the use of uniform textbooks, and the development of a common curriculum helped create an internal structure of educational standards that produced a greater measure of stability and accountability. Beyond all this, however, the whole exercise was to take place within a philosophy calculated to promote religion, piety, and obedience and designed to foster private and public morality. Schools opened and closed each day with prayer, readings from the Scripture took place regularly, and teachers were urged to impress upon their students the principles of piety, justice, and truth, love of country, industry, and frugality, chastity, moderation, and temperance. Poor children and children of immigrant parents particularly, the School Committee emphasized in its 1850 report, should receive sufficient moral and religious teaching to keep them "in the right path amid the moral darkness which is their daily and domestic walk."

One of the outstanding leaders in the early drive for a better organized and more professional statewide system of public schools was Horace Mann of Franklin, Massachusetts, who moved on from a promising career in law to service in the state legislature. As president of the senate during his final term of office, he signed a significant education bill that became law on April 20,1837, providing for the establishment of a state board of education, which was empowered to appoint a secretary. Through the influence of Edmund Dwight, a prominent textile manufacturer and noted philanthropist from Springfield, Horace Mann himself was appointed to the new post of secretary. During his years of service, from 1839 to 1848, he almost completely transformed the moribund school system in Massachusetts.

Mann's first task was to arouse the awareness of the general public to the purpose, the value, and the needs of public education. He was able to achieve this by organizing a series of annual educational conventions in every county throughout the Commonwealth. He made sure that these conventions were attended not only by teachers and school officials, but also by members of the general public. He also arranged for prominent civic leaders and persons of intellectual distinction from the various communities to address as many of these meetings as possible. Mann also edited and published a semimonthly magazine called *The Common School Journal*, as well as prepared a series of detailed annual reports designed to persuade his fellow citizens to recognize public education as the best hope of preserving democratic institutions in the United States. He repeatedly defended the school system as the route to social stability and equal opportunity. It had never happened, he argued, and never could happen, that an educated people could be permanently poor. "Education then, beyond all other devices of human origin, is a great equalizer of the conditions of men," wrote Mann, "the balance wheel of the social machinery," thus encouraging further support from those members of the conservative establishment who saw public education as one more way to avert social unrest in an increasingly diverse urban society.

It is not surprising that during the Civil War, little more than a dozen years later, after Union forces captured the Sea Islands along the South Carolina coast in 1862, Massachusetts dispatched the Boston Educational Commission to set up schools for the freed slaves whose white owners had abandoned them and moved to the mainland. Under the direction of Edward Everett Hale and other well-known Bostonians, the commission determined to instill in the former slaves the self-discipline and Protestant work ethic they saw in Horace Mann's program in Massachusetts. According to Richard Abbott's *Cotton and Capital*, the Northerners believed the former slaves could become an efficient part of the American free labor force if they received instruction in temperance, self-respect, neatness and order, and they saw "system in work" as an essential part of the Boston model.

In his post as secretary of the Massachusetts Board of Education, Horace Mann conducted an unrelenting campaign for better school buildings, textbooks, libraries, and equipment. He was able to establish a six-month's minimum school year, insisted on dividing pupils into grades, and succeeded in getting the state legislature to double the educational appropriations. Under his vigorous direction, fifty new schools were founded, standardized curricula developed, teaching methods revamped, and teachers' salaries substantially increased. To improve the teaching profession itself, he brought about the establishment of teachers' institutes, and created the first three state "normal schools" in the United States devoted specifically to the professional training of teachers. In keeping with the ideas of other progressive educators in the area, such as Bronson Alcott and George Ripley, Mann also declared himself opposed to flogging and other forms of corporal punishment, encouraging teachers to reply upon what he called "moral suasion" in disciplining their students.

In the course of their preparations, teachers were heavily dependent upon textbooks for guidance and instruction, and in this respect received support from several publishers of the period. In 1783, a twenty-five-year-old schoolteacher named Noah Webster, declaring that "America must be as independent in *literature* as she is in *politics*, as famous for *arts* as for *arms*," published the first edition of his famous *Blue Back Speller*, that would sell millions of copies and help prospective teachers in their efforts to standardize the American language. Webster was convinced that the use of his textbooks in the common schools would allow a benevolent society to enlighten the lower classes and, in the process, "render them harmless." In 1836, William Holmes McGuffey, a professor from Ohio, also provided assistance to the classroom with a series of graded works called *Eclectic Readers*. These books taught children to recite and memorize popular poems of the day, as well as the patriotic words and sayings of such famous American figures as George Washington, Patrick Henry, and Daniel Webster. McGuffey's *Readers* were replete with inspirational stories and parables calculated to instill in children such basic American values as thrift, morality, sobriety, and patriotism.

Mann's determination to completely reform the state's educational system, however, was not without its critics. Some objected to the higher taxes that would be required to implement his ambitious programs; others objected to his use of progressive German and Swiss educational techniques; still others were opposed to the nonsectarian Christian philosophy he adopted in order to accommodate children of all Protestant denominations who would attend classes together. Thirty-one schoolmasters of Boston issued a 144-page pamphlet challenging Mann's critical assessment of the prevailing common schools, objecting to the "new kind of influence and teaching" he was introducing, and criticizing his theory of moral discipline. By challenging the traditional use of corporal punishment, the masters claimed, the secretary had effectively undermined their "rightful authority," thereby inviting anarchy into the classroom. The Reverend A. W. McClure, an influential Boston minister, used the pages of his monthly publication, the *Christian Observatory*, to denounce this new infatuation with what he called the "Heresy of Love" and called upon Bostonians to restore the sterner faith of their Pilgrim fathers. Mann was not deterred by these attacks from Calvinist critics, however, and fought back with pamphlets supporting his own position, and in the fall of 1844 he saw a number of his friends and supporters, including Dr. Samuel Gridley Howe, elected to seats on the Boston school board. From that vantage point Mann's allies launched a vigorous campaign to discredit the rebel schoolmasters, ridicule their outmoded methods of corporal punishment, and condemn the old-fashioned system of rote learning they used in the classroom.

Slowly and gradually, the movement for a system of free, tax-supported, public education gained wider support. Members of the working class wanted free schools to give their families an equal chance to pursue the American dream; newly arrived immigrants welcomed the opportunity to provide their children with the kind of education they never could have received in the Old Country; even orthodox critics were willing to admit the need for increased literacy as a means of avoiding the demagoguery of illiterate voters and uninformed mobs. Gradually the tide changed, and by 1860 the principle of free, tax-supported, public education—at least at the elementary level—had been generally accepted throughout most of the Northern states.

More than simply a better organized and more efficient method of turning out literate citizens who could participate responsibly in the democratic process and industrious workers who could labor diligently in the factories and counting houses of the city, Boston's new public schools were also regarded as an essential part of the social-reform spirit of the period that sought to elevate minds, inspire the spirit of inquiry, and achieve new levels of accomplishment. Taught to be more humane and compassionate Christians, boys could learn to become "good and virtuous" patriots, while girls would be ready to assume their duties as the teachers of a coming generation of Americans who would face a much more modern and complex age.

CHAPTER 6 } PROGRESS & POPERY

In the enthusiasm of Bostonians to raise their city to such an elevated level of intellectual achievement and human accomplishment that it would be universally recognized as the Athens of America, the emergence of the Roman Catholic Church as a recognizable influence was the source of considerable anxiety. Most Protestants regarded the city's growing Irish Catholic immigrant community as one of the most serious obstacles to almost every single aspect of their humanitarian reforms as well as to their idealistic endeavors to improve the lives of individual citizens and establish the moral vigor of a Christian and decidedly Protestant Republic.

Anti-Catholicism had been a constant theme in Boston history, going back to earliest colonial times. Five centuries of mutual hatred and almost uninterrupted warfare between the English and the Irish accounted for the cold, even violent, reception faced by the first Irish emigrants who came ashore on the Shawmut Peninsula, where John Winthrop and his Puritan followers, in 1630, had established the Massachusetts Bay Colony. Despite the fact that most of the Irish settlers who arrived during the seventeenth century were Presbyterians from the northern counties of Ireland, their strong Protestant convictions did little to make them acceptable to the Puritans, who regarded the Irish universally as a barbaric, inferior, and unmanageable race of people. Despite a cool reception and early difficulties, however, the Ulster Irish (often referred to as the "Scotch-Irish"), who spoke English, demonstrated an admirable work ethic and eventually supported the colonial rebellion, were gradually accepted into the general Puritan community by the end of the century.

No such receptive attitude was ever held toward those Irish people who emigrated from the southern counties and followed the Roman Catholic religion. To Anglo-Saxons in general, but to the Puritans in particular, Irish Catholics were not only from an inferior race, but they were also members of a detested religion that was blasphemous and heretical, and one whose members had also conspired with foreigner enemies like the Spaniards and the French to overthrow the English monarchy. The unsuccessful attempt in 1605 by a group of disgruntled Catholics, among them Guy Fawkes, to blow up the leaders of the government—the so-called Gunpowder Plot— only made the English more certain than ever that Catholics were engaged in a Papist conspiracy of cosmic proportions.

Under these circumstances, Puritan authorities took every measure to see that no Irish Catholics ("St. Patrick's Vermin") were allowed into the Bay Colony, especially when they were also seen as potential allies of the French, who were in the process of colonizing neighboring Canada during the eighteenth century. In a further attempt to discourage Catholic immigration, in June 1700, the Massachusetts General Court passed a law forbidding any Catholic priest from coming into Massachusetts territory, under the penalty of life imprisonment or—if he escaped and was recaptured— death. In the absence of priests, it was assumed that Catholics would not turn up anywhere they could not hear Mass, receive the sacraments, or make their annual Easter duty. The spectre of the pope and the stereotype of every Catholic as a potential subversive agent continued to inflame the Puritan imagination, and for generations on Guy Fawkes Day, every November 5, the Protestants of Boston took part in an elaborate anti-Catholic demonstration called "Pope's Night" that always ended with the pope being burned in effigy.

Even when England defeated France in the Seven Years' War in 1763, and ordered a relaxation of its official anti-Catholic policies in order to accommodate its newly acquired French Catholic population in Canada, the Puritans of Massachusetts showed no signs of easing their fiercely anti-Papist attitudes. Regardless of what the British government said, young John Adams still viewed "popery" as incompatible with liberty. Catholicism was a "Roman system" that had kept humanity in chains "for ages," he said, and therefore had no right to enjoy any form of recognition or toleration. Only the coming of the American Revolution, the desire to develop better relations with Canada, and the necessity of developing a military alliance with France forced many Bostonians to subordinate their prejudice against everything Catholic to their fervent desire for national independence.

During the wartime period of comparative tolerance, a handful of French and Irish Catholics in the town formed a small congregation of their own and began to practice their religion openly. After using the services of several transient priests, they were provided with a permanent curate in the person of Fr. François Matignon, who was joined in 1796 by Fr. Jean-Louis de Cheverus, another French refugee from Revolutionary France. By that time, the growth of the town's Catholic population to nearly a thousand required the construction of a church in 1803, and only five years later Fr. Cheverus was appointed the first Bishop of Boston. Although the number of Catholics continued to increase slightly every year, the newcomers were still manageable enough in numbers, and useful enough in the services they provided, to ensure a continued attitude of acceptance, if not outright tolerance. Bishop Cheverus proved to be a gracious and surprisingly popular churchman, and there appeared little reason to consider the small Catholic community a serious threat to the life and society of the Puritan capital. By the 1820s, however, things had changed dramatically.

The colossal debt after the end of the Napoleonic Wars in 1815 had led the government of Great Britain to force landowners either to raise rents on their properties or to convert their fields into pasture for the more profitable grazing of sheep and cattle. One result of this preemptive land policy was a marked acceleration of bankrupt farmers and displaced tenants from all parts of Ireland, but especially from the rural counties of the south and the west. From 1825 through 1830, approximately 125,000 people emigrated from Ireland to the United States—with more than 30,000 of them coming to the Commonwealth of Massachusetts. By 1830, there were nearly 8,000 Irish Catholics residing in Boston.

The sudden growth in the city's Irish Catholic population during the early 1820s immediately brought back the old sense of fear and foreboding among native Bostonians whose traditional Puritan suspicions concerning the dangerous and subversive character of "popery" had never completely disappeared. A welcome source of labor only a few years earlier when they were cutting down the hills and filling in the coves, the foreigners were now viewed as a danger to the livelihood of native-born American workers. During the 1820s there were sporadic outbreaks of violence against persons and property in the Irish sections of town along Ann Street and Broad Street, and in 1834 city leaders were shocked by the burning of the Ursuline convent in Charlestown. Members of the city's upper classes—the lawyers, the businessmen, the bankers—might have regarded the growing influx of these foreigners as both distasteful and alarming, but they certainly did not anticipate losing their homes, their businesses, or their incomes. The same, however, was not true of the day laborers, the streetsweepers, the lamplighters, the stablemen, the brickyard workers, or the truckmen. Poor workingmen who made a meager living from unskilled occupations could easily see the "Paddies" as potential rivals, whose depressed standard of living would impel them to take over the native workers' livelihoods. Even members of the police and fire departments, whose ranks were jealously reserved for able-bodied "American" candidates, could foresee the obvious economic consequences when immigrants eventually moved up the political ladder and demanded their rightful places on the city payroll. Men confronted with such frightening possibilities were ready to lash out at any tangible evidence of growth or increasing prosperity in the immigrant population. Certainly political and economic resentment was apparent on the part of those workers who toiled at the local brickyard for a dollar or two a day, when they savagely attacked and burned the Ursuline Convent. And in the Broad Street Riot three years later, it was no coincidence that members of the fire companies vented their rage against the members of an Irish funeral procession who had the temerity to block their return to the station.

Increasingly, however, prejudice against Catholics in Boston began to turn from sporadic and often spontaneous acts of violence to more institutionalized and systematized forms of action, directed by a number of influential and conservative Protestant groups in the area. This happened at a particular moment in time when leaders of older and more conservative Protestant denominations in New England were beginning to recover from the initial shock of having been ousted from their longtime positions of power and influence by those who supported newer, more liberal, and more humanistic religious organizations such as the Unitarians and the Universalists. Conservatives believed that the greatest challenges to old-time Calvinist morality had come in the late 1790s, with the outbreak of the French Revolution abroad and the emergence of Jeffersonian liberalism at home. They were convinced that evil people had employed radical ideas, atheistic philosophies, and anticlerical prejudices to cut deeply into the revealed truths of the Christian message and had come up with new denominations that abandoned their earlier beliefs in the Divinity and the Bible in favor of secular, humanistic issues such as social harmony and human progress. "Wicked and artful men in foreign countries," announced Rev. Jedidiah Morse, a Congregational minister, in November 1798, were determined to undermine the foundations of Christianity, and to "overthrow its Altars." These warning by well-known conservative spokesmen like Morse were heeded throughout New England, wrote historian Richard Hofstadter, "wherever Federalists brooded about the rising tide of religious infidelity or Jeffersonian democracy."

Determined to restore the preeminence of "orthodoxy" in America, the older leaders prepared to launch a series of counterattacks in order to preserve the Christian moral values upon which America had been founded, as well as to root out those subversive elements they felt were conspiring against the basic ideals of the Constitutional republic. An early attempt by conservative Protestant groups to prevent the further dissemination of radical theological views took place in 1801, when New England Congregationalists and Presbyterians formed a "Plan of Union" to confront the inroads that were already being made by the advocates of Unitarianism. In 1808, various Congregational groups took a further step to restore the Calvinist influence by establishing the Andover Seminary in Massachusetts, which reinforced orthodoxy and the revival spirit so forcefully under the direction of Rev. Jedidiah Morse that its location came to be known as "Brimstone Hill." To avoid the kind of liberal ideas that had taken hold at Harvard, Morse and his associates made professors subscribe to an Andover Creed of what one writer has called "double-distilled Calvinism." And when Rev. Lyman Beecher came to Boston in 1826 to assume the position of pastor at the new Hanover Street Church, he expanded his familiar sermons on the evils of intemperate drinking to include fierce tirades against Unitarians, Freemasons, Catholics, and other "infidels" who were endangering orthodox Protestantism and American freedom.

In their ongoing struggle to restore the principles of orthodoxy, however, Protestants realized that they needed a more permanent organizational structure and more effective lines of communication with other sympathetic religious groups. During the 1820s, therefore, many Congregationalists and Presbyterians, supported by various groups of Methodists, Baptists, and Episcopalians, banded together to form several interdenominational associations, designed to foster the evangelical spirit that was sweeping through the western counties as part of the Second Great Awakening, but also to ensure that fundamental Protestant teachings were not weakened or watered down in the process. Their American Education Society provided subsidies for church-related colleges and seminaries, while the American Home Missionary Society paid the expenses of many pastors traveling to new settlements in the West and helped poor congregations support their ministers in rural areas. The American Sunday School Society dispatched missionaries to all parts of the country and supplied them with lesson plans, books, tracts and other forms of teaching aids. The American Tract Society published millions of edifying religious pamphlets and booklets to promote moral virtues and high ethical standards, and the American Bible Society took on the task of distributing literally millions of copies of the Bible to all parts of the nation to ensure the continued influence of the scriptures. Although the conservatives did not actually discourage the emotional evangelism that was characteristic of so many camp meetings of the period, they did urge that wherever possible such meetings should be carried on by resident pastors among their own congregations. If itinerant evangelists were needed, the missionary societies announced themselves capable of providing a more educated and dignified variety of preachers to suit the purpose.

Allowing for slight differences in doctrinal views within the individual sects and denominations, these national societies represented a forceful common effort by the leading American churches of the period to disseminate the Gospel, to promote the basic Anglo-Saxon virtues, and to apply the Christian doctrine of brotherhood to specific social problems in a manner consistent with traditional, orthodox traditions. Serious concern with improving social conditions in the community led many conservative Protestants to work closely with such movements as temperance and prison reform where they felt that serious moral issues were involved; but they generally stayed clear of more "radical" efforts at institutional reform which they felt were conducted in ways that were contrary to accepted modes of conduct and dangerous to the established social order. The roots of true reform, they felt, lay not merely in improving physical conditions or changing the social environment, but in returning America to the old moral values of fundamental Calvinism. Most of the work of these associations was carried out by dedicated laymen, especially prominent political leaders and wealthy businessmen and merchants, who took pains to inculcate such virtues as sobriety, frugality, and hard work, which they saw as an integral part of the Christian message. Such leisurely pastimes as card playing and dancing were branded as frivolous, but the use of tobacco and alcoholic beverages was denounced as harmful self-indulgence. Recreational activities or amusements on the Sabbath were looked upon as a violation of the spirit of the Lord's Day. If America was to achieve its God-given mission, if order and stability were to be preserved in a democratic nation, as historian W. David Lewis has summarized it, then individual social behavior had to be brought into line with proper standards and values.

In addition to their mission of preserving traditional Protestant morality, promoting civilization, bringing the Gospel to the frontier, and enkindling a general moral renewal, many leaders of conservative Protestant organizations also turned to the more pragmatic task of protecting America from dangerous ideologies and other "foreign" influences that ran counter to what they considered to be those traditional Anglo-Saxon–Puritan virtues, which had given the nation its unique and distinctive character.

These fears and anxieties about what many believed to be deliberate and widespread conspiracies by foreign, radical, and alien groups to pervert conservative religious values and radicalize the American system of republican government first took political form with the emergence of the Anti-Mason movement of the late 1820s and early 1830s. The movement actually began in 1826, in upstate New York, when a man named William Morgan was kidnapped, and presumably murdered, after it was discovered that he planned to reveal the secrets of the Masonic Order. This incident provided a rallying point for a movement that drew much of its support from members of conservative Protestant groups who had long believed that members of the Masonic Order were not only destroying Christianity by promoting the kinds of rational and atheistic ideas they had acquired from the radical doctrines of the French Revolution, but were also acquiring such extraordinary political influence in the United States that they posed a serious threat to the American democratic system. Determined to stamp out both godless atheism as well as special privilege—both of which they regarded as totally un-American—conservative religious spokesmen joined with a number of active political leaders to forge the Anti-Mason movement into a bona fide political party, a third party, in fact, that gained considerable grassroots support throughout the Northeast during the early 1830s in opposition to the rising power of the Jacksonian Democrats. Following the victory of the Democrats and the reelection of Andrew Jackson in 1832, however, the Anti-Mason Party quickly dissolved, and most of its members made their way into the conservative Whig Party. Despite its devastating defeat, the Anti-Mason Party was an early example of a growing determination by orthodox groups to take concerted action against organizations whose "foreign" ideologies, dangerous alliances, and secular principles threatened the fundamental Protestant religious values upon which the nation was founded.

The same exaggerated fears and apprehensions that characterized the conservative response to the spread of Masonry were also evident in its reaction to the growth and expansion of Roman Catholicism during the first half of the nineteenth century. Directed by a number of conservative Protestant groups in the area, the fundamentalist assault against popery took on a broader and more systematic form called "nativism," to more clearly differentiate their own purposes and goals from those they regarded as foreign and essentially un-American. By the late 1820s and early 1830s, a regular campaign of vituperation was being carried on in sermons, lecture programs, and public speeches, denouncing popery as a false religion, the fruit of "the great apostasy." Catholics, claimed conservative speakers, had refused to accept the Bible as the rule of faith and, instead, had substituted a system of "soul-destroying superstitions" and "senseless absurdities." During the winter of 1830–31, Rev. Lyman Beecher, now pastor of Boston's Hanover Street Church, delivered a series of Sunday evening lectures at the nearby Park Street Congregational Church on the subject of "Political Atheism," in which he vigorously belabored the evils of Catholicism and the dangers that popery represented to the American way of life. Local Catholics were indignant over what they regarded as Beecher's unfair and outrageous sermons, and Bishop Benedict Fenwick arranged a course of fifteen lectures of his own. They were presented at the small Catholic church on Franklin Street by him and by a well-educated priest from Ireland, Fr. Thomas J. O'Flaherty, who had studied medicine at Philadelphia before going into the priesthood, and who was always referred to as "Dr. O'Flaherty." The two men delivered their rebuttals on alternate evenings, from January 16 to May 1, 1831, setting forth to large audiences, composed of both Catholics and Protestants, the true beliefs of Catholics and refuting what they regarded as Rev. Beecher's deliberate and hostile misrepresentations.

In the meantime, the various conservative Protestant associations were using their tracts, broadsides, journals, and newspapers to further publicize what they saw as the errors implicit in Roman Catholic theology. Local weekly publications, such as the Boston *Recorder*, the Congregational weekly newspaper, the Baptist *Christian Watchman*, the Unitarian *Christian Register*, and the Methodist *Zion's Herald*, worked in close association with a variety of New York–based newspapers and magazines to launch further assaults against the insidious ideologies and alien influences they felt would surely undermine the Christian foundations of American freedom. The *Protestant Magazine* announced to its readers that it intended to defend the "great truths of the gospel opposed by popery, and to exhibit those doctrines and practices of Roman Catholics which are contrary to the interests of mankind."

Determined not to allow undocumented charges and scurrilous innuendos to go unchallenged, Bishop Fenwick of Boston authorized the creation of a weekly newspaper of his own, *The Jesuit, or Catholic Sentinel*, as a means by which he could "explain, diffuse, and defend the principles of the One, Holy, Catholic, and Apostolic Church." His predecessor, Jean Lefebvre de Cheverus, the first Catholic bishop of Boston, had been a French émigré, a small and somewhat delicate man, who had won the admiration and respect of Boston Protestants with his Gallic charm and gracious manner. Benedict Fenwick, however, had come from a prominent Maryland family, and, at the age of forty-three, he was nearly six feet tall and weighed well over 250 pounds, was proud of his American heritage, and was not prepared to back down from a fight. In the first issue of *The Jesuit*, dated September 5, 1829, he announced that, in defending the doctrines of the Catholic Church, he and his editors would not "seek battle"; at the same time, however, he warned that they would not shrink from it "when forced upon us." Generally, however, most of the early Catholic newspapers begun during this period in Boston and in several other American cities were too few in number, too inefficiently operated, and too weakly funded to compete effectively with the large-scale efforts of the conservative Protestant press. In many cases, too, the Catholic papers' methods and techniques proved counterproductive, especially when their articles and editorials adopted the same shrill, angry, and argumentative tone as those of their adversaries. In one editorial, for example, "Dr. O'Flaherty" referred to Protestants as "mercenary Bible mongers" and "modern Pharisees," while he excoriated those "foul libelers" and "scurrilous scribblers" who exhausted the "armory of falsehood" in their efforts to injure the Catholic Church. The result was that very soon the influence of *The Jesuit* and similar publications was restricted almost exclusively to their own Catholic readers, while their lecture programs all too often degenerated into raucous shouting matches in which very few minds were changed or opinions altered. Bishop Fenwick soon realized that his newspaper was not achieving its purposes of defending the faith and explaining Catholic doctrines, so in 1843 he transferred ownership to a layman named Patrick Donahoe, who changed the name of the paper to the *Boston Pilot* and proceeded to publish it as a general weekly newspaper that catered to a predominantly Irish Catholic readership.

By that time, too, efforts at using newspapers to develop some type of ecumenical dialogue and catechetical instruction were being completely overshadowed by further aggressive assaults by nativist critics who had now moved on from condemning the doctrinal beliefs of Roman Catholics to exposing what they saw as the total immorality of a system they charged with promoting all sorts of personal vice and immoral behavior. During the 1830s, several American publishing houses revived a series of older anti-Catholic polemics, most of them originally published in Europe at least a century earlier, many of which focused on bizarre stories about the Spanish Inquisition. The suggestive titles and subtitles of these books pointed up a more subtle and even more vicious trend in the nativist crusade. Although most of these works purported to expose the hidden rituals, the secret rites, and the elaborate intrigues of the church they referred to as the "whore of Babylon" and the "abomination of abominations," many of them actually made a special point of elaborating on the allegedly licentious attributes of convents and nunneries, where "lecherous" priests and "compliant" nuns were engaged in almost continuous sexual depravity. "Escaped nuns" such as Maria Monk, who in 1836 published a totally fabricated story called *Awful Disclosures,* describing the terrible things that supposedly happened to her at the Hotel Dieu Nunnery at Montreal, found a ready-made market for their revelations among those readers who were prepared to believe the worst about Roman Catholics.

Boston saw its own version of what historian Richard Hofstadter has called the "pornography of the Puritans," when a woman named Rebecca Reed went about claiming that she had "escaped" from the Ursuline Convent located in nearby Charlestown. An enterprising publisher put the young woman's harrowing tales of life behind convent walls between the covers of a book, with the provocative title of *Six Months in a Convent,* that sold two hundred thousand copies within a month of its publication. To many Bostonians who had been brought up on a traditional Anglo-Saxon–Protestant diet of Spanish Inquisition, Jesuit threats, Irish uprisings, gunpowder plots, and papal schemes, the lurid details of this imaginative story seemed entirely plausible and terrifying, despite the fact that Rebecca Reed, like Maria Monk, was an unfortunate psychopath whose stories proved to be without any semblance of truth. Indeed, the rumors about the terrible things going on at the Ursuline Convent caused already inflamed anti-Catholic feelings in the Boston community to reach fever pitch when Rev. Lyman Beecher appeared on the scene. Beecher had recently left his post at the Hanover Street Church to accept the presidency of Lane Theological Seminary in Ohio, but had returned to Boston on a fund-raising tour. The conservative churchman delivered a series of thunderous anti-Catholic sermons in three different Protestant churches on the night of Sunday, August 10, 1834, repeating his earlier denunciations of Catholicism and calling upon his listeners to take decisive action against the resurgence of popery in America.

Given the general anti-Catholic sentiment of the time, the prolonged newspaper campaign, the rash of exposé literature, the dreadful stories of Rebecca Reed, and the persistent rumors of what was going on behind the walls at the Ursuline Convent, the inflammatory sermons of Rev. Beecher provided the final goad to violence. It was on the following night, Monday, August 11, 1834, that the mob of forty or fifty brickmakers and truckmen stormed the gates of the Ursuline Convent and burned the property to the ground. Although there were formal protests from prominent Bostonians and leading Protestant journals about the use of violence in the anti-Catholic crusade, there was little indication that such sentiments of regret reflected any basic change of attitude on the part of those who were obviously delighted to see the offensive symbol of the Catholic presence gone from the scene. Although eight of the ringleaders were eventually brought to trial for the capital offense of arson, all of them were found not guilty—a verdict greeted with cheers of delight by friends and neighbors who packed the courtroom and greeted the defendants as heroes in the fight to save America from the false religious beliefs and eccentric behavioral practices of foreign Papists.

Despite the prevailing hostility of Protestant Americans toward Roman Catholics and their religious beliefs, however, there was a tentative sense in some quarters that quite possibly Catholicism, as it began to develop in the uniquely free American environment, might gradually assume more democratic characteristics that would eventually make it more acceptable to native-born Americans. Charles Carroll of Carrolton, for example, a distinguished Catholic from Maryland, had been a member of the Continental

Congress and a signer of the Declaration of Independence. His cousin, John Carroll, although a priest—and a Jesuit at that—had been approved to work among the people of Canada during the Revolution, and in 1790 he was the first American to be named a Catholic bishop in the United States, thus helping to dispel the prevailing notion that American Catholics were totally under the control of a foreign and "alien" power. Bishop Carroll had accommodated himself to the prevailing Protestant practice of placing church property in the hands of lay boards of trustees, who were responsible for administering it and representing the congregation before the courts of law. In the town of Boston, the first congregation was composed of Catholic laypeople, since no Catholic priests had been allowed in the Massachusetts Bay Colony, and organized their community along the lines of the traditional congregational model, with laymen serving as trustees and assuming legal responsibility for church finances and property rights. This was a situation that Jean-Lefebvre de Cheverus, the town's first bishop, pretty much accepted, asking his parishioners for a "universal show of hands" in the American fashion when it came time to approve the construction of a church. As early as 1831, as John McGreevy has pointed out in his study *Catholicism and American Freedom,* Alexis de Tocqueville, the observant French visitor, felt that he could make out a new "Catholic style" in America and held out the possibility that in time Catholicism might well become a powerful contributor to the "maintenance of a Democratic Republic in the United States." And about the same time, another visitor, Harriet Martineau, encouraged her British readers to believe that the Catholic religion in America was being modified by the "spirit of the time," and that its members were no longer a set of men "who can be priest-ridden to any fatal extent."

These fitful expectations of a more liberal and democratic Catholicity in America proved very short-lived, however, and the results were even more controversial than before. After the death of Bishop John Carroll in 1815, a number of French bishops were sent to replace what some people called the "American" bishops in several of the country's new dioceses. Ambrose Marechal, for example, replaced John Carroll at Baltimore; Jean Du Bois came to serve in New York; Louis Du Bourg was assigned to New Orleans; Benedict Flaget went to Kentucky. Indeed, the appearance of so many "foreign" bishops caused such distress among Irish and German Catholics that many of them actually contemplated establishing an "Independent Catholic Church of America," until the Vatican quickly stepped in and appointed more acceptable candidates. Bishop Patrick Kelly, for example, was sent to Richmond, Virginia; Bishop John England was assigned to Charleston, South Carolina; and Bishop Benedict Fenwick came north to Boston.

These new appointments were more than merely changes in name and nationality, however; they were representative of a more serious desire on the part of Rome to bring the Catholic Church in America back into much closer conformity with traditional administrative procedures and ecclesiastical lines of authority. Historian John McGreevy has suggested an interesting similarity between the orthodox revival that had been set in motion among the various conservative Calvinist-Protestant denominations in the United States in an effort to counteract the liberal effects of Unitarianism and the kind of "revivalism" that was directed by conservative members of the Catholic hierarchy in America during the 1820s and 1830s. In many respects, this new orthodoxy reflected the response of Catholic leaders in Rome to present a solid front against the frightening upsurge of liberalism, nationalism, and secularism throughout Europe—much of it anti-Catholic, most of it decidedly anticlerical—that was threatening to topple monarchies, establish republican governments, and break the political power of the Catholic Church. European Catholic leaders recoiled in alarm at the increasing power of the "ultra-radical" insurgents and called upon loyal members of the faithful to stand together against what Bishop John Bernard Fitzpatrick of Boston called the "red-republican" activities of those who would tear down centuries of traditional Christian culture.

This unsettling wave of radical change and progressive reform throughout Western Europe also caused the Holy See to become even more apprehensive about reports that, in the United States, many Catholics were calling for the Church in America to operate in a much more democratic manner and insisting that laypeople have a greater degree of participation in such administrative matters as the conduct of parish affairs, the appointment of pastors, the management of finances, and the ownership of church property. Indeed, in many parts of the country it had become common practice for prosperous landowners, influential lawyers, and successful businessmen to serve their Catholic parishes as lay trustees and property administrators.

Neither members of the Roman hierarchy, nor an increasing number of the newly appointed American bishops who had been trained in European seminaries, found the "congregational" style of lay involvement in diocesan affairs acceptable as a permanent arrangement for the governance of

BISHOP JOHN BERNARD FITZPATRICK

*Born in Boston and educated at the Boston Latin School, where his classmates
included the sons of Boston's leading citizens, John Bernard Fitzpatrick studied for
the Catholic priesthood at Montreal and Paris, and in 1846 became the third Bishop
of Boston. At a time of great tension and possible violence with the wave of Irish
Catholic immigration that followed the Great Famine, Fitzpatrick proved to be an
effective mediator between the Irish, who fondly regarded him as a friend and
protector, and the Yankees, who respected him as a churchman of learning and
culture. (Courtesy, Archdiocese of Boston)*

the Catholic Church in the United States. There was hardly an American parish or diocese during the 1820s and 1830s that did not feel the effects of the ensuing strains and tensions between those who wanted to retain the earlier democratic procedures they had started out with, and those "ultramontanes" who looked ("beyond the mountains") to Rome for guidance and sought to impose a more centralized form of governance. In New York City, for example, bitter strife persisted for many years between the lay trustees who served St. Peter's Church and the irascible Bishop John Hughes ("Dagger John"), who eventually formed his own administrative board and brought church affairs directly under his personal control. "Episcopal authority comes from above, and not from below," he announced in no uncertain terms. "Catholics do their duty when they obey their bishop." Philadelphia also experienced all kinds of divisions between German priests and Irish parishioners, Irish bishops and native trustees, members of the hierarchy and an eccentric priest named William Hogan. When Bishop Henry Conwell finally excommunicated Hogan in 1821, a wholesale brawl broke out on the steps of St. Mary's Church that had to be quelled by the city police. In Charleston, South Carolina, and in Norfolk, Virginia, Irish boards of trustees not only rose up against their newly appointed French pastors, but also openly confronted Archbishop Marechal of Baltimore.

And in Boston itself, St. Mary's Church in the North End of the city became the scene of an unsavory and prolonged dispute between two priests each of whom had organized his own group of supporters and fought openly for the right to exercise primary control of the parish. This scandalous tug-of-war dragged on for so long that, finally, in 1847, the new bishop, John Bernard Fitzpatrick, sent both priests to new assignments and brought in a Jesuit priest, Fr. John McElroy, who had just finished a brief tour of duty as an Army chaplain during the Mexican War, to take control of the troublesome parish. Slowly, but gradually, one American bishop after another either seriously modified or totally eliminated lay boards of trustees and assumed sole episcopal authority for the administration and management of their respective dioceses.

The emerging ecclesiastical authority of the American bishops, the development of a much more centralized hierarchical structure, and the influence of Romanist theological views during the 1830s and 1840s persuaded many conservative Protestants that they were no longer contending with the nuisance of a small, diffuse, and essentially pathetic cult of misguided immigrants, but a growing organism of sinister and potentially dangerous proportions that was an even more serious threat than false religious doctrines and eccentric personal behavior. The sight of American bishops coming together for a Plenary Council at Baltimore in 1829, for example, to discuss such things as canonical directives, ecclesiastical management, and the establishment of a parochial school system, convinced many critics that the very foundations of the American Republic were imperiled by a deliberate, well-planned conspiracy designed by the Vatican for the purpose of establishing a whole new base of Catholic power in America.

American Protestants, it should be recalled, were descended from people who left their homes in England during Elizabethan times, who made the hazardous journey across the Atlantic, and who faced wilderness, wolves, and Indians in order to start a new life in a world free from the evils of "Papism" they believed existed in the Church of England. Just when most of then felt they had achieved the kind of society they had envisioned—a clearly Protestant nation, with a constitutional system based on the theory of natural rights as well as sound Anglo-Saxon precedents—they suddenly saw their beloved nation being flooded by literally millions of Catholics. Most of this immigration, to be sure, was the unfortunate result of adverse political and economic forces in the British Isles; but much of it, many were convinced, was the result of a deliberate plot, directed by the Pope and engineered by the Jesuits, to reestablish the kind of authoritarian institutions that would inevitably eradicate those freedoms and liberties guaranteed by the American constitutional system.

Adding significantly to the fierce spirit of orthodox religious reaction against the steady growth of Roman Catholic influence in the United States was the impact of the eminent historians of the period whose works also reflected the strong anti-Catholic views of the period—but for different reasons. "All the romantic historians regarded Spain and New France as grim historical exhibits of the Roman Church's influence on government and society," wrote David Levin in his study *History as Romantic Art*. While orthodox Calvinists usually emphasized the theological errors and doctrinal superstitions that made Papism such an insidious danger to America's religious values and Christian traditions, the Unitarian writers were more concerned with those moral and ethical failings of the Catholic Church they felt were completely contrary to the secular ideals of liberty, humanity, and progress. The central target of the romantic criticism, according to Dr. Levin, was authoritarianism—"absolutism," "regal and sacerdotal despotism"—not so much religious doctrine, as temporal policy. From the fanaticism and monkish intrigues of the Spanish Court of Ferdinand and Isabella to the cruelties and savagery of Cortés and Pizarro in the forests of Mexico and Peru, William Hickling Prescott made it clear to his readers that Catholics were more concerned with the "external rites and forms" of their religion than with the "spirit of Christianity itself." In a similar vein, John Lothrop Motley saw in the efforts of Philip II of Spain to suppress the struggle of Dutch Protestants for independence, the same vicious, cold-blooded ruthlessness of "priestcraft" working hand-in-hand with "kingcraft" in a diabolical manner. When Francis Parkman published his volumes on the French in New France, he often expressed admiration for the courage and fortitude of the Jesuit martyrs. He deplored, however, the ways in which Catholics broke the natural laws by preventing religious and intellectual freedom, entering into unholy "conspiracies," using Jesuitical "duplicity" to bring Christianity to the Indians, and inciting savages to attack Protestant women and children. And George Bancroft, when he wrote about the Seven Years' War, asked his readers to consider what it would have meant for the future of North America if Catholicism and France's "tottering legitimacy" had prevailed, rather than the forces of Protestantism and "popular liberty." Historians' negative descriptions regarding the authoritarian role the Catholic Church had played in the course of American history might have been expressed in the measured terms of academic scholars, rather than in the thunderous polemics of Calvinist preachers, but there was no question that they viewed Catholicism as a consistent reactionary force impeding both political liberty and intellectual freedom.

Written in a more popular vein, and appealing to a much wider audience, two books appeared in 1835 that described in great detail the new dangers a revived Roman Catholic Church posed to the American way of life. The first, *Foreign Conspiracy against the Liberties of the United States*, came from the pen of the celebrated painter and inventor of the telegraph, Samuel F. B. Morse, the son of Rev. Jedidiah Morse. "A conspiracy exists, and its plans are already in operation," Morse proclaimed. "We are attacked in a vulnerable quarter which cannot be defended by our ships, our forts, or our armies." In Apocalyptic terms, Morse described the a coming of a "great war" in the Western World between the Protestant forces of "political and religious liberties" on the one hand, and the Catholic forces of "political reaction and

GEORGE BANCROFT

George Bancroft was a prolific writer who was convinced that he could be a successful historian as well as an active public official. His ten-volume History of the United States *became a huge success among American readers. Imbued with the Jacksonian philosophy, the work was strongly nationalistic and enthusiastically democratic. As a member of the Democratic Party, Bancroft served as Secretary of the Navy under President James K. Polk, and in 1846 was appointed Minister to Great Britain. (Courtesy, Bostonian Society/Old State House)* ultramontanism" on the other, that would determine the ultimate fate of the nation. The only way to prevent this calamity, he wrote, was to put an end altogether to foreign immigration. "Awake! To your posts! Place your guards . . . shut your gates!" At the very same time, Rev. Lyman Beecher, now back at Lane Theological Seminary in Ohio, produced the second book, *A Plea for the West*, in which he also saw Protestantism engaged in a life-or-death struggle with Catholicism and predicted that the Christian millennium might well come about in the New World—with the Mississippi Valley as the critical danger zone. Conjuring up the idea of a great international conspiracy directed from Rome, Beecher saw a rising tide of immigration that was hostile to free institutions sweeping in upon America, subsidized and dispatched by "the potentates of Europe." Creating tumult and violence, filling the jails, crowding the poorhouses, and quadrupling taxation, these Catholic immigrants, warned Beecher, would send increased thousands of voters to the polls "to lay their inexperienced hand upon the helm of our power."

If the influx of Roman Catholics caused native-born Americans grave concern for the future safety of American institutions, the unprecedented flood of immigrants coming from Germany and Ireland during the late 1840s and early 1850s shocked them into the need for more concerted action. When a devastating fungus struck the potato crop in Ireland in 1846, it touched off a succession of famine years that caused widespread starvation, disease, and death throughout the land. It was this awful famine that brought a million and a half Irish people across the Atlantic during the next fifteen years. During the same period, hundreds of thousands of immigrants from the various German states, escaping political oppression and military conscription, also sought refuge in America. Altogether, during the twenty years between 1840 and 1860, over four and a half million immigrants came pouring into the United States—three-fifths of them from Ireland and Germany, many of them Roman Catholics, and all of them presenting serious problems of assimilation. As early as 1850, Mayor John Prescott Bigelow was warning the citizens of Boston about the large number of "aged, blind, paralytic, and lunatic immigrants" who were rapidly accumulating there and turning Massachusetts into a "moral cesspool." The increase in foreign-born pauperism in our midst "is an evil," agreed the *Boston Daily Advertiser*, which called for a "remedy" before it was too late.

Such a remedy to deal with this new and greatly enlarged "Catholic menace" was concocted during 1852–53, when a number of local patriotic groups and associations combined to form the American Party, a national political organization designed to protect the United States from the "insidious wiles of foreigners." Highly secret, complete with handshakes, passwords, and rituals, this new organization was commonly referred to as the Know-Nothing Party because its members were instructed to comment "I know nothing" if asked any questions about the party's organization, finances, membership, or intentions. The primary goal of the new party was to elect its members to federal offices so that they could eventually pass new laws severely restricting foreign immigration. Meanwhile, members were pledged not to hire immigrants for responsible jobs, not to vote them into political office, and generally to keep them as second-class citizens in menial and subordinate positions.

In an amazingly short period of time, political power in such East Coast cities as Boston, New York, Philadelphia, and Baltimore swung to the new party. In Massachusetts, the American Party succeeded in electing the governor, all the state officers, the entire state senate, and all but four members of the house; Jerome Van Crowninshield Smith, a longtime nativist, became mayor of Boston. Once its members were sworn into office, the anti-Catholic spirit of the movement became evident: the Know-Nothing legislature announced itself ready to eliminate "Rome, Rum, and Robbery" and lost little time in pushing forward a program of "Temperance, Liberty, and Protestantism." In addition to proposing a so-called Twenty-One-Year Law that would prevent any immigrant from becoming a voter until he had been a Massachusetts resident for at least twenty-one years, the reading of the Protestant Bible (the King James version) was made compulsory in all public schools, and, in February 1855, a joint committee of the state legislature was formed to inquire into "certain practices" alleged to be taking place in nunneries and Catholic schools. Members of what was called the Nunnery Committee undertook inspections of local Catholic schools with such heavy-footed insensitivity, however, that the committee lost all credibility and was quickly dissolved—especially when it was discovered that the members had charged their liquor bills to the Commonwealth.

In recent years, historians have correctly explored more complex political and economic motives that help explain the swift and remarkable success of the Know-Nothing movement in the Bay State. John R. Mulkern's recent study, *The Know-Nothing Party in Massachusetts*, for example, makes clear the political effects of the social and economic dislocations that occurred throughout Massachusetts as a result of rapid industrialization. Certainly the new party reflected a major effort on the part of rural voters in western Massachusetts to break the political stranglehold of the upper-class Whig politicians, lawyers, and judges in the eastern counties. Then, too, the economic tensions between the agrarian interests of the western farmers and the commercial interests of the eastern maritime and industrial families— tensions going back to the days of Shays's Rebellion—also helped shape the populist agenda of the American Party. But it would be a mistake to overlook or diminish the strong anti-Catholic bias that permeated the entire organization. In written instructions to new recruits applying for membership in a local Know-Nothing chapter in Boston, dated October 13, 1854, for example, the prospective members were told that the American tradition of the Citizen Soldier was being "contaminated" by putting arms in the hands of men who "cannot be relied upon in the hour of danger, are foes to civil and religious liberty, acknowledging as they do a higher authority in the person of the Pope of Rome than any civil or military power in this Republic." The new members not only swore absolute secrecy concerning all aspects of the party's organization, but they also vowed to defend "our Republic Institutions" against the encroachments of "the Church of Rome its Popes Cardinals Priests and its ignorant and deluded followers in any form whatever." In taking the final pledge, each initiate not only raised his right hand to salute the American flag, but also placed his right foot on "the emblem of the Church of Rome and all other despotism." It was certainly in keeping with these sentiments that, in his inaugural address after taking the oath of office as governor of Massachusetts in January 1855, Governor Henry Gardner declared that "the honor of the American flag should be confided only to those who are born on the soil hallowed by its protection," and announced that he would propose to disband all military companies composed of persons of foreign birth. A short time later, the state legislature disbanded all Irish militia companies in Massachusetts, occupied their armories, and confiscated all their military equipment.

As the presidential election of 1856 approached, the high-riding American Party made plans to organize a national convention and put a Know-Nothing candidate in the White House. In the spring of 1856, however, startling reports from the Kansas Territory brought to national attention the explosive events of the slavery struggle in that western region. On May 21, pro-slavery forces sacked the "Boston abolition town" of Lawrence, Kansas, and carried off a number of Free-Soil leaders. Three days later, a Free-Soil defender named John Brown and several of his followers hacked to death five pro-slavery settlers in bloody retaliation. And then came the news from the nation's capital that Massachusetts senator Charles Sumner had been severely beaten on the floor of the Senate Chamber after an impassioned speech against slavery. By the summer of 1856, it was clear that the issue of slavery was the all-consuming preoccupation of voters over all the country—not something so elusive and contrived as a "Catholic menace." In the November elections, the Know-Nothing candidate, Millard Fillmore, received only eight electoral votes from the state of Maryland, and the American Party faded away into the mists of history. For a brief time, however, it had been a dramatic and frightening example of the fear with which Protestant, native-born Americans, in Boston and in many other parts of the country, regarded the influx of Roman Catholic immigrants, and the lengths to which they would go to keep the outsiders in their place. Even at this point, despite the depressing and unexpected breakup of their political organization, many conservatives were still confident that they had been successful in awakening the American public to the dangers Catholicism posed to the political institutions of the Republic as well as to the ongoing efforts to cleanse American institutions of all traces of foreign ideas and alien philosophies. The way to true intellectual freedom obviously lay in cultivating in a new generation those New World characteristics that were uniquely Protestant and exclusively American.

In dealing with the anti-Catholic movement in mid-nineteenth century Boston, however, the question inevitably arises as to whether this was simply one more example of the extreme religious prejudice that had preoccupied the Puritan mind since colonial days, or a more sincere and conscientious attempt to root out the dangers standing in the way of enlightened progress and reform. Many of the historians who have specialized in the antebellum reform period have asked this question—and have come up with different answers. Alice Felt Tyler, in her invaluable synthesis, *Freedom's Ferment* (1944), readily admitted that anti-Catholicism manifested "blind prejudice and mass hatred," but nevertheless believed that it should be considered a reform movement. Arthur M. Schlesinger Sr., in *The American as Reformer*

(1951), denied that anti-Catholicism was a reform movement at all and considered it an example of a type of bigotry that was contrary to the principles of America. John R. Bodo, on the other hand, in his *Protestant Clergy and Public Issues, 1812–1848* (1954), insisted that anti-Catholicism was not only a reform movement, but a defensible one, since it was opposing a religion it considered hostile to civil and religious liberty. In a more recent study of the period, *The Ferment of Reform, 1830–1860* (1967), C. S. Griffin suggests that anti-Catholicism might be considered both a moral reform and a social reform at the same time. A movement that was intended to convert Catholics to the ideals of Protestantism, he writes, was designed to help "purify" American society and to protect it from the "evils of the institutionalized hierarchy." To encourage Protestants to hate the Catholic Church was to help destroy that institution and, as a result of that process, to bring about the moral reformation of individuals. Since reform was the final objective, therefore, Griffin suggests that the anti-Catholic movement would have to be included as a significant part of the reform movement itself.

This judgment would seem to be the conclusion of John McGreevy also in his recent study *Catholicism and American Freedom* (2003). McGreevy provides an even stronger and more dramatic contrast between mid–nineteenth-century Protestant revivalism, with its emphasis on individualism, liberty of conscience, and democratic freedom, and the Catholic revival in the Romanist tradition during the same period, with its sense of communitarianism, mysticism, and authoritarianism. In this respect, the anti-Catholicism of antebellum America can be seen as much as a calculated intellectual and political judgment as a purely emotional and essentially bigoted response to a different set of religious beliefs. The issue that caused the sudden and total collapse of that movement, however, the fierce struggle over the expansion of slavery, was a clear signal that times were changing, new voices were being heard, and different concerns were beginning to challenge the reasons for Boston's image of itself as the Athens of America.

CHAPTER 7 } *A* 'N'EW G'ENERATION

The intensity of the efforts to prevent the religious beliefs and social attitudes of Roman Catholics from impeding the progressive
reforms of the Boston establishment was just one indication of changing
attitudes and disturbing impulses. Up to a certain point, Boston's serious
and self-conscious efforts to achieve an exalted status as the modern version
of the ancient Athenian city-state were carefully and thoughtfully guided
by a wealthy, educated, and well-placed citizen elite, most of whose distinguished members had grown to maturity during the formative years of the
early American Republic. Prominent Bostonians like Josiah Quincy, Harrison Gray Otis, Samuel Eliot, John Collins Warren, William Ellery Channing,
and Joseph Tuckerman had all been born before the year 1800. Descendants
of old New England families, their earlier Calvinist views had been tempered
by the more compassionate ideals of Unitarianism, and after the election of
Thomas Jefferson in 1800, their previous Federalist political principles had
been gradually adjusted into a slightly more genteel form of Whiggery.

Still viewing themselves as members of a natural aristocracy—a modern
Unitarian version of the Calvinist "elect"—this leadership espoused a new
political morality of social responsibility for the future of their city. Utilizing
the structures of existing institutions such as churches and hospitals, colleges
and clubs, banks and businesses, they considered themselves in a unique
position to save Boston from the kind of popular demagoguery—whether
Jeffersonian or Jacksonian—that threatened to upset the social order and
moral traditions. Influenced by the rational ideas of the Enlightenment, as
well as by the Christian principles of Unitarianism, they clearly believed in
progress—as long as they were the ones who had control of things and saw
that progress took place slowly and gradually, without upsetting the established social order or flying in the face of accepted moral traditions. Care-
ful, thoughtful, and reflective, these men used the power and profits they
derived from their families' diversified economy of commerce, manufacturing, banking, and railroading to foster a broad array of social, intellectual,

and institutional reforms. These were positive and measurable achievements they hoped would complete the goals of the Revolution by creating the ideal republican community—their City Upon a Hill—that would display many of the idealized characteristics of ancient Athens. Refurbishing the two-hundred-year-old city, cleaning its streets and modernizing its buildings, assuring the safety and security of its citizens, assisting the poor and the homeless, promoting temperance, rehabilitating the criminal, offering medical care for the sick and the disabled, providing a public education for all children, advancing the cause of knowledge among the general public— these were among the many ways in which they sought to make it possible for Americans to improve their lives gradually, broaden their horizons, raise their intellectual standards, and achieve their ideal of a free and open democratic society that they felt, would exceed even the glories of ancient Athens.

Material progress and cultural change often produce unexpected and unintended consequences, however, and there were a number of Americans who felt that the new spirit of redemption and salvation, the inspiring visions of perfectibility, and the exciting new opportunities for knowledge also created possibilities for much more imaginative forms of social living that would be communal and "utopian" in nature—reaching far beyond the individualistic and materialistic limitations of the prevailing capitalistic society. During the mid-1820s and early 1830s, several hundred utopian communities sprang up throughout the West and the Northeast, involving men and women committed to the idea of the perfectibility of human beings, and dedicated to the goal of creating a more perfect society in which such people could live and flourish. Some of the more successful of these utopian communities were formed by leaders of various religious groups, whose members usually shared their goods in common, abandoned the unnatural and artificial trappings of the modern world, and sought to lead lives of primitive simplicity. European pietistic sects—Moravians, Rappites, and Amish—established small communities in the Pennsylvania region. Farther to the north, in the "Burned-Over District" that stretched from western Vermont across the Mohawk Valley, were similar groups, whose property was held in common and whose organized plans for living were often made without benefit of traditional marriage arrangements. It was in this region that "Mother" Ann Lee attempted to establish the rule of celibacy with her "Shaker" and "Universal Friend" communities at Lebanon, New York. It was at Hampton, New York, that a pious New England Baptist named William

Miller worked out his theories that the end of the world was at hand and that the Second Coming of Jesus Christ would take place on March 21, 1834. When the fateful day of judgment came and went without catastrophic results, especially after many of the faithful had sold off their worldly goods and waited in white robes on rooftops and hilltops, the number of "Millerites" or "Adventists" declined sharply. The fall-off in the number of local adherents caused the original wooden tabernacle that Miller's followers had built in Boston's Scollay Square to be replaced in 1846 with a Gothic-style granite structure designed by Isaiah Rogers, architect of the Tremont House. Called the Howard Athenaeum, the new building served for many years as a legitimate theater, with a richly decorated interior and the first cushioned seats in a Boston theater.

Even Boston's Catholic bishop was caught up in the reformist spirit of utopian experiments. Convinced that his poor Irish immigrants would be happier, and certainly much healthier, far away from the squalid slums of the city's waterfront, in 1833, Bishop Benedict Fenwick proposed what he called the Benedicta Community, a Catholic colony located in the fresh outdoors environment of rural Maine. He envisioned the construction of a sawmill and other enterprises where Irish workers could learn useful trades and marketable skills, and he looked forward to building a college and a seminary to serve the needs of his diocese. Unfortunately, however, the gregarious immigrants from Ireland showed little enthusiasm for moving to the rural isolation of Aroostook County, preferring to remain in Boston, close to their family, friends, and churches. Fenwick was forced to conclude that his noble experiment was a total failure, but he used some of his remaining funds to purchase sixty acres of land in Worcester, some forty miles west of Boston, where he built the College of the Holy Cross, named after the original church on Franklin Street in Boston.

But there were a number of secular groups, too, that also came up with unorthodox experiments in social planning and group living. In 1825, for example, a Scottish manufacturer named Robert Owen, despairing of social reform in Great Britain, purchased property in Indiana, where he organized a short-lived cooperative community called New Harmony along the socialist principle of "from each according to his ability, to each according to his needs." Another utopian experiment developed from the theories of a French mathematician named Charles Fourier, who proposed to find social harmony in a scheme of living that combined the right number and kind of individuals carefully organized in a series of groups called *phalanxes*. In this system, a form of socialism was practiced, with the highest returns going to those members of the community who did the most unpleasant jobs. More than forty of these groups arose during the 1830s, including the North American Phalanx near Red Bank, New Jersey; Ceresco, near Ripon, Wisconsin; and the well-known Brook Farm, just outside Boston.

The spirit of radical reform was clearly in the air, directed to bringing about substantial changes in the existing middle-class social order—if not to replacing it completely. In demonstrating their opposition to the existing fashions and restrictive artificialities of straight-laced, middle-class American society, young men started growing beards; took up wearing robes and sandals; ate fruits, nuts, berries, and other natural foods; gathered together in rustic communes; worked on utopian plans for a brave new world. "We are all a little wild here with numberless projects of social reform," Ralph Waldo Emerson explained to the visiting English historian Thomas Carlyle in the fall of 1840. "Not a reading man but has a draft of a new Community in his waistcoat pocket." All this restless change and novel experimentation was disturbing to members of Boston's conservative establishment—and occasionally frightening when groups of these young radicals gathered together, as they did in November 1840, to attend a convention on the subject of "universal reform" at Boston's Chardon Street Church. Addressing themselves to such controversial issues as perfectionism, pacifism, communitarianism, socialism, birth control, civil disobedience, and the repeal of the Sabbath Laws, they formed what Edmund Quincy, son of the former mayor, called "the most singular collection of strange specimens of humanity that was ever assembled." Emerson was even less charitable in his description of the radical extremists who rushed to the podium to sound off for their particular causes: "Mad-men and mad-women, men with beards, Dunkers, Muggletonians, Come-outers, Groaners, Agrarians, Seventh-Day Baptists, Quakers, Abolitionists, Calvinists, Unitarians, and Philosophers, all came successively to the top and seized the moment, if not the hour, wherein to chide, or pray, or preach, or protest."

With the gradual aging of the old Federalist generation during the 1830s and 1840s, however, a new generation of civic-minded Brahmins had become old enough to begin taking an active role in many of the reform activities and benevolent projects already initiated by their fathers and grandfathers. "We are all young men now," observed the editor of the *Boston*

Transcript on June 30, 1836. "Nobody wears a wig, not a cocked hat, nor powder, nor small-clothes and silk stockings and buckles, nor white-topped boots, nor a queue, nor a gold-headed cane. We have changed all that. The 'Gentlemen of the Old School,' those patterns of manly elegance, are fast passing away." Most of these younger men and women (historian David Donald puts their median age at twenty-nine) generally found the civic and intellectual improvements initiated by the older generation commendable enough, but they also made it clear that their fathers' reforms were much too shallow and superficial to create the truly free and open democratic society they envisioned as the eventual goal of America. Although it is true that the older generation of civic leaders wanted to help the poor and the homeless, for example, its members had failed to address themselves to the basic causes of poverty itself. They were willing to construct more humane prisons for criminals and even made provisions for their rehabilitation, but they had done nothing about attacking the social causes of crime itself. They came to the assistance of the alcoholic and the addict, but they had not dealt with the fundamental reasons for the depressing economic conditions and harmful environmental forces that had created those addictions in the first place. And they had done virtually nothing to address the depressed status of women or, even worse, the brutal condition of African American slaves.

The new thrust in the reform impulse, however, was not only generational, but ideological as well. A growing number of social activists in Boston felt that the rationality and objectivity of the Unitarian elite deprived the Christian message of its emotional content and its mystical inspiration. For this reason, that message no longer reflected the strong moral imperative they considered essential in confronting the fundamental evils throughout American society that denied to all men and women the full freedom and equality that was their birthright. Theodore Parker, a controversial clergyman once dubbed "Roxbury's Friar Tuck," was one of those scholarly intellectuals of the period who shared this view and sought to develop a new and more transcendental faith based, not on scriptural texts or theological doctrines, but upon the kind of intuition that would bring an individual immediately in touch with God.

Born in Lexington in 1810, the grandson of Captain John Parker, who had fought with the minutemen at Lexington Green on the morning of April 19, 1775, and the son of a local farmer, young Parker was largely self-educated until he went to Harvard and eventually graduated from the Divinity School

WILLIAM LLOYD GARRISON

Born in the North Shore town of Newburyport, William Lloyd Garrison moved to Boston, where he became active in the antislavery movement. On January 1, 1831, Garrison published the first issue of his newspaper, The Liberator, *which denounced slavery as a moral evil and demanded the total and immediate emancipation of slaves. For many years, Garrison and his followers were regarded by most Bostonians as troublemakers who were perverting the moral law, defying the Bible, and endangering financial relations with Southern slaveholders. (Courtesy, Bostonian Society/Old State House)* in 1856. A close friend of Ralph Waldo Emerson, Parker often walked the short distance from his church in West Roxbury to Brook Farm, and frequently traveled to Concord to meet with Emerson, Bronson Alcott, Margaret Fuller, and the other members of the Transcendental Club. An immensely popular preacher, lecturer, and writer, Parker compiled one of the largest personal libraries in the Boston area, and mastered an incredible number of foreign languages, among them Russian, Chaldaic, and Arabic.

Parker, as did Emerson, became skeptical of the calm and dispassionate views of Unitarianism, with its emphasis on rationalism that he felt did not adequately reflect the mystical and individual encounter between man and God. He came to believe that religious truths were derived from individual intuition and personal feelings, rather than from divine revelation and theological study. He wanted to make Unitarianism a more idealistic faith whose members would make a moral commitment to social justice. His demand for a new kind of theology, based on the immanence of God in nature as well as in human experience, created intense controversy in religious circles and caused the leaders of the Unitarian clergy in Boston to withdraw from him, even though he insisted on remaining a member of that denomination until his death.

Resigning his West Roxbury pastorate in 1845, Theodore Parker became a minister of a new "free church," the Twentieth-Eighth Congregational Society in Boston, where he proceeded to use his pulpit to speak out in support of William Lloyd Garrison and his Abolition movement, attacking both the slaveholding aristocracy of the South and the merchant-manufacturing establishment in the North and denouncing the mainline Protestant churches of the North for having become what he called "the sworn ally of slavery."

Convinced that human perfection could not be achieved fully by either progressive institutional reform or by the work of well-meaning benevolent agencies, but only by a complete ideological transformation of social values based on a strict observance of biblical injunctions, members of the new generation of reformers broke away from established traditions and from old conservative institutions in their determination to achieve what they considered to be their higher moral purposes. Positive, passionate, and impatient, these young men and women took an absolutist approach in rejecting the use of gradualism or moderation to achieve their goals, resorting to public demonstrations to publicize their controversial issues and to dramatize their nonnegotiable demands.

Reformers of the new generation displayed not only a new urgency, a new sense of passion, but also introduced a degree of personal confrontation that was not often present in an earlier generation where—except for a few eccentrics—the formalities of good manners and gentlemanly conduct were usually observed. But now there was a ferocity, even a savagery, in their dissension that left little room for discussion and practically no chance for compromise. Previously, opponents would use tact, discussion, and diplomacy to seek some common ground, some middle way, to resolve differences or to work out solutions that would be satisfactory—at least to some extent—to both parties in a dispute. Now there was no common ground, no attempt to resolve positions, to compromise issues. Convinced that morality was on their side, they could not possibly see themselves compromising with evil or modifying anything that was good.

An early indication of the practical effects of this way of thinking could be seen when Charles Sumner, a young Harvard Law School graduate who had recently returned from a three-year trip to Europe, began showing an interest in several of the city's ongoing social reform programs. Through his friendship with Dr. Samuel Gridley Howe, he frequently visited the Perkins Institution in South Boston, observed the doctor's work with the blind, and made the acquaintance of Howe's most famous student, Laura Bridgman, who later perceptively complained, according to Ernest Freeberg, that she had not found her visitor "gentle." Through Howe, Sumner became acquainted with the work Horace Mann was doing in rejuvenating the public schools of the Commonwealth, and he was particularly impressed by Mann's efforts to develop a new system of nonsectarian education. The Boston Prison Discipline Society was another reform activity of the period whose humane work attracted Sumner's interest. Not long after becoming a member of the society, however, he began challenging the leadership of Louis Dwight, who had been the society's influential secretary for some twenty years. Sumner accused Dwight of being lazy, inefficient, and provincial in his administration of the organization, but focused his sharpest attacks on the older man's decision to support the Auburn penitentiary system used at Sing Sing, New York, where prisoners were locked in cells at night but allowed to work and engage in recreation during the day. Sumner insisted that a much superior system was the Pennsylvania system, where each prisoner was separated from the other inmates and placed in an individual cell, pointing out that this was the system favored by major European penologists at the

CHARLES SUMNER

This 1846 crayon portrait of Charles Sumner by Eastman Johnson displays the youth and attractiveness of the Harvard Law School graduate just one year after he delivered his controversial Fourth of July address denouncing the evils of war and the wastefulness of national defense. Elected to the United States Senate from Massachusetts, in 1856 Sumner was severely beaten by a Southern congressman after a speech against the Kansas-Nebraska Act in which he denounced the "slavocracy" of the South. (Courtesy National Park Service, Longfellow National Historic Site) time. At the annual meting of the Society at the Park Street Church in May 1845, as described by David Herbert Donald in his outstanding biography, Sumner issued a public assault against Dwight's administrative leadership as well as his policies regarding prisons and spoke in favor of setting up a special committee to visit Philadelphia and inspect the Pennsylvania system at firsthand. Through 1846, Sumner continued an unceasing attack on Louis Dwight, becoming so offensive in his personal references that he lost the support of many Bostonians who were shocked and repelled by his lack of common courtesy. Convinced of the righteousness of his cause, however, and undeterred by the protests of his critics, Sumner spoke out again against Dwight at the society's annual meeting at Tremont Temple in May 1847. Although Dwight was reelected to his position as director, the debates had become so violent and the language so strident that the following year, at the suggestion of George Ticknor, members agreed that future public meetings of the Boston Prison Discipline Society should be discontinued. Although Sumner was satisfied that the end of the society meant that more attention would be given to the Pennsylvania system, his shocking performance, his lack of good manners, and his outrageous personal insults to an older man who was held in high esteem by the conservative leaders of Boston, caused him to be shunned by proper Boston society and, according to David Donald, denied a professorship at the Harvard Law School.

At almost the same time that Charles Sumner was becoming acquainted with the workings of the Boston Prison Discipline Society, but before he began his agitation against Louis Dwight, the young Harvard lawyer, was invited to deliver the City of Boston's 1845 Fourth-of-July Oration—an honor reserved for "young men of promising genius." In the past, such prominent Bostonians as Harrison Gray Otis, John Quincy Adams, and Josiah Quincy had delivered the oration; more recently Charles Francis Adams, George Hillard, and Horace Mann had been selected for the same honor. After some hesitation, Sumner informed Mayor Thomas A. Davis of his acceptance, and indicated that he would speak on the subject of International Peace.

The question of war and peace had become a topic of some discussion in Boston circles in the years following the second war with Great Britain. Although there had always been some Americans who had written wistfully about the virtues of peace and the horrors of war, the need for colonial defenses against incursions of the French and the Spanish, the sporadic wars with the Indians, and the national struggle for independence from Great

Britain, kept the necessity for armed power and military defense very much in the foreground of national policy. With the end of the War of 1812, however, and what looked like the permanent security of America's national boundaries against foreign invasion, Bostonians began to harbor more serious antiwar sentiments—especially since many of them had been opposed to the second war with England in the first place. The decision by Congress, in 1821, to economize after the Panic of 1819 by reducing the size of the United States Army from ten to six thousand men, provided stimulus to an organized peace movement, the Massachusetts Peace Society, which was founded by Rev. William Ellery Channing and Noah Worcester in response to what they felt were the militaristic implications of the war. Worcester used the pages of his magazine, *Friends of Peace*, to attack the policy of conscription and the idea of a standing army, claiming that such measures would cause the United States to follow in the footsteps of European countries. For his part, Channing not only emphasized the special responsibility of the Christian clergy to speak out against the "miseries and horrors of war," but also pointed to what he regarded as the unique role of the United States itself, with its republican form of government and its historic democratic mission, in leading such a crusade. The Massachusetts peace movement had considerable appeal among such members of the intellectual classes as former mayor Josiah Quincy, now president of Harvard College and the poet James Russell Lowell. In 1838, Ralph Waldo Emerson delivered an "Address on War" in praise of universal peace, which he regarded as inevitable as the prevalence of "civilization over barbarism." In typical Transcendental fashion, however, he cautioned that peace would not be achieved by laws or manifestos but by "private opinions" and "earnest love."

A greater step in making the pursuit of peace a more practical reality came with the efforts of William Ladd of Exeter, New Hampshire, a retired sea captain and wealthy businessman, who devoted his time and money for the rest of his life to banishing war from civilized society. After joining the Massachusetts Peace Society, and helping to establish several new branches in neighboring states. Ladd became convinced that a broader and more inclusive organization was necessary and took the lead in forming the American Peace Society. The objective of the society was to promote peace by establishing a "congress of Christian nations" that would arbitrate disputes and settle national controversies by rational means instead of by war. Starting in 1829, the American Peace Society offered a prize for the best paper written on the subject of "A Congress of Nations for the Preservation of Peace." Although no single prize was ever awarded, six of the best essays dealing with the subject of a congress of nations were published in 1840 in a volume that had a wide circulation both in the United States and in Europe. The American Peace Society continued, under the leadership of William Ladd and others, developing close relations with numerous pacifist organizations in Europe and persistently appealing to the United States Congress, as well as to various state legislatures, to declare an annual "concert of prayer" on behalf of universal peace. For every contribution sent to the Society by a church organization, the New York headquarters refunded half the donation in the form of booklets promoting peace.

Despite the nation's increasing demands for territorial expansion and joyous shouts of "Manifest Destiny" that marked the 1830s and 1840s, peace advocates in the United States stepped up their opposition to militarism and war. They called for the abolition of compulsory duty in the state militia, which they claimed took unfair advantage of the poor and working classes, and often criticized the military academy at West Point as a useless extravagance that had the effect of creating a military aristocracy. After his return from Europe in 1840, when he began interesting himself in various local reform movements, Charles Sumner also attended the meetings of the Peace Society that Rev. William Ellery Channing had founded and soon became a member of its executive committee. During the 1840s, he shared with many Bostonians a concern over the American saber-rattling during the Canadian boundary disputes with Great Britain in the Northwest ("Fifty-four forty or fight"), and in the Southwest with Mexico ("Remember the Alamo"), and deplored what he called the "insidious" plan of the South to use war with Mexico as a means of annexing Texas and using its vast territory to create several "great slaveholding states." "For myself," he wrote to his friend George Putnam, "I hold all wars unjust and un-Christian." War and peace were very much on Sumner's mind, therefore, when in 1845 he accepted the mayor's invitation to deliver to the annual Fourth-of-July Oration.

There certainly was no reason for apprehension or concern on the part of city officials and high-ranking military officers that morning, as they settled in their seats in Boston's Tremont Temple and watched the young speaker make his way to the podium. Tall, handsome, and self-assured, Charles Sumner appeared an ideal choice as the day's speaker, and certainly the title of his oration, "The True Grandeur of Nations," seemed most appropriate for such a patriotic occasion. Once he began speaking, however, it quickly became obvious that things were not going according to plan. After opening with a denunciation of the annexation of Texas and the demands for the Oregon Territory, Sumner launched into an all-out condemnation of the evils of war that wasted lands, ruined and famished cities, slaughtered armies, and ruined human nature itself. Ignoring the surprised expressions and angry whispers among the military men sitting before him, he continued, placing the blame for the continuance of war upon those Americans whose exaggerated sense of patriotism led them to support their country "right or wrong." He saved his most blistering attacks, however, for the nation's military system, and its "costly *preparations* for war." He ridiculed the army officers who had been trained at West Point—that "seminary of idleness and vice"—the naval officers who served in a navy that "had no purpose," and the members of the state militia, with their gaudy uniforms, who were not even competent to put down a street riot. The *true* grandeur of the nation, the young orator concluded, lay not in warfare, but in "moral elevation, enlightened and decorated by the intellect of man." Then, he declared, in a final burst of rhetoric that called to mind the city's remarkable series of social reforms, "shall the naked be clothed and the hungry fed. Institutions of science and learning shall crown every hill-top; hospitals for the sick . . . shall nestle in every valley; white spires of new churches shall leap exulting to the skies."

When it was all over and the city officials, together with their military guests, walked out of Tremont Temple and made their way to Faneuil Hall for the customary Fourth-of-July dinner, they made little effort to contain their angry reactions to Sumner's provocative speech. Members of Boston's leading families, whose ancestors had fought for independence at Lexington, Concord, and Bunker Hill were particularly furious at the implications of Sumner's blanket denunciation of all war as "dishonorable"; representatives of the military establishment voiced their disgust at his depiction of military men as little more than wild beasts; city officials were outraged at their invited speaker's delivering an oration that was both inappropriate for the patriotic occasion and embarrassing to the city. "The young man has cut his own throat," announced former mayor Samuel A. Eliot, clearly voicing the general opinion of Beacon Hill.

Even many of Charles Sumner's close friends, such as Nathan Appleton, Josiah Quincy, Horace Mann, and William Hickling Prescott, were distressed by the extremism of Sumner's views and the lack of civility with which he expressed them. But Sumner himself seemed oblivious of the "apple of discord" that he had thrown out to the public with such abandon. He chose to believe that, although some listeners might have objected to what he had to say, there were many others who received his words with praise and applause. And, indeed, there were a number of Bostonians who welcomed what they regarded as Sumner's brave and outspoken position on behalf of world peace. The members of the Peace Society, for example, quickly republished Sumner's oration, sent copies to each member of the United States Congress, as well as to leading members of the British government, in hopes that it would help avert a threatened war between the United States and Great Britain over the Oregon Territory. And leading antislavery spokesmen in the city, too, welcomed the moral approach and blunt words of Sumner that were so much in line with those of William Lloyd Garrison, who had come out publicly in 1831 with demands for the total and immediate emancipation of slaves. Surely, during such an intense period of social reform, when the city's intellectual elite was calling for such humanitarian improvements as the relief of the sick, provisions for the mentally ill, assistance for the addicted, and rehabilitation of the imprisoned, it was almost inevitable that reformers would begin focusing on the terrible plight of human beings in the bondage of slavery.

Indeed, in the years after Independence, when the Northern states drew up their constitutions eliminating slavery, and the Southern states elected to preserve that institution, there were a number of Americans who still objected to its continued existence and who engaged in various efforts for its gradual removal. For this purpose, numerous organizations were formed, many of them located below the Mason-Dixon Line, and with impressive Southern memberships. These early antislavery societies were largely apologetic in their attitudes toward slavery, admitting that they regarded it as an undesirable institution, inherited from their forefathers, that should be done away with in the course of time. Although various organizations differed considerably as to just how emancipation could be achieved, for the most part they were similar in their general attitude and approach. First, emancipation was to be a gradual process—slavery would not be abandoned immediately, but over the course of many years and generations to avoid the sudden shock to the prevailing white social structure. Second, it was to be effected gradually—a small percentage of slaves would be set free at regular intervals over a long period of time, again providing further assurance that there would be no abrupt changes. And third, it would be a compensatory process—slavery represented a major capital investment running into the hundreds of millions of dollars, and the slaveholders would have to be compensated for the grave economic losses they would suffer.

A prominent example of this early type of antislavery organization was the American Colonization Society, which proposed to reduce the population of slaves in the United States by purchasing the freedom of a number of slaves each year and sending them back to Africa. Founded at Washington, D.C., during the winter of 1816–17, this association acquired a piece of territory on the coast of West Africa, called Liberia, as the place to which the freed slaves would be sent; its capital would be called Monrovia, in honor of James Monroe of Virginia, former president of the United States. Boasting a membership that included such prominent Virginia slaveholders as Monroe, Judge Bushrod Washington, John Randolph of Roanoke, and John Marshall, as well as Henry Clay of Kentucky and Francis Scott Key of Maryland (author of "The Star Spangled Banner"), the Colonization Society proved to have widespread appeal to those, in both the North and the South, who were looking for some kind of rational, sensible, and peaceful resolution to the increasing national racial problem. Despite the fact, as historian James B. Stewart has pointed out in his *Holy Warriors*, that the Colonization Society was actually "wildly impractical" as well as a "financial and organizational impossibility," many Bostonians saw it not only as a sensible way of eventually transforming the United States into a "white man's country," but also of sending blacks who had been exposed to the white culture back to Africa to Christianize the "dark continent." Amos Lawrence, the Boston textile magnate, for example, stated his opinion that the colonization movement was destined to make "a greater change in the condition of the blacks than any other event since the Christian era."

There were other Americans, however, who regarded the institution of human bondage with the utmost horror and disgust, who regarded any attempts to solve this problem in a partial or gradual manner as hypocritical; they demanded, instead, its immediate and total abolition. The attitude of such critics was translated into action on January 1, 1831, when William Lloyd Garrison ran off the first issue of a newspaper called *The Liberator* from a small handpress in a little office in downtown Boston. Although Garrison was by no means the first person to call for the abolition of slavery, he was certainly the most articulate spokesman for a militant and immediatist approach to the problem. The traditional strategy of quiet reason, rational discussion, and genteel moderation that had characterized so much of the early social reformers' approach in Boston was rudely thrust aside by this outspoken man who declared publicly that he had no intention of using moderation "in a cause like the present." He admitted that there were those who objected to the "severity" of his language, but he did not heed them. "Is there not cause for severity?" he asked. "I will be as harsh as truth, and as uncompromising as justice," he declared. "I am in earnest—I will not equivocate—I will not excuse—I will not retreat a single inch—AND I WILL BE HEARD."

But the obvious differences between the new Abolition movement and the earlier antislavery organizations went far beyond the external differences in character, attitudes, and approaches. To understand the passionate thrust and absolutist position of the Abolition movement, and the almost fanatical zeal of its proponents, one must appreciate that its opposition to slavery—like Charles Sumner's opposition to war—was based solidly on moral grounds. Garrison and his followers took the unequivocal position that slavery was a sin and a crime against humanity, a moral evil that went against all the fundamental religious principles of a decent Christian society. Seen in this light, the Abolitionists viewed every slaveholder as a sinner and a criminal, according to the moral law, who disregarded statutory or constitutional sanctions of every kind, and hence they refused to accept any solution to the slavery question that did not call for total and immediate emancipation. Garrison refused to countenance any delay in freeing the slaves and condemned what he sneeringly called "that popular but pernicious doctrine of gradual abolition." He went out of his way to deplore the idea that slavery could be brought to an end by transporting or "colonizing" slaves to Africa or to any other part of the world—an idea that still had the support of many prominent Bostonians. Charging that the American Colonization Society had been deliberately organized by Southern slaveholders, Garrison claimed that the organization was "solemnly pledged not to interfere with a system that was "unfathomly deep in pollution, nourished on fear and selfishness, and encrusted with corroding evil."

Because of the fierceness of his attack and the harshness of his words, the early days of Garrison and his small band of followers were far from peaceful, and the results were anything but encouraging. Garrison himself complained that he found "contempt more bitter, opposition more active, and apathy more frozen" in New England "than among slave owners themselves." To his dismay, the early issues of his *Liberator* appeared to cause hardly a ripple upon the smooth surface of Boston society. "Suspicion and apathy," moaned Garrison, were the reactions to his paper, and the rent on his hole-in-the-wall office on Washington Street became harder to meet every day. Even when apathy gave way to curiosity, and Bostonians did begin to take notice of Garrison and his small band of followers, the Abolitionists were generally perceived as radicals, agitators, anarchists, and troublemakers, and were certainly not socially acceptable in most respectable circles. "They did not go to work like Christian gentlemen," observed the Congregational minister Rev. Horace Bushnell, while the gentle Unitarian spokesman, Rev. William Ellery Channing, agreed that they only served to stir up "bitter passions and fierce fanaticism." Financial opinion, reflected in the pages of the influential commercial publication *Nile's Register*, complained that Garrison was "doing all possible injury to the cause of emancipation," and the *Washington National Intelligencer* accused him of "poisoning the waters of life to the whole community."

The prosperous merchants and businessmen of Boston were especially outraged at what they considered an irrelevant issue, dragged in by the heels, that might well upset the peace and prosperity of the Commonwealth. Already they had heard ominous rumblings from angry planters in the Cotton Kingdom who threatened serious economic reprisals unless their financial partners in the North put an end to the dangerous ravings of the Abolitionists. "The people of the North must go to hanging these fanatical wretches, if they would not lose the benefit of Southern trade," warned the *Richmond Whig*, while *De Bow's Review* out of New Orleans, began to conjure up the awful picture of grass growing in the streets of Northern cities if the South became angry enough to withhold its indispensable supplies of cotton. Fearful that a disorganized group of maniacs and anarchists might disrupt the cordial relations that Boston textile magnates had so carefully built up with their Southern friends over the years (the "lords of the lash" and the "lords of the loom" Charles Sumner had labeled them), local business interests realized the need to take positive steps to control the activities of the offending elements before the situation got out of hand. Former mayor Harrison Gray Otis, himself a heavy investor in cotton manufacturing, wrote to his friend Nathan Appleton, then a representative in the U.S. Congress, pleading with him to pursue legislation for a program of federally subsidized colonization. A system of dividing up an annual appropriation among the various Plantation States, which would then be used, "*in its own mode,*" to colonize slaves would, argued Otis, cut the ground out from under the present demands for abolition. Otis repeated his proposals in a similar letter to Daniel Webster, then serving in the Senate, adding ominously: "there will be no peace or security for us until you buy up the Virginia negroes & send them off."

Writing letters was obviously not enough to ease rising tensions, however, and so a huge meeting of some fifteen hundred citizens was called for Faneuil Hall on August 21, 1835, to address the problem further and reassure Southern planters of the good intentions of their friends in the North. Presided over by Mayor Theodore Lyman Jr. and Abbott Lawrence, it was attended by leading members of Boston society, as well as by numerous "Southern gentlemen" who came north to attend this well-publicized meeting. With nods of approval, the assembly listened closely to the words of Harrison Gray Otis, now seventy years old, as he warned his Boston friends that slaveowners would regard any attempt at immediate abolition as "war in disguise upon their lives, their property, their rights and institutions, an outrage upon their pride and honor, and the faith of contracts." By the close of his eloquent address, the audience was on its feet cheering his final patriotic appeal that "the thirteen stripes may not be merged in two dismal strains of black and red!"

By this time, denunciations of local Abolitionists were coming so fast and furiously that Garrison's friends, fearing for his safety, pleaded with him to leave the city. Reluctantly he consented, and for about a month he and his wife stayed away from Boston. In October, however, Garrison made known his return, and the *Liberator* announced that the regular meeting of the Boston Female Anti-Slavery Society would be held at three o'clock on October 21, 1835. Garrison apparently felt that the recent Faneuil Hall meeting had given the conservative elements an opportunity to vent their spleen against the Abolitionists and placate the "fiery spirits" of their friends in the South.

Now that the storm had passed, he felt that it was safe to return to Boston and resume operations.

Despite his feeling of confidence, however, trouble was already brewing. Reports had spread through the city that George Thompson, a well-known British emancipationist (an "infamous scoundrel" one local critic called him), would be addressing the scheduled meeting of the Boston Female Anti-Slavery Society. A menacing crowd was already at the doors of 46 Washington Street when Garrison arrived at his office, which adjoined the small lecture hall where the women were holding their meeting. Promptly at three o'clock, the mob burst in, broke up the ladies' meeting and then began searching for Garrison, who had just escaped through a rear window. The shouting mob finally caught up with the Abolitionist leader, pummeled him severely, threw a rope around him, and dragged him triumphantly through the streets. Ragged and torn, he was finally rescued from the mob and spirited off to jail for his own protection—after being booked as a "rioter." The next day Mayor Lyman dismissed the charges, released Garrison, but advised him to get out of town immediately. Garrison decided to follow the mayor's advice and journeyed to Providence with his wife for a much-needed rest.

Of the nature of the mob that had attacked him, Garrison had no doubts. "It was planned and executed," he insisted, "not by the rabble, or the workingmen, but by 'gentlemen of property and standing' from all parts of the city." Wendell Phillips, son of Boston's first mayor, had been a nonpartisan witness to the event, and he later gave a classic description of the assault being conducted by the "gentlemen" of the city—in "broadcloth and in broad daylight." The conservative character of the rioters was further confirmed by a visitor from Baltimore, Mr. T. L. Nichols, who chanced to see the historic outburst as he walked through the city: "Merchants and bankers of Boston, assembled on 'Change in State-Street," he related, "and believing him [Thompson] to be at the office of Garrison's *Liberator*, they gathered tumultuously, and came around from State-Street into Washington Street, determined to put a stop to the eloquence of the English Abolitionist." Although the evidence is largely circumstantial, there is little doubt that Boston's leading merchants and businessmen had desired to demonstrate their goodwill to their "Southern brethren" in deeds as well as by words.

Garrison's potentially fatal encounter in Boston was only one of a number of bloody episodes that occurred during the mid-1830s, indicating the violent and almost hysterical nature of the anti-Abolitionist sentiment on the part of conservative forces in the North. Under continuing pressure from the Southern states that demanded the suppression of the radical movement, Northerners often resorted to desperate measures in their attempts to stamp out the dangerous agitation. In New York City, for example, angry mobs sacked the home of Lewis Tappan, a local emancipationist, wrecked a number of churches, and destroyed houses in the black section of the city. Although the mayor of the city called out the militia, it took three days for the riots to be put down. In Cincinnati repeated attacks were directed against the *Philanthropist*, an Abolitionist newspaper published by James G. Birney, a converted Alabama slaveholder, who headed the Ohio Anti-Slavery Society. The final blow came with the news that Elijah Lovejoy, a prominent Presbyterian minister who edited the Alton *Observer*, had been shot and killed by an Illinois mob while he was trying to prevent his printing presses from being wrecked—for the fourth time.

Those who expected that the years of "terror" would intimidate the Abolitionists into inactivity and provide a strong deterrent to further membership were doomed to disappointment. The violence of 1835–36 not only failed to halt the Abolitionist movement, it actually served as a positive incentive to membership and growth by providing more sympathy and more converts than the movement had been able to achieve through its own exertions. "Mob actions, as it turned out, not only created a sympathy for their victims," writes historian James B. Stewart, "but brought a number of important new people directly into the movement." Garrison's movement had already attracted members of some of the oldest and "best" families in the Bay State. The young minister from Connecticut Samuel May could trace his ancestry back to the Sewalls and the Quincys; Samuel Sewall, another member, was a promising young Boston lawyer and a direct descendant of old Judge Samuel Sewall himself; Ellis Gray Loring, a highly respected lawyer with a prominent Boston clientele, could trace his family back to 1634; and Amasa Walker, whose forebears had come to New England in 1630, would soon be lecturing at Harvard in the field of political economy.

The murder of Rev. Elijah Lovejoy was particularly influential in inflaming public indignation and rousing many hitherto complaisant Bostonians out of their lethargy. More people of wealth, background, and position now began to join Garrison's cause, as Rev. William Ellery Channing headed a petition signed by one hundred prominent citizens, requesting the use of Faneuil Hall for a protest meeting. Wendell Phillips, Harvard '31, a young lawyer and son of John Phillips, Boston's first mayor, had never been particularly interested in abolition until the afternoon he saw Garrison being hauled through the streets of Boston at the end of a rope. Still not converted, he became more interested in the cause after he fell in love with an ardent Abolitionist, Miss Ann Terry Green, and the following spring he publicly joined the Massachusetts Antislavery Society. The news of Lovejoy's murder completed the transition. Burning with outrage, Phillips ascended the platform at the Faneuil Hall meeting and delivered a thundering oration on behalf of human liberty and freedom that not only brought the audience to its feet, cheering wildly, but also marked him from that moment on as the foremost antislavery orator in the United States.

The list of new Abolitionists grew alarmingly. Edmund Quincy, son Josiah Quincy, Boston's second mayor, joined the movement; Dr. Henry Ingersoll Bowditch, who had witnessed the downtown Boston mob scene, "from that moment on became an abolitionist" and subscribed to Garrison's *Liberator*. Even the influential merchant and railroad magnate John Murray Forbes, confessed that, although he had been indifferent to the issue of slavery, Lovejoy's death and Phillips's speech "changed my whole feeling with regard to it," although he still would not join Abolition societies because of what he described as the "bigotry and pigheadedness" of Garrison and his followers. James Russell Lowell was soon adding his writing abilities to the antislavery movement, and by the 1840s Ralph Waldo Emerson had become a vocal adherent of the cause. Together with John Greenleaf Whittier, who had been one of Garrison's first disciples, the "literary Abolitionists" were destined to become an influential force in the drive for emancipation. The movement continued to mushroom. By 1838, there were more than two hundred antislavery societies in the state of Massachusetts alone, with funds enough to send out propagandists and supply Abolitionist literature to all parts of the country. Membership was increasing every day, and the *Liberator*'s circulation continued to go up. "We are becoming Abolitionists at the North fast," exulted Charles Sumner, as the fortunes of the antislavery crusade were clearly in the ascendancy.

Indeed, Sumner made a further name for himself as a radical reformer by attacking racial discrimination, not just in the South, but right in the heart of Boston itself. In the fall of 1849, he agreed to support the interests of a five-year-old African American girl named Sarah Roberts, whose father had brought suit against the City of Boston for denying his daughter admission to a nearby white school solely on the basis of her color, thus forcing her to attend the school for black children some distance away from her home. With Sumner as cocounsel with Robert Morris, the only black member of the Massachusetts Bar, the case of *Sarah Roberts v. The City of Boston* was argued before the Supreme Judicial Court of Massachusetts. Although Sumner made an eloquent plea for "equality before the law," arguing that both white children and black children suffered from attending separate schools, Chief Justice Lemuel Shaw ruled against the plaintiff. Despite this setback, black and white Abolitionists renewed their efforts for integrated schools in Boston and switched their attacks from the judicial chambers to the political arena where they were able to bring enough public pressure to bear on state legislators to repudiate the decision of the court. On April 18, 1854, the Great and General Court of Massachusetts passed a law stating that no child, on account of "race, color, or religious opinions," could be excluded from any public school in the Commonwealth. Following passage of this statute, a number of boys from the all-white Phillips School were transferred to the all-black Smith School, while a corresponding number of black students were marched over to take their seats at the Phillips School.

Despite their growing numbers and occasional victories, however, William Lloyd Garrison and his small band of devoted followers in Boston were beginning to encounter various forms of resistance from within their own ranks. There were a number of prominent Abolitionist leaders outside the immediate Boston circle, for example, who were not at all as optimistic as Charles Sumner about the ultimate success of their crusade and who had become disenchanted with Garrison's highly personalized brand of abolition, which they felt was often doing more harm than good. Some objected to Garrison's harsh words and rigid confrontational attitude that, they believed, repelled conservative listeners and turned away many prospective members who might otherwise have been persuaded to join the antislavery cause. Others found Garrison's continued refusal to involve the Abolition movement as an influential player in the nation's political-party system both naïve and self-defeating. Despite efforts to get Garrison to change his mind and adopt a more reasonable attitude, the Boston leader remained steadfast in his insistence that, even though the Constitution of the United

JOHN MURRAY FORBES

A prominent member of Boston's financial establishment, John Murray Forbes made his early profits in the lucrative China trade but became increasingly involved in the construction of railroads. Along with other investors, Forbes bought and completed the Michigan Central Railroad, and later financed roads that eventually became the Chicago, Burlington & Quincy, as well as the Hannibal & St. Joseph lines. Forbes was one of the first conservative Whigs to support the antislavery cause, not so much for moral reasons but as a means of preventing the slaveholding states from controlling the Congress. (Courtesy, Bostonian Society/Old State House)

States had sanctioned the institution of slavery, the document was nothing more than "a covenant with death and an agreement with hell." Because of this conviction, he absolutely refused to allow his movement to become involved in any part of the badly tainted American political process. And his outspoken rejection of the importance of organized religion, together with his condemnation of American Christianity for "huge perversions of God's will" in refusing to speak out against the evils of human slavery, were viewed by such evangelical Abolitionists as Lewis Tappan of New York and Theodore Weld of Ohio as nothing short of heresy.

And there were Abolitionists who were genuinely alarmed by Garrison's efforts to further radicalize the movement by opening the base and developing a "broad platform" that would welcome into Abolitionism many other types of radical reform groups whose members had their own agendas—Sabbatarians who wanted to forbid the transport of the mails on Sunday, advocates of nonresistant pacifism, women who demanded legal and civil rights—so long as they also agreed to denounce slavery as a sin and accept black equality as one of their goals. Many Abolitionists feared that opening up the tent this way and bringing in all sorts of radical groups would inevitably weaken the single focus of the antislavery movement and water down the unique significance of its message. Political abolitionists like Tappan of New York and James G. Birney of Kentucky, soon to be the presidential candidate of the new Liberty Party, were anxious to attract a larger and more conservative membership into the antislavery cause so that they could politicize the movement and create an effective antislavery party in the North. They feared the effects of a distraction that could well splinter the group, turn off prospective members, confuse the issue, and undermine their political appeal. The incorporation of women, especially into the antislavery movement on the basis of full equality, was seen as a serious "tactical disaster," according to historian James Stewart, citing the antifeminist remark by Elizur Wright, editor of the *Massachusetts Abolitionist* and a conservative opponent of Garrison, to the effect that "tom-turkeys," not "hens," were the ones who should "do the gobbling" in discussing such a serious issue of the day as slavery.

Whether Wright realized it or not, however, the time had passed when women would be content any longer to remain cooped up in a henhouse, or in any other institution that confined their movements, muzzled their speech, or limited their thoughts. In an era of numerous social reforms, religious revivals, increased political suffrage, and stimulating literary expression, it would have been impossible any longer to suppress the natural feelings of self-confidence and self-expression that were becoming an evident part of the growing feminist spirit. The participation of women in the Abolition movement would prove to be the final straw in breaking the fetters that had kept them in their own long and oppressive state of bondage. According to Blanche Glassman Hersh, in her study *The Slavery of Sex,* women's involvement in Garrison's Abolitionist movement "served as the catalyst which transformed latent feminist sentiment into the beginnings of an organized movement."

CHAPTER 8 } THE POLITICS OF RIGHTEOUSNESS

The decision of a number of well-educated, fiercely determined, upper-class Boston women to involve themselves in the controversial Abolition movement marked a distinct change not only in the activities of females well outside the strictly defined limits of their "domestic sphere" but also in the character of the Boston abolition movement itself.

It is true that many of the city's well-known wives and mothers had already involved themselves in a variety of local social and charitable organizations, participating in religious and missionary work, assisting widows, orphans, and "fallen women," joining groups for prison reform, and taking an active role in temperance efforts. But most of these activities were still seen as somehow safely contained within the invisible boundaries of a woman's narrow circle of domestic concerns, and, for the most part, members of conservative Boston society looked favorably upon these benevolent efforts. They were clearly charitable and compassionate; they were often related to the humanitarian work of local church groups; they were directed at curing social ills and moral evils; and they were made up exclusively of women who were associated with other women—not with members of the opposite sex. These voluntary associations for reform, however, not only strengthened middle-class women's sense of sisterhood and common purpose, but also provided them with many essential administrative talents and political skills they would not usually have developed in purely domestic settings. They wrote constitutions, they recruited new members, they elected officers, they coordinated meetings, they raised funds—skills they would use as they gradually redefined for themselves what historian Sara Evans has called "the meaning of public and private life."

Within a year after William Lloyd Garrison had published his *Liberator* in 1831, calling for the total and immediate emancipation of slaves, women had formed female antislavery societies throughout New England, and by 1838 they had created over a hundred such societies in the region. Garrison not only permitted women to join him in his moral crusade, but he strongly encouraged them to do so, becoming, as Blanche Glassman Hersh has written in *The Slavery of Sex*, "the catalyst" who not only changed the nature of the antislavery movement, but also helped to transform the role and consciousness of the women who took part in that movement. Garrison saw to it that a "Ladies Department" was included in the early issues of the *Liberator*, and he made a point of imploring the "Women of New England" to take special note of the one million black women in bondage, "exposed to all the violence of lust and passion," and urged them to join him in working for immediate emancipation.

One of the first women to respond to Garrison's appeal was Maria Weston Chapman, a strong and dynamic personality, and a member of one of Boston's leading families. In 1832, Maria and three of her sisters organized the Boston Female Anti-Slavery Society to serve as an auxiliary to Garrison's all-male New England Anti-Slavery Society. Chapman was clearly the driving force of the female society, and originally concentrated on raising funds for the cause by organizing highly profitable yearly antislavery fairs and selling a gift book called the *Liberty Bell*, which contained articles and poems by well-known Abolitionists. From these "auxiliary" activities, Chapman moved on to what were usually considered "male" roles, such as initiating petition campaigns, publishing the annual report of the Society and, whenever Garrison himself was out of town, editing the *Liberator*. Garrison's crusade for the immediate emancipation of slaves also changed the life of another Boston woman, Lydia Maria Child, who had acquired a reputation as a popular novelist and author of a highly successful cookbook called *The Frugal Housewife*. Capitalizing on this woman's literary talents, Garrison inspired Child to write *An Appeal on Behalf of that Class of Americans Called Africans* (1833), the first antislavery work to be published in book form in the United States. Although it had a strong appeal to those in the city who were sympathetic to the Abolitionist cause, the book aroused extensive controversy among members of the general public, because Child not only attacked slavery in the South, but also condemned the various forms of racial discrimination that flourished in the schools, churches, and public institutions in Northern cities like Boston.

After several years of activity, there were indications that many women involved in the abolitionist movement, especially in Boston and Philadelphia, were becoming increasingly dissatisfied with the routine and essentially subsidiary roles they were playing in their auxiliary organizations.

These feelings surfaced when Sarah and Angelina Grimké, two sisters from a slaveholding family in South Carolina, moved north to take up the antislavery cause. The two reformers addressed the convention of antislavery women in 1837 and challenged women to break their own bonds if they expected to aid those of their sex in the bondage of slavery. Following the convention, the Grimké sisters addressed the Boston Female Anti-Slavery Society at the invitation of Maria Weston Chapman, and then went on to address other women's groups in the New England area, on many occasions speaking to audiences of both men and women.

The idea of women speaking in public about the controversial subject of abolition, especially before "mixed" gatherings, aroused the wrath of the orthodox clergy in Massachusetts. The General Association of Congregational Ministers issued an edict to all its member churches condemning the Grimké sisters for going beyond the boundaries of acceptable female behavior in addressing "promiscuous" audiences. The ministers cited the New Testament as their authority in stating that it was "unnatural" for a woman to assume the "place and tone of a man as a public reformer," and they claimed that it opened the way to "degradation and ruin." The Grimké sisters refused to be intimidated by these clerical denunciations, however, and stood firm in their conviction that men and women had the same moral right and duty to oppose slavery. And their position was supported by Maria Weston's sister, Anne Warren Weston, who pointed out that the same ministers who had used the Scriptures to justify slavery in the first place were now using the same sacred text to sanction woman's inferiority and subordination. In a clear display of feminist consciousness, Weston concluded that, in working to aid the antislavery movement, the Grimké sisters were occupying "the very sphere to which God has appointed every Christian."

One young woman who heard the ministers' letter read in the Congregational church in North Brookfield, where she was teaching school, was Lucy Stone. Already sensitive to her inferior position as a female, having been denied permission to vote or join in discussions at her church, in 1843 she enrolled at Oberlin College in Ohio, an institution noted for its antislavery views as well as for its willingness to accept females as students. After graduation, Stone became a lecturer with Garrison's Society in Boston, but found that her responsibilities to the abolition cause clashed with her commitment to women's rights. "I was a woman before I was an abolitionist," she explained, and eventually worked out an arrangement that allowed her to lecture on women's rights on her own during the week, so long as she lectured for the Anti-Slavery Society on the weekends. The notoriety of her public appearances before large, mixed audiences caused her church to expel her for what it called "conduct inconsistent with her covenant engagements."

Although she had earlier decided not to marry so that she would never have to acknowledge any man as "master," Stone was successfully courted by Henry Brown Blackwell, a Cincinnati hardware merchant who was both antislavery and profeminist. At their marriage ceremony, on May 1, 1855, they both read a manifesto against the prevailing marriage laws, and the bride announced that in order to preserve her identity she would keep her own name, calling herself "Mrs. Stone." In the years that followed, a number of Lucy Stone Leagues were established in various parts of the country by sympathetic groups of feminists, who became known as "Lucy Stoners" in their desire to preserve their own separate identities.

While Lucy Stone was trying to balance her commitment to the feminist cause with her responsibilities to emancipation, other women in Garrison's movement were becoming increasingly dissatisfied with their subordinate position as auxiliaries in the Abolition movement, especially after listening to the Grimké sisters lecturing on the equality of the sexes. In 1839, the Garrison-dominated American Anti-Slavery Society, after a long and often acrimonious discussion, decided to interpret the word "person" in its constitution as including women as well as men. An examination of the votes—180 yeas, 140 nays—shows that there were many more nays coming from the New York delegates than from those who represented Boston.

As plans began to develop for the upcoming annual meeting of the American Anti-Slavery Society, which was to be held in New York City the following year, there were rumors that the New Yorkers planned to flood the hall with their members, capture control of the Society, and reverse the vote that was recently taken to admit women on an equal basis. The Bostonians, thereupon, went all-out to get as many as possible of their own delegates to the New York meeting. Indeed, the Garrison people went so far as to charter a special steamboat to take their representatives from Providence to New York. More than a thousand Abolitionists came to New York City to attend the annual meeting, when it convened in the Presbyterian church on Madison Avenue. The nomination of one of Garrison's female members for a seat on the executive board, a young Quaker named Abby Kelley, also a graduate of Oberlin College, touched off an intense debate between the New

LUCY STONE

A graduate of Oberlin College, the first Massachusetts woman to be awarded a college degree, Lucy Stone became a public lecturer for both the Abolition movement and the movement for women's rights. Although she appeared young and innocent, she spoke with a fervor that captivated friendly audiences and often neutralized audiences which were aggressively hostile. When she decided to keep her maiden name after her marriage in 1855, she became a model to many other young women who formed "Lucy Stone Leagues" in her honor. (Courtesy, Bostonian Society/Old State House)

Yorkers and the Bostonians over the "woman question." Despite demands by the conservative delegates for her resignation, Kelley adamantly refused to resign and, as the Grimké sisters had done, defended her position on the ground that men and women had the same moral rights and responsibilities. Kelley was finally approved for the post by a vote of 557 to 451, at which point, according to the critical view of Oliver Johnson, an eyewitness to the proceedings, Garrison's Anti-Slavery Society had transformed itself into a "woman's rights" association that would seek to overturn traditional family values and destroy man's faith in the Bible.

The election of Abby Kelley was the last straw for many conservative Abolitionists, especially those from New York, who were already chafing under what they had come to regard as Garrison's autocratic leadership and his self-defeating measures. His refusal to become involved in national politics, his policy of pacifism and nonviolence, his attacks on organized religion, and now his insistence on including women in the antislavery cause were seen as detrimental to the organization and destructive of its goals. Shortly after the vote admitting Abby Kelley as a member of the executive committee had been taken, Lewis Tappan of New York invited those who had voted against the appointment to meet with him in an adjoining room for the purpose of forming a new antislavery organization. A large number of the ministers present, according to Oliver Johnson, accepted the invitation and subsequently helped organize a new society, with a constitution that specifically guarded against the "intrusion" of women. Known as the Massachusetts Abolition Society, the rival organization hoped to attract a new following of orthodox clergymen, conservative businessmen, and "men of influence" generally, who would be attracted to the antislavery cause without being forced into "swallowing Garrison." In order to communicate their message, they founded a new publication, *The Massachusetts Abolitionist*, which they hoped would supersede Garrison's *Liberator* in attracting new members to the cause. The impasse over Kelley's appointment was more than a tempest in a teapot; it was a critical ideological crisis that split the association in two and increasingly radicalized the Garrison-dominated group into a smaller and more marginalized part of the reform movement in the North.

Following the fight over Abby Kelley's appointment and the troublesome woman question, Garrison and his people faced a similar and even more bitter confrontation at the World's Anti-Slavery Convention that met in

London in 1840. Having decided to admit women to membership, the Garrisonian antislavery societies felt honor-bound to include females as delegates to the international conference. Those who were commissioned as delegates from these societies included Ann Green, the bride of Wendell Phillips, Lucretia Mott, Sarah Pugh, Mary Grew, Elizabeth Neall (now Mrs. Sydney Howard Gay), and Emily Winslow (now Mrs. Taylor). Anticipating such a development, Garrison's conservative critics in the Massachusetts Abolition Society took steps to prevent it. According to Oliver Johnson, in his recollections called *William Lloyd Garrison and His Times*, Garrison's opponents "had the ear" of the members of the British and French Society, who were responsible for framing rules for the conference, and who arranged to exclude the female delegates from America on the ground that their admission would be contrary to "British usage." Wendell Phillips, at the prompting of his young wife, who urged him to be "brave as a lion," made strenuous efforts to persuade organizers of the convention to repeal this rule and admit the women delegates, but his efforts were to no avail.

The convention had been in session for about a week when William Lloyd Garrison arrived in London, accompanied by fellow delegates N. P. Rogers, William Adams, and Charles Lenox Remond, an African American from Boston who had become prominent in the national abolition movement. When he learned that the credentials of the women delegates had not been honored, Garrison refused to take his place on the floor with the other delegates to the convention, but took a seat in the galleries as a spectator, while other male delegates framed a formal protest against the exclusion. Charles Remond, rose to speak in protest against the exclusion of female delegates and subsequently participated in a boycott of the convention staged by a number of the Abolitionists. Once again, however, the organizers of the convention refused to yield, with members of the English clergy citing Holy Scripture as the authority for relegating women to their "God-ordained" sphere. To give the vote to females, they argued, would be to act in opposition to the word of God. They also felt it would be improper to expose the "shrinking nature of woman" to the tasteless indelicacies involved in a discussion of slavery. The only final concession was to allow the women to view the proceedings from behind a screened-off area, where they were joined by Garrison and several other male supporters, and asked to have "no unpleasant feelings over the outcome."

Far from agreeing to have "no unpleasant feelings," the women returned to the United States outraged at their humiliating experience at the London convention. Elizabeth Cady Stanton called the experience a "fresh baptism into woman's degradation," especially since it had come at the hands of men who were supposed to be committed to the cause of freedom and emancipation. Now, more than ever, women were painfully aware of the obstacles and discrimination that continued to confront them at all levels and in every walk of life—refusing them educational opportunities, professional advancement, legal rights, political liberties, and even equality of status in humanitarian reform movements. Clearly the time had come for women to speak out on their own behalf and make other women conscious of just how limited they were in what they could do, how far they could go, and what they could achieve.

During the summer of 1848, Lucretia Mott visited with her friend Elizabeth Cady Stanton in upstate New York, and in the course of their conversations, they made plans to hold a Woman's Rights Convention in July in the Wesleyan Chapel in Seneca Falls, New York. When July 19 arrived, a large number of men and women discovered that the doors of the chapel were locked, and they could not enter until they boosted a small boy through an open window to let them in. With Stanton's husband James presiding, the convention opened; several women read their prepared speeches, Lucretia Mott explained the purpose of the convention, and then Elizabeth Cady Stanton proceeded to read the Declaration of Sentiments that had been composed by members of the committee and modeled on the original Declaration of Independence "We hold these truths to be self-evident," said the women, "that all men and women are created equal," substituted the word "man" in those places where "King George" had been mentioned, and listed a series of "grievances," similar to those of the Colonies against the Crown, as the basis for their demands. The Declaration of Sentiments concluded with a request for immediate admission to all the rights and privileges pertaining to citizens of the United States. The reading of the Declaration was followed by a series of twelve resolutions, the most controversial of which was a call for women's "sacred right to the elective franchise." Indeed, although all the other resolutions passed unanimously, observes historian Blanche Hersh, the demand for suffrage was considered so radical that it passed by only a small majority. Interestingly enough, Frederick Douglass, the leading black spokesman for emancipation and an advocate of women's rights, was the only male present at the convention to endorse Elizabeth Cady Stanton's resolution calling for women's suffrage.

Confident and self-assured, the new feminists proceeded to abandon their "proper sphere" and went about the serious and all-consuming business of emancipating women from what Hersh has called "the slavery of sex." After nearly three decades of associating with one another in female Bible societies, missionary societies, charitable societies, maternal societies, and literary societies, whose pious goals and humanitarian purposes lent them a certain legitimacy, Boston women went on to acquire additional skills and organizational insights during their auxiliary work with Garrison and the Abolition movement. Engaging in petition campaigns, organizing national conventions, speaking on public platforms to "mixed" audiences provided them with the methods, language, and techniques they used in rejecting the authority of a male-dominated society and asserting their own demands for full participation in the public and civic life of the nation.

These challenges to the established traditions of middle-class order and decorum, of course, opened women up to social ostracism, loss of reputation, and a steady diet of ridicule and denunciation. Ministers of mainline churches argued from the "sin of Eve" and the masculinity of Jesus that the subordination of women was permanently ordained by God and, therefore, not subject to change. Those who would reject the authority of Scripture, they charged, would bring about nothing but "strife, discord, anger, and division." Newspapers regularly cast aspersions on the femininity of women's rights advocates, referring to them as unattractive "old maids," "badly mated" wives, "mannish women" who crowed like hens, while questioning the masculinity of their male supporters, and suggesting that "hen-pecked" husbands ought to wear petticoats. Because of her outspoken style of speaking, Abby Kelley was denounced as "unsexed" and "immodest"; Susan B. Anthony was regarded as "unwomanly" and "aggressive"; Lucy Stone was often maligned and vilified at meetings and in newspaper columns. Gales of laughter usually greeted those women who appeared in public in the masculine-style attire designed by Amelia Jenks Bloomer as a practical and sensible alternative to the decorative frills, flounces, and bows of the current female fashion that hampered women's movement and emphasized their purely decorative function in society.

Despite the negative aspects of public opinion, however, most of the female reformers fought on, believing that, with enough time, hard work,

JULIA WARD HOWE

During her early years, Julia Ward Howe was recognized as the wife of Dr. Samuel Gridley Howe, director of the Perkins Institution for the Blind. Howe had literary ambitions of her own, however, and during the Civil War she became famous in her own right as the author of the stirring poem "The Battle Hymn of the Republic." After the war, Howe continued to follow a literary career but became better known as a powerful force in women's politics and an eloquent spokesperson for women's suffrage. (Courtesy, Bostonian Society/Old State House) dogged persistence, fanatical devotion, and tireless energy, they would eventually, if not inevitably, bring about the changes and reforms to which they were devoting their lives. But it was a losing cause. Although women's rights advocates were able to make some limited gains in the area of legal rights (control of their own earnings, larger inheritance rights for widows), their demands for the suffrage were completely ignored. Part of the reason for this was that, by the 1850s, the movement for women's rights, along with most of the other social-reform movements that had dominated national interest and local headlines for so long, were fast being overshadowed by the national political debate over the future of slavery in the United States. Activities such as the temperance movement, prohibition, prison reform, utopianism, nativism, the lyceum movement, universal education, pubic libraries, help for the disabled, care for the insane, and the women's movement, all of which had been so prominent during the 1830s and 1840s, were now submerged by the growing struggle over the territorial expansion of slavery in the aftermath of the war between the United States and Mexico.

The attention of the nation became so focused on such controversial political issues as the disposition of the lands in the Southwest acquired from Mexico, the question of statehood for California, the status of slavery in the District of Columbia, and the question of fugitive slaves that all other matters took a back seat. Many Americans hoped that the Compromise of 1850 would satisfactorily resolve the thorny issues and set the stage for a nation whose slave and free-soil populations would agree to lead a form of uneasy but essential peaceful coexistence on either side of the 36° 30' latitude line along the southern boundary of Missouri, preventing slavery from moving north into the Louisiana Territory. This conspiracy of silence was rudely broken four years later, however, when Congress passed Senator Stephen A. Douglas's Kansas-Nebraska Act that provided for two new territories above that line to enter the Union "with or without slavery," as determined by its future settlers. The ground rules had been broken; the dividing line between free soil and slave soil had been erased—the fight was on! Douglas's bill brought the slavery issue back into national politics with a vengeance, and made Kansas Territory the national testing ground for whether slavery could be contained below the 36° 30' line or allowed to expand throughout the free lands of the West. Things were never the same after 1854. Relations between the North and the South deteriorated rapidly, and every bitter incident between angry settlers, every savage slaughter on the bloody plains of Kansas, aroused public reaction nationally and pushed the two sectors farther and farther apart.

Like a gigantic vacuum, the politics of slavery sucked up the energy that had, for so long, vitalized so many of the social and humanitarian reform movements of the antebellum era. Direct political action overshadowed and overpowered the older movements that had relied upon what C. S. Griffin, in his study *The Ferment of Reform, 1830–1860*, called "traditional means," like institutions, churches, voluntary associations, and humanitarian volunteers, and that had insisted that success was possible through rational discussion and moral suasion instead of social upheaval or public violence. In the whirlwind of venom and violence that now enveloped the nation, however, moral absolutism and ideological confrontation left no further room for discussion or debate. It was no longer possible, for example, for Northerners to discuss slavery as a complex labor system, a serious sociological problem, or a difficult political issue that could be resolved over a long period of time. No! Slavery was a sin, a moral evil, a crime against humanity that must be stamped out totally and immediately. It was an evangelistic resurgence of old fundamental Protestantism, directed at what was seen as an all-consuming source of immorality that eventually forced all Americans to take a stand between right and wrong, good and evil, regardless of the political or social consequences.

And the irony of it all was that in pursuing their ambitious goal of reforming American standards and turning America into a modern version of ancient Athens, the Boston leadership elite only contributed further to the deep cultural division that separated the Northern states and the Southern states as they squared off against the explosive slavery issue. Its members had abandoned the religious fundamentalism of orthodox Congregationalism in favor of the more tolerant and rational views of the "Boston religion." They had established hospitals and asylums, patronized great literature and the fine arts, and encouraged the pursuit of science and technology. They had restructured old cities, modernized police and fire departments, and offered all kinds of humane assistance for the poor and the homeless. While they supported new educational opportunities for boys and girls, they also advanced knowledge in the treatment of those with mental illnesses and physical disabilities. These were the creative, orderly, and systematic reforms the Unitarian leadership felt would transform Boston into the kind of Athenian republic that would serve as a model for the rest of the nation.

But they were to find, much to their dismay, that the rest of the country did not want Boston as their model, not did those citizens want their own life and culture to reflect the society they saw in the New England region. One person who had the opportunity to witness at firsthand this cultural dichotomy was thirty-year-old Frederic Law Olmsted. Long before he designed the public park system of Boston, popularly known as the Emerald Necklace, Olmsted had been a civil engineer, a gentleman farmer, and a casual writer, who was asked by Henry Raymond's *New York Daily Times* to visit the South and send back reports on his observations of the Cotton Kingdom. On December 11, 1852, Olmsted set out on a fourteen-month tour of the slave states, sending back reports that were first printed in the *Times* and then published in book form.

Olmsted's principal concern, and certainly that of his New York publisher, was to investigate the omnipresent institution of slavery in the region and to comment upon its vast social impact on Southern social and economic life. The young reporter, however, was also keenly sensitive to many other aspects of Southern life, especially the ways in which various representatives of the South spoke proudly and defensively about their own distinctive way of life. For the most part, Olmsted observed, the average white Southerner was perfectly content with things as they were, always had been, and as they *ought* to be. He was reluctant to get involved with conflicting interests or to see his particular section of the country become subject to the new kind of social experiments he heard were taking place in the Northern states at that time. "The Southerner can understand nothing of all this," Olmsted wrote. "He naturally accepts the institutions, manners, and customs in which he is educated as necessities imposed on him by Providence."

In several parts of the South, especially in the Baptist regions, where the fundamental beliefs of Protestantism were strongly opposed to the sin of drunkenness, Olmsted found some sympathy for Northern temperance activities. Most other reform movements of the period, however, found little interest or support in a region that put greater store on states' rights, personal liberties, and fiscal conservatism. Prison-reform movements and prison-discipline societies, with their fancy theories about penology and their sympathetic plans for the "reformation" of felons and criminals, found little appreciation among a people who believed in simple frontier justice and the presence of a hangman's noose. Stories about such liberal innovations as utopian communities, experiments in eccentric styles of social living, and programs of pietistic religious reforms found little interest among Southerners who preferred the changelessness of their community and the homogeneity of their people and who followed an evangelical Protestantism that emphasized the infallibility of the Bible. More radical reform movements, such as concerns for universal peace, women's rights, and, of course, the abolition of slavery, were regarded as both outrageous and flagrantly dangerous by Southerners who ridiculed the idea of having "long-haired men" being bossed around by "short-haired women" in their efforts to violate the laws of nature and reject the word of God.

The lyceum movement, so prevalent in the North during the 1820s and 1830s, did not flourish in the South whose citizens preferred the hardy and romantic novels of Sir Walter Scott to the effete Transcendentalism of Northern writers like Ralph Waldo Emerson. Educational reforms involving government authority and state appropriations for schools, supplies, equipment, and the professional training of teachers seemed both prodigal and unnecessary in rural communities where there was little everyday need for much more than the three Rs. Wealthy families could pay for private schools or hire special tutors for their younger children, if they chose, and then send their older sons off to college in England and Scotland, or to such Northern institutions of higher learning as Harvard, Dartmouth, and Princeton. Education was regarded as a private option for the upper classes, not an unnecessary and wasteful system by which the government would educate people in rural areas who had no other future but tilling the soil and planting the crops.

Nor was there any inclination on the part of most leading Southerners to develop in their own region the type of industrial economy, driven by aggressive and mercenary Yankees, that was powering the economy of so much of the North. Ugly factory buildings, dirty smokestacks, noisy steam engines, and hordes of slovenly laborers contrasted sharply with the Southerners' idyllic dreams of the agrarian virtues of the old Republic, with open green fields, sparking streams, and unpolluted air. Olmsted reported that many people he talked with in Virginia believed that slavery was justified on noneconomic grounds precisely because it protected the South from the class conflicts and radical "isms" they found prevalent in the North—such as rent riots, factory strikes, immigrant unrest, "diseased" philanthropy, radical democracy, and the advance of all kinds of socialist ideas. The South, wrote Olmsted, saw crowded Northern cities as the natural habitat of agitators and wild-eyed reformers and "uniformly rejected the isms which infest Europe and the Eastern and Western States of this country." The hordes of illiterate and impoverished immigrants they read about in their newspapers flooding into the cities of the North, during the 1840s and 1850s, contrasted sharply with what they saw as the homogeneous white population of the South, as people who knew their place in the natural order of things and were content to remain in that place. This clear division of ideology between the Southern view of social and intellectual reform movements and that of the Northern states makes it abundantly clear that there were two separate and distinct societies—two different cultures—that made up the Union.

Historians of the Civil War have rightly pointed out the many factors that separated the two sections of the country and eventually led to the final crisis of the Union. There were contrasting theories over federal power and states' rights; tensions between competitive economic systems; a breakdown in the prevailing political-party structure. But perhaps nowhere were the differences between the Northern states and the Southern states so striking as in their conflicting cultural views regarding the future direction of the nation. The Boston view of a rational and progressive Christianity, as a commitment to science and technology, a highly educated citizenry, a creative literary culture, advanced social and medical services, and an expanding view of human rights and social freedom, was not at all acceptable to the people of the South. They tended to regard most of these radical Northern ideas as a callous rejection of fundamental Christian morality, a flagrant violation of states' rights, an unwarranted intrusion into personal liberties, and a reckless disregard for the stability and security guaranteed by the continuance of long-established social systems, class structures, and racial barriers.

There was no point to further discussion; there was no common ground between the principles of good and evil. The ideal of an "Athens of America," based upon the idea of educated gentlemen engaged in civil discussion with a tolerant regard for the differing opinions of others, was no longer a concept that had any meaning or relevance amid the raucous voices of ideological adversaries and the violent clash of arms that would eventually bring the Union to its tragic conflict.

SOURCES

CHAPTER 1

Thomas H. O'Connor and Alan Rogers, in *This Momentous Affair: Massachusetts and the Ratification of the Constitution of the United States* (Boston, 1987), provide a summary of the arguments for and against ratification. Also see James Truslow Adams, *New England in the Republic, 1776–1850* (Boston, 1926); Joyce Appleby, *Capitalism and a New Social Order: The Republican Vision of the 1790s* (New York, 1984). Gavin Weightman's *The Frozen-Water Trade* (New York, 2003) is a dramatic example of Yankee entrepreneurship in the early Republic. Walter Muir Whitehill, in *Boston: A Topographical History* (Cambridge, 1959), offers a fascinating overview of topographical and architectural changes in Boston; Harold Kirker's, *Bulfinch's Boston, 1787–1817* (New York, 1964) is a standard history of Bulfinch's influence on the city; his later book, *The Architecture of Charles Bulfinch* (Cambridge, 1998) concentrates on his technical work and supplies a copy of his architectural library. Douglass Shand-Tucci, *Built in Boston: City and Suburb, 1800–1950* (Amherst, Mass.: 1988; rev. rpt., 2001); George M. Cushing Jr., *Great Buildings of Boston* (New York, 1982); and Jane Holtz Kay, *Lost Boston* (Boston, 1980).

For works that cover major religious trends in the early colonial period, see Perry Miller, *The New England Mind: The Seventeenth Century* (New York, 1939); Herbert W. Schneider, *The Puritan Mind* (New York, 1939); and Kenneth Murdock, *Increase Mather: The Foremost American* (Cambridge, 1925). Alan Heimert, *Religion and the American Mind from the Great Awakening to the Revolution* (Cambridge, 1966), and William W. Sweet, *Religion in Colonial America* (New York, 1942), bring the story up to the Revolutionary period. Henry F. May, in *The Enlightenment in America* (New York, 1976), provides a stimulating assessment of the influence of the New Science in colonial America. Also see Gerald R. Cragg, *From Puritanism to the Age of Reason* (Cambridge, rpt., 1966); Albert Post, *Popular Freethought in America* (New York, 1943); and Herbert M. Morais, *Deism in 18th Century America* (New York, 1934), for explanations of the influences of the new science on traditional American thought.

On Unitarianism in America, Conrad Wright's *The Beginnings of Unitarianism in America* (Boston, 1955) offers a useful historical background for the new religious movement. More recent studies are Conrad Wright, ed., *A Stream of Light: A Sesqui-centennial History of American Unitarianism* (Boston, 1975); David Robinson, *The Unitarians and the Universalists* (Westport, Conn., 1985); and Daniel Walker Howe, *The Unitarian Conscience: Harvard Moral Philosophy, 1805–1861* (Cambridge, 1970). Also see Conrad Edick Wright, ed., *American Unitarianism: 1805–1865* (Boston, 1989), for a series of scholarly essays on the role of the Unitarian Church in antebellum America. See also David P. Edgel, *William Ellery Channing: An Intellectual Portrait* (Boston, 1955).

Sydney E. Ahlstrom's *A Religious History of the American People* (New York, 1972) is helpful on antebellum religious movements. Also see William W. Sweet, *Religion in the Development of American Culture, 1765–1840* (Cambridge, 1953), and William McLoughlin, *New England Dissent, 1630–1833: The Baptists and the Separation of Church and State* (Cambridge, 1971). Barbara M. Cross, ed., *The Autobiography of Lyman Beecher* (Cambridge, 1961), and H. Shelton Smith's *Changing Conceptions of Original Sin* (New York: 1955) are works that examine changes in religious orthodoxy.

Interpretations of the political changes from Federalism to Jeffersonian Republicanism may be found in Stephen G. Kurtz, *The Presidency of John Adams: The Collapse of Federalism, 1795–1800* (Philadelphia, 1957); David Hackett Fischer, *The Revolution of American Conservatism: The Federalist Party in the Age of Jeffersonian Democracy* (New York, 1965); Paul Goodman, *The Democratic-Republicans of Massachusetts* (Cambridge, 1964); Ronald Formisano, *The Transformation of Political Culture: Massachusetts Parties, 1790s–1840s* (New York, 1983); and Linda Kerber, *Federalists in Dissent: Imagery and Ideology in Jeffersonian America* (Ithaca, N.Y., 1970). Jacqueline Barbara Carr, *After the Siege: A Social History of Boston, 1775–1800* (Boston, 2005), is a cultural study of the transformation of Boston from war to peace.

CHAPTER 2

Changing political structures following the War of 1812 are examined in James M. Banner, *To the Hartford Convention: The Federalists and the Origin of Party Politics in Massachusetts, 1789–1815* (New York, 1970); Shaw Livermore Jr., *The Twilight of Federalism: The Disintegration of the Federalist Party, 1815–1830* (Princeton, 1962); and George Dangerfield, *The Era of Good Feelings* (New York, 1952), and his *The Awakening of American Nationalism, 1815–1828* (New York, 1965). Arthur B. Darling's *Political Changes in Massachusetts, 1824–1848: A Study in Liberal Movements in Politics* (New Haven, Conn., 1925) is an older standard view of state politics, while Harlow W.

Sheidley, *Sectional Nationalism: Massachusetts Conservative Leaders and the Transformation of America, 1815–1836* (Boston, 1998), is a more recent interpretation of Bay State politics during the postwar period.

Political and economic forces brought many changes to Boston life and society. Robert Remini, *John Quincy Adams* (New York, 2002); Lynn Parsons, *John Quincy Adams* (Madison, Wisc., 1998); and Mary Hargreaves, *The Presidency of John Quincy Adams* (Lawrence, Kans., 1985) offer studies of John Quincy Adams. Works about Andrew Jackson include Robert Remini's *The Jackson Era*, 2nd ed. (Wheeling, Ill., 1997); Edward Pessen, *Jacksonian America: Society, Personality, and Politics*, rev. ed. (Urbana, Ill., 1985); Glyndon Van Deusen, *The Jacksonian Era* (New York, 1959); and Claude Bowers, *Party Battles of the Jackson Era* (New York, 1929). Arthur M. Schlesinger Jr.'s *The Age of Jackson* (Boston, 1945) is an older study, but it is still valuable for its insights into Democratic politics in Massachusetts. The economic and social effects of the postwar textile industry are treated in Thomas H. O'Connor, *Lords of the Loom: The Cotton Whigs and the Coming of the Civil War* (New York, 1968); Robert F. Dalzell, *Enterprising Elite: The Boston Associates and the World They Made* (Cambridge, 1987); William F. Hartford, *Money, Morals, and Politics: Massachusetts in the Age of the Boston Associates* (Boston, 2001); and Frederic Jaher, "The Politics of the Boston Brahmins, 1800–1860," in *Boston, 1700–1980: The Evolution of Urban Politics*, ed. Robert Formisano and Constance Burns (Westport, Conn., 1984). For an analysis of the professional and philanthropic characteristics of the Boston elite, see Peter Dobkin Hall, *The Organization of American Culture, 1700–1900: Private Institutions, Elites, and the Origins of American Nationality* (New York, 1982).

The observations of visitors provide graphic descriptions of early nineteenth-century Boston. Mrs. Royall, for example, set down her impressions of the city in her *Sketches of History, Life, and Manners in the United States* (New Haven, Conn., 1826). Alexander McKay, an English lawyer and journalist, visited America and provided a similar description in his *Western World: Travels in the United States in 1846–47*, 3 v. (London, 1849). A convenient introduction to the writings of foreign visitors can be found in Allan Nevins, ed., *America through British Eyes* (New York, 1948), and in Oscar Handlin, ed., *This Was America* (Cambridge, 1949), which records the observations of European travelers. Warren S. Tryon, in *A Mirror for Americans: Life and Manners in the United States, 1790–1870, as Recorded by American Travelers*, 3 v. (Chicago, 1952), provides excerpts from the writings of Americans from one part of the country about another.

Background material for the establishment of Boston's African American community can be found in George A. Levesque, *Black Boston: African-American Life and Culture in Urban America, 1750–1860* (New York, 1994); James O. Horton and Lois E. Horton, *Black Bostonians: Family Life and Community Struggle in the Antebellum North* (New York, 1979); Robert C. A. Hayden, *A History of the Black Church in Boston* (Boston, 1983); and Carol Buchalter Stapp, *Afro-Americans in Antebellum Boston: An Analysis of Probate Records* (New York, 1993). The beginnings of Boston's Irish American community can be found in James B. Cullen, *The Story of the Irish in Boston* (Boston, 1889); James Haltigan, *The Irish in the American Revolution and Their Early Influence in the Colonies* (Washington, D.C., 1907); Dale T. Knobel, *Paddy and the Republic: Ethnicity and Nationality in Antebellum America* (Middletown, Conn., 1986); and Thomas H. O'Connor, *The Boston Irish: A Political History* (Boston, 1995). Oscar Handlin, *Boston's Immigrants, 1790–1880* (Cambridge, 1941), is a valuable source for understanding the city's immigrant community.

The indispensable source for materials on the active life and career of Josiah Quincy still remains Josiah Quincy, *A Municipal History of the Town and City of Boston During Two Centuries, from September 17, 1639, to September 17, 1830* (Boston, 1852). Robert A. McCaughey, in *Josiah Quincy, 1772–1864: The Last Federalist* (Cambridge, 1974), updates the much earlier biography by Edmund Quincy, *The Life of Josiah Quincy of Massachusetts* (Boston, 1867). The most recent study of the new market is John Quincy Jr., *Quincy's Market: A Boston Landmark* (Boston, 2003). Also see Samuel Eliot Morison, *Harrison Gray Otis, 1765–1848: The Urbane Federalist* (New York, 1969); Kenneth W. Porter, *The Jacksons and the Lees*, 2 v. (Cambridge, 1937); Ferris Greenslet, *The Lowells and Their Seven Worlds* (Boston, 1946); Francis W. Gregory, *Nathan Appleton: Merchant and Entrepreneur, 1779–1861* (Charlottesville, Va.: 1975), and Frank O. Gatell, *John Gorham Palfrey and the New England Conscience* (Cambridge, 1963) for additional biographies of prominent Bostonians.

CHAPTER 3

On the subject of poverty and homelessness, see Louis B. Wright, *The Cultural Life of the American Colonies* (New York, 1957); Robert H. Bremmer, *From the Depths: The Discovery of Poverty in the United States* (New York, 1956); Margaret James, *Social Problems during the Puritan Revolution, 1640–1660* (London, 1930); Josiah Benton, *Warning Out in New England, 1656–1817* (Boston, 1917); Eric G. Nells, "The Working Poor in Pre-Revolutionary Boston," *Historical Journal of Massachusetts* 17 (1989); Thomas H. O'Connor, "To Be Poor and Homeless in Old Boston," *Massachusetts and the New Nation*, ed., Conrad E. Wright (Boston, 1992). The extensive records of the Boston Overseers of the Poor may be found in the archives of the Massachusetts Historical Society. Josiah Quincy, in *Remarks on Some of the Provisions of the Laws of Massachusetts Affecting Poverty, Vice, and Crime* (Cambridge, 1822), offers a political view of the problem, while Ellery Channing, *The Ministry of the Poor: A Discourse before the Benevolent Fraternity of Churches on their First Anniversary* (Boston, 1835), and Daniel T. McColgan, *Joseph Tuckerman: Pioneer in American Social Work* (Washington, D.C., 1940), give a religious view. See David Rothman, *The Discovery of the Asylum* (Boston, 1971), and Clifford S. Griffin, *Their Brothers' Keepers* (New Brunswick, N.J., 1960), for prevailing views concerning public welfare and private philanthropy.

For studies related to the Woman's Sphere in the postrevolutionary period, see Nancy F. Cott, *The Bonds of Womanhood: "Woman's Sphere" in New England, 1778–1835* (New Haven, Conn., 1977); Michael K. Grossberg, *Governing the Hearth: Law and the Family in Nineteenth Century America* (Chapel Hill, N.C., 1985); Steven Mintz and Susan Kellogg, *Domestic Revolutions: A Social History of American Family Life* (New York, 1986); and Karen Halttunen, *Confidence Men and Painted Women: A Study of Middle-Class Culture in America, 1830–1870* (New Haven, Conn., 1982). On the subject of education, see Carl Degler, *At Odds: Women and the Family in America: From the Revolution to the Present* (New York, 1980); Barbara M. Cross, ed., *The Educated Woman in America* (New York, 1905); Jeanne Boydson, Mary Kelley, and Anne Margolis, eds., *The Limits of Sisterhood: The Beecher Sisters on Women's Rights and Women's Sphere* (Chapel Hill, N.C., 1988); and Kathryn Kish Sklar, *Catharine Beecher: A Study in American Domesticity* (New Haven, Conn., 1973).

The literary and cultural influences of women in the nineteenth century have been explored by Ann Douglas, in *The Feminization of American Culture* (New York: 1977); Mary Kelley, in *Private Women, Public Stage: Literary Domesticity in Nineteenth-Century America* (New York, 1984), and David S. Reynolds, in *Beneath the American Renaissance: The Subversive Imagination in the Age of Emerson and Melville* (New York, 1988). For the early involvement of women in medicine, see Mary Roth Walsh, *"Doctors Wanted: No Women Need Apply": Sexual Barriers in the Medical Profession, 1835–1975* (New Haven, Conn., 1977); Catherine Scholton, *Childbearing in American Society, 1650–1850* (New York, 1985); Judith Walzer Leavitt, *Brought to Bed: Childbearing in America, 1750–1950* (New York, 1986); and Amalie Kass, *Midwifery and Medicine in Boston: Walter Channing, M.D., 1786–1876* (Boston, 2002).

For the role of religion in the development of feminine consciousness in nineteenth-century America, see Barbara Leslie Epstein, *The Politics of Domesticity: Women, Evangelism, and Temperance in Nineteenth Century America* (Middletown,

Conn., 1981); Ann Boylan, *Sunday School: The Formation of an American Institution, 1790–1880* (New Haven, Conn., 1988); Keith Melder, *Beginnings of a Sisterhood: The American Women's Rights Movement, 1800–1850* (New York, 1977); Barbara J. Berg, *The Remembered Gate: Origins of American Feminism: The Woman and the City, 1800–1860* (New York, 1978); and Lori D. Ginzburg, *Women and the Work of Benevolence: Morality, Politics, and Class in the Nineteenth Century* (New Haven, Conn., 1990).

Works on crime and punishment include Jack Tager, *Boston Riots: Three Centuries of Racial Violence* (Boston, 2001); Alan Lupo, *Liberty's Chosen Home: The Politics of Violence in Boston* (Boston, 1977); and Leonard L. Richards, *"Gentlemen of Property and Standing": Anti-Abolition Mobs in Jacksonian America* (New York, 1970), which provide good general coverage, while Nancy L. Schultz, in *Fire and Roses: The Burning of the Charlestown Convent, 1834* (New York, 2002), has provided the most recent scholarly account of the famous event. Roger Lane's *Policing the City: Boston, 1822–1885* (New York, 1971) is a valuable survey of the changing nature of urban security in the nineteenth century, while Edward H. Savage, *Police Records and Recollections: or Boston by Daylight and Gaslight* (Boston, 1873), is a fascinating collection of anecdotes and events. W. David Lewis, *From Newgate to Dannemora: The Rise of the Penitentiary in New York, 1796–1848* (Ithaca, N.Y., 1965); Adam J. Hirsch, *The Rise of the Penitentiary: Prisons and Punishment in Early America* (New York, 1992); Andrew Kotnicki, *Religion and the Development of the American Penal System* (Lanham, Md., 2000); James M. Moynahan, *The American Jail: Its Development and Growth* (Chicago, 1980); Thomas Dunn, *Democracy and Punishment: Disciplinary Origins of the United States* (Madison, Wisc., 1987); and Blake McKelvey, *American Prisons: A Study in American Social History prior to 1915* (Chicago, 1936), provide background for changing systems of prison reform, while Nicole Rafter, *Partial Justice: Women, Prison, and Social Control* (New Brunswick, N.J., 1990), and Estelle Freedman, *Their Sisters' Keepers: Women's Prison Reform in America, 1830–1930* (Ann Arbor, Mich., 1981), give a feminist view.

The growing problem of alcoholism in an increasingly urban society has been treated by Ian Tyrall, *Sobering Up: From Temperance to Prohibition in Antebellum America, 1800–1860* (Westport, Conn., 1979); W. J. Rorabaugh, *The Alcoholic Republic: An American Tradition* (New York, 1979); Joseph R. Gusfield, *Symbolic Crusade: Status Politics and the American Temperance Movement* (Urbana, Ill., 1963) are comparatively recent studies. John Allen Krout's *The Origins of Prohibition* (New York, 1925), and D. Leigh Colvin, *Prohibition in the United States* (New York, 1926), are older studies. Carol Mattingly, *Well-Tempered Women: Nineteenth Century Temperance Rhetoric* (Carbondale, Ill., 1998), and Barbara Epstein, *The Politics of Domesticity: Women, Evangelism, and Temperance in Nineteenth-Century America* (Middletown, Conn., 1981), emphasize the influence of women.

CHAPTER 4

Henry Viets, *A Brief History of Medicine in Massachusetts* (Boston, 1930); and Samuel Green, *The History of Medicine in Massachusetts* (Boston, 1881), provide general summaries of the topic. Philip Cash, Eric Christianson, and J. Worth Estes, eds., *Medicine in Massachusetts, 1620–1820* (Boston, 1980); Richard H. Shyrock, *Medicine and Society in America, 1660–1860* (Ithaca, N.Y., 1960); Maurice B. Gordon, *Aesculapius Comes to the Colonies*, rpt. ed. (Ventnor, N.J., 1970); and Philip Cash, *Medical Men at the Siege of Boston, April 1775–April 1776* (Philadelphia, 1973), cover the colonial and revolutionary periods. Studies regarding the establishment of the medical profession in the Boston area may be found in Robert W. Greenleaf, ed., *An Historical Report of the Boston Dispensary for One Hundred and One Years, 1796–1877* (Brookline, Mass., 1898); Walter L. Burrage, A *History of the Massachusetts Medical Society* (Norwood, Mass., 1923); Joseph F. Kett, *The Formation of the American Medical Profession: The Role of Institutions, 1780–1860* (New Haven, Conn., 1968); and Henry K. Beecher and Mark D. Altschule, *Medicine at Harvard: The First Three Hundred Years* (Hanover, N.H., 1977). Peter Dobkin Hall, *The Organization of American Culture, 1700–1900* (New York, 1980), is especially perceptive in his analysis of the connections between politics and the profession of medicine in the early nineteenth century.

The early nineteenth century saw remarkable advances in medical knowledge, as well as in the treatment of the physically and emotionally disabled. Joseph E. Garland, *Every Man Our Neighbor: A Brief History of the Massachusetts General Hospital, 1811–1961* (Boston, 1961); Frederick Washburn, *The Massachusetts General Hospital* (Boston, 1939); and Rhoda Truax, *The Doctors Warren of Boston: First Family of Surgery* (Boston, 1968), provide the background for the first general hospital, while Sylvia Sutton, *Crossroads in Psychiatry: A History of the McLean Hospital* (New York, 1986), and Alex Beam, *Gracefully Insane: The Rise and Fall of America's Premier Mental Hospital* (New York, 2001), trace the history of work with the mentally ill. Leonard K. Eaton's *Early New England Hospitals, 1700–1833* (Ann Arbor, Mich., 1957) is a convenient summary, while *Aesculapian Boston* (Boston, 1980) contains a series of scholarly essays on hospitals, institutions, and medical societies written by members of the Paul Dudley White Medical History Society.

The larger question of the role of medicine in American society has been treated by Richard H. Shryock in his *Medicine and Society in America, 1660–1860* (Ithaca, N.Y., 1960), while John B. Blake, *Public Health in the Town of Boston, 1630–1822* (Cambridge, 1959), and Barbara G. Rosenkrantz, *Public Health and the State: Changing Views in Massachusetts, 1842–1936* (Cambridge, 1972), concentrate on the Bay State. Amalie M. Kass's *Midwifery and Medicine in Boston* is a fascinating study of medicine and obstetrics during the antebellum period. Charles E. Rosenberg's *The Cholera Years: The United States in 1832, 1849, and 1866* (Chicago, 1962) is the major work dealing with a major pandemic in nineteenth-century America.

Harry Best, *Blindness and the Blind in the United States* (New York, 1934); Katharine E. Willkie, *Teacher of the Blind: Samuel Gridley Howe* (New York, 1965); Harold Schwartz, *Samuel Gridley Howe: Social Reformer, 1801–1876* (Cambridge, 1956); and Laura Richards, *Samuel Gridley Howe* (New York, 1935) are biographies of the reformer. Ernest Freeberg, *The Education of Laura Bridgman: First Blind Person to Learn Language* (Cambridge, 2001), and Elisabeth Gitter, *The Imprisoned Guest: Samuel Howe and Laura Bridgman, the Original Deaf-Blind Girl* (New York, 2001), are recent studies of Howe's most famous patient.

For prevailing attitudes toward the care and treatment of the mentally ill, see Gerald Grob, *Mental Institutions in America: Social Policy to 1875* (New York, 1973); David Rothman, *The Discovery of the Asylum* (Boston, 1971); Norman Dain, *Concepts of Insanity in the United States, 1789–1865* (New Brunswick, N.J., 1964); and Clifford S. Griffin, *Their Brothers' Keepers: Moral Stewardship in the United States, 1800–1865* (New York, 1957). Charles Rosenberg, in *The Care of Strangers: The Rise of America's Hospital System* (New York, 1987), is also helpful on this subject. Thomas J. Brown, *Dorothea Dix: New England Reformer* (Cambridge, 1998), and David Gollaher, *Voice for the Mad: The Life of Dorothea Dix* (New York, 1995), are recent studies that have updated the earlier work of Helen E. Marshal, *Dorothea Dix: Forgotten Samaritan* (New York, 1937).

CHAPTER 5

For a collection of the writings of the major Transcendentalists, see Perry Miller, ed., *The Transcendentalists: Their Prose and Poetry* (New York, 1957). Ralph Waldo Emerson, *Essays* (Boston, 1903), is essential to an understanding of his social and philosophical ideas. For historical treatments of the movement, see Anne Rose, *Transcendentalism as a Social Movement* (New York, 1981); Philip Gura, *The Wisdom of Words: Language, Theology, and Literature in the New England Renaissance* (Middletown, Conn., 1981); Lawrence Buell, *Literary Transcendentalism: Style and Vision in the American Renaissance* (Ithaca, N.Y., 1973); Paul Boller, *American Transcendentalism, 1830–1860* (New York, 1974); Warren S. Tryon, *Parnassus Corner* (Boston, 1963); William R. Hutchinson, *The Transcendentalist Ministers: Church Reform in the New England Renaissance* (New Haven, Conn., 1959); and Van Wyck Brooks, *The Flowering of New England* (New York, 1936).

Studies on individual writers include Mary K. Cayton's *Emerson's Emergence: Self and Society in the Transformation of New England, 1800–1845* (Chapel Hill, N.C., 1989); David Robinson, *Apostle of Culture: Emerson as Preacher and Lecturer* (Philadelphia, 1982); Gay Wilson Allen, *Waldo Emerson: A Biography* (New York, 1981); and Joel Porte, *Representative Man: Ralph Waldo Emerson in His Time* (New York, 1979); Robert D. Richardson, *Henry Thoreau: A Life of the Mind* (Berkeley, Calif., 1986); Joseph W. Krutch, *Henry David Thoreau* (New York, 1948); Leo Stoller, *After Walden: Thoreau's Changing Views on Economic Man* (Stanford, Calif., 1957); and Sherman Paul, *The Shores of America: Thoreau in Inward Exploration* (Urbana, Ill., 1957); James R. Mellows, *Nathaniel Hawthorne in His Time* (New York, 1980); and Randall Stewart, *Nathaniel Hawthorne: A Biography* (Hamden, Conn., 1970); William Ellery Sedgwick, *Herman Melville: The Tragedy of Mind* (New York, 1944); Newton Arvin, *Longfellow* (Boston, 1963); Charles Capper, *Margaret Fuller: An American Romantic Life* (New York, 1992); Paula Blanchard, *Margaret Fuller: From Transcendentalism to Revolution* (Cambridge, 1978); and Katherine Anthony, *Margaret Fuller: A Psychological Biography* (New York, 1920).

For studies that analyze the work of the nation's first school of American historians, see George Callcott, *History in the United States, 1800–1860: Its Practice and Purpose* (Baltimore, 1970); Bert J. Lowenberg, *American History in American Thought: Christopher Columbus to Henry Adams* (New York, 1972); David Levin, *History as a Romantic Art: Bancroft, Prescott, Motley, and Parkman* (New York, 1959); John S. Bassett, *The Middle Group of American Historians* (New York, 1917); and Michael Kraus, *A History of American History* (New York, 1937). Herbert B. Adams, *The Life and Writings of Jared Sparks*, 2v. (Boston, 1893); Mark De Wolfe Howe, *The Life and Letters of George Bancroft*, 2v. (New York, 1908); and Russel Nye, *George Bancroft: Brahmin Rebel* (New York, 1944).

For the development of the Boston Public Library, see Jesse H. Shera, *Foundations of the Public Library: The Origins of the Public Library Movement in New England, 1629–1855* (Chicago, 1949); C. Seymour Thompson, *Evolution of the American Public Library, 1653–1876* (Washington, D.C., 1952); Horace Wadlin, *The Public Library of the City of Boston: A History* (Boston, 1911); and Walter Muir Whitehill, *The Boston Public Library: A Centennial History* (Cambridge, 1956). Josiah Quincy, *The History of the Boston Athenaeum* (Cambridge, 1951); Alexander Williams, *A Social History of the Greater Boston Clubs* (Barre, Mass., 1970); Reginald Fitz, *The Thursday Evening Club of Boston, 1846–1946: An Historical Sketch* (Boston, 1946); Mark De Wolfe Howe, *Later Years at the Saturday Club* (Boston, 1921); Harriette Knight Smith, *The History of the Lowell Institute* (Boston, 1898); and Carl Bode, *The American Lyceum: Town Meeting of the Mind* (New York, 1956) provide information on other cultural institutions of the period. Robert V. Bruce's *The Launching of Modern Science, 1846–1876* (New York, 1987) is particularly informative on the influence of science among members of Boston's intellectual community.

On the subject of public education, Stanley Schultz's *The Culture Factory: Boston Public Schools, 1789–1860* (New York, 1973) is one of the best studies of the Boston public school system. Also see Richard D. Brown, *The Strength of a People: The Idea of an Informed Citizenry in America, 1650–1870* (Cambridge, 1986); Lawrence Cremin, *American Education: The Colonial Experience, 1607–1783* (New York, 1970); Samuel Eliot Morison, *The Intellectual Life of Colonial New England* (Ithaca, N.Y., 1956); Michael B. Katz, *The Irony of Early School Reform: Educational Innovation in Mid-Nineteenth-Century Massachusetts* (Cambridge, 1968); and Lawrence A. Cremin, *The Republic and the School: Horace Mann and the Education of Free Men* (New York, 1957). Robert B. Downs, *Horace Mann: Champion of Public Schools* (New York, 1974); Jonathan Messerli, *Horace Mann: A Biography* (New York, 1971); Lawrence A. Cremin, *The Republic and the School: Horace Mann and the Education of Free Men* (New York, 1957); and Louise Hall Tharp, *Until Victory: Horace Mann and Mary Peabody* (Boston, 1953), are biographical studies of Mann himself.

CHAPTER 6

The indispensable source for the history of the Roman Catholic Church in Boston remains Robert H. Lord, Edward T. Harrington, and John E. Sexton's *History of the Archdiocese of Boston*, 3v. (New York, 1944), while Thomas H. O'Connor, in *Boston Catholics: A History of the Church and Its People* (Boston, 1998), provides an updated one-volume survey. Jay Dolan, *The American Catholic Experience: A History from Colonial Times to the Present* (Garden City, N.Y., 1985), and James Hennesey, *American Catholics: A History of the Roman Catholic Community in the United States* (New York, 1981), are readable and informative general histories of the church in the United States.

Scholarly accounts of the Catholic Church during the colonial period and the early Republic include John Tracy Ellis, *Catholics in Colonial America* (Baltimore,

1975); Mary A. Ray, *American Opinion of Roman Catholicism in the Eighteenth Century* (New York, 1936); and Charles H. Metzger, *Catholics and the American Revolution: A Study in Religious Climate* (Chicago, 1962). John Gilmary Shea, *The Life and Times of the Most Rev. John Carroll, Bishop and First Archbishop of Baltimore* (New York, 1888); Arthur T. Connolly, *An Appreciation of the Life and Labors of Rev. Francis Matignon* (Boston, 1908); and Annabelle M. Melville, *Jean Lefebvre de Cheverus, 1768–1836* (Milwaukee, 1958), bring the story of the church into the early days of the Republic.

Accounts of the Protestant orthodox revival in the early nineteenth century may be found in G. G. Atkins and F. L. Fagley, *History of American Congregationalism* (Boston, 1942); Andrew Zenos, *Presbyterianism in America* (New York, 1937); and Perry Miller, *Orthodoxy in Massachusetts* (Cambridge, 1933). Barbara M. Cross, ed., *The Autobiography of Lyman Beecher* (Cambridge, 1961); James K. Morse, *Jedidiah Morse* (New York, 1939); and William B. Sprague, *The Life of Jedidiah Morse* (New York, 1874), provide biographical material on two prominent orthodox church leaders. Also see John R. Bodo, *The Protestant Clergy and Public Issues, 1812–1848* (Princeton, N.J., 1954); William G. McLoughlin, *Revivals, Awakenings, and Reform* (Chicago, 1978); Charles C. Cole, *The Social Ideas of Northern Evangelists, 1826–1860* (New York, 1954); Whitney H. Cross, *The Burned-Over District: The Social and Intellectual History of Enthusiastic Religion in Western New York, 1800–1850* (Ithaca, N.Y., 1950); and Peter G. Mode, *The Frontier Spirit in American Christianity* (New York, 1923).

Older works such as Gustavus Myers's *History of Bigotry in the United States* (New York, 1943); Ray Allen Billington, *The Protestant Crusade, 1800–1860* (New York, 1938); and Richard Hofstadter, *The Paranoid Style in American Politics* (Chicago, 1979), are still useful for their views on religious prejudice and nativism. The second volume of *The History of the Archdiocese of Boston* deals at length with Bishop Benedict Fenwick's efforts to respond to hostile attacks by orthodox Protestant critics; and Nancy L. Schultz, *Fire and Roses: The Burning of the Charlestown Convent, 1834* (New York, 2000), is the most recent account of the event. Leo Ruskowski, in *French Émigré Priests in the United States, 1791–1815* (Washington, D.C., 1940), discusses the influence of the European clergy in America, and John McGreevy's *Catholicism and American Freedom* (New York, 2003) gives a modern and sophisticated analysis of changing Catholic thought in the nineteenth century.

The early years of the Catholic Church in Boston were marked by tension and controversy. Loven P. Beth, *The American Theory of Church and State* (Miami, Fla.,

1958), and Evarts B. Greene, *Religion and the State* (Ithaca, N.Y., 1959), discuss religion in a democratic republic; Jerome Kerwin, *The Catholic Viewpoint on Church and State* (Garden City, N.Y., 1960), focuses on Catholic issues; Patrick W. Casey, in *People, Priests, and Prelates: Ecclesiastical Democracy and the Tensions of Trusteeism* (Notre Dame, Ind., 1987), updates the earlier work of Peter Guilday, *Trusteeism* (New York, 1928). Thomas H. O'Connor, in *Fitzpatrick's Boston, 1846–1866: John Bernard Fitzpatrick, Third Bishop of Boston* (Boston, 1984), provides a study of the Catholic Church in Boston from the Great Famine to the Civil War; Dale T. Knobel, in *Paddy and the Republic: Ethnicity and Nationalism in Antebellum America* (Middletown, Conn., 1986), is especially good in analyzing the stereotypes of Irish Catholics in America; Oscar Handlin's *Boston's Immigrants* (Cambridge, 1941) is a classic study of the social and economic adjustments of Irish immigrants in Boston; Thomas H. O'Connor, *The Boston Irish: A Political History* (Boston, 1995), focuses on the political aspects of the city's Irish population. John Mulkern's *The Know-Nothing Party in Massachusetts: The Rise and Fall of a People's Party* (Boston, 1990) analyzes the many forces that led to the creation of the American Party.

CHAPTER 7

Territorial expansion provided the background for many of the nation's social and reform movements. Thomas R. Hietala's *Manifest Design: Anxious Aggrandizement in Late Jacksonian America* (Ithaca, N.Y., 1985) and Robert W. Johannsen's *To the Halls of Montezumas: The Mexican War in the American Imagination* (New York, 1985) are recent interpretations of the expansionist impulse during the mid-nineteenth century. Also see Reginald Horsman, *Race and Manifest Destiny* (Cambridge, 1981); John H. Schroeder, *Mr. Polk's War: Opposition and Dissent: 1846–1848* (Madison, Wisc., 1973); and Frederick Merk, *Manifest Destiny and Mission in American History* (Cambridge, 1963, 1995), which is still regarded as a classic. For antebellum peace movements, see Peter Brock, *Pacifism in the United States, from the Colonial Era to the First World War* (Princeton, N.J., 1968); Merle Curti, *The American Peace Crusade: 1815–1860* (Durham, N.C., 1929). Arthur A. Ekirch Jr., *The Civilian and the Military* (New York, 1956) provides a history of antimilitarism in the United States. Highlights of Sumner's involvement in the peace movement, as well as in other local reform movements have been drawn from David Herbert Donald's *Charles Sumner and the Coming of the Civil War* (New York, 1961). Also see Henry Steele Commager, *Theodore Parker: Yankee Crusader* (New York, 1947).

Winthrop Jordan's *White over Black: American Attitudes toward the Negro, 1550–1812* (New York, 1968) is essential for an analysis of racism; Eugene Genovese, in

Roll, Jordan, Roll: The World the Slaves Made (New York, 1975), explores the complexity of the master-slave relationship; Kenneth Stampp's *The Peculiar Institution: Slavery in the Antebellum South* (New York, 1956) analyzes the profitability of slavery; David Brion Davis, in *The Problem of Slavery in the Age of Revolution, 1770–1823* (Ithaca, N.Y., 1975), views slavery in an international context. Philip J. Staudenraus, *The African Colonization Movement* (New York, 1961), is valuable for its account of attempts at gradual emancipation.

James B. Stewart's *Holy Warriors: The Abolitionists and American Slavery* (New York, 1976), and Merton Dillon's *The Abolitionists: The Growth of a Dissenting Minority* (1973) are scholarly works that build upon such well-known earlier studies of abolitionism as Dwight L. Dumond, *Antislavery: The Crusade for Freedom in America* (Ann Arbor, Mich., 1961); Louis Filler, *The Crusade against Slavery, 1830–1860* (New York, 1960); Russel B. Nye, *William Lloyd Garrison and the Humanitarian Reformers* (Boston, 1955); and Gilbert H. Barnes, *The Antislavery Impulse, 1830–1844* (New York, 1933). The best works on Garrison are John L. Thomas, *The Liberator: William Lloyd Garrison, A Biography* (Boston, 1963) and Walter M. Merrill, *Against Wind and Tide: A Biography of William Lloyd Garrison* (Cambridge, 1963). Irving H. Bartlett, *Wendell Phillips: Brahmin Radical* (Boston, 1961), is also helpful in understanding the movement's leader. Stephen Kendrick and Paul Kendrick, *Sarah's Long Walk: The Free Blacks of Boston and How Their Struggle for Equality Changed America* (Boston, 2004), is a recent study of the Sarah Roberts case. For differences and conflicts within the abolition movement, see Aileen Kraditor, *Means and Ends in American Abolitionism: Garrison and His Critics on Strategy and Tactics, 1834–1850* (New York, 1969); Gerald Sorin, *The New York Abolitionists: A Case Study of Political Radicalism* (New York, 1971); Carleton Mabee, *Black Freedom: The Nonviolent Abolitionists from 1830 to the Civil War* (New York, 1970); Bertram Wyatt-Brown, *Lewis Tappan and the Evangelical War Against Slavery* (Cleveland, 1969); and Betty Fladeland, *James Gillespie Birney: Slaveholder to Abolitionist* (New York, 1955). Richard H. Sewall, *Ballots for Freedom: Antislavery Politics in the United States, 1837–1860* (New York, 1976); Joseph G. Rayback, *Free Soil: The Election of 1848* (Lexington, Ky., 1970); and Frederick J. Blue, *The Free-Soilers: Third-Party Politics, 1848–1854* (Urbana, Ill., 1973), trace the development of antislavery politics before the Civil War.

CHAPTER 8

The subject of women making the transition from abolitionism to suffrage has been treated by Eleanor Flexner, *Century of Struggle: The Women's Rights Movement in the United States* (Cambridge, 1959); Blanche G. Hersh, *The Slavery of Sex:*

Feminist-Abolitionists in America (Urbana, Ill., 1978); Ellen Dubois, *Feminism and Suffrage: The Emergence of an Independent Women's Movement, 1848–1869* (Ithaca, N.Y., 1978); Alma Lutz, *Crusade for Freedom: Women of the Antislavery Movement* (Boston, 1968); and Aileen Kraditor, *Up from the Pedestal: Selected Writings in the History of American Feminism* (Chicago, 1968). Also see Gerda Lerner, *The Grimké Sisters from South Carolina: Pioneers for Women's Rights and Abolition* (New York, 1967): Milton Meltzer, *Tongue of Flame: The Life of Lydia Maria Child* (New York, 1968); Dorothy Sterling, *Ahead of Her Time: Abby Kelley and the Politics of Antislavery* (New York, 1992); Elinor Rice Hays, *Morning Star: A Biography of Lucy Stone, 1818–1893* (New York, 1961); and Odelia Cromwell, *Lucretia Mott* (Cambridge, 1958).

INDEX

A native of South Boston, THOMAS H. O'CONNOR graduated from the Boston Latin School in 1942. After three years' service in the U.S. Army, he received his A.B. and M.A. degrees from Boston College, and his Ph.D. from Boston University in 1958. Dr. O'Connor began teaching at Boston College in 1950, served as chairman of the history department, and currently holds the title of University Historian.

Dr. O'Connor's teaching concentrated on the Age of Jackson and the Civil War, and in these areas he published *Lords of the Loom* (1968) and *The Disunited States* (1972). His increasing interest in the history of Boston led to the publication of such works as *Building a New Boston* (1993), *The Boston Irish* (1995), *Civil War Boston* (1997), and *Boston Catholics* (1998).

Dr. O'Connor is a member of the board of directors of the Bostonian Society, a resident fellow at the Massachusetts Historical Society, and a recent member of the Massachusetts Archives Commission. He was awarded the Gold Medal in History from the Daughters of the American Revolution, the Distinguished Irish-American Award from the Charitable Irish Society of Boston, and the Gold Medal of the Eire Society of Boston.

Dr. O'Connor has a daughter, Jeanne, and a son, Michael, and currently lives with his wife, Mary, in Braintree, Massachusetts.